Library Daylight

Tracings of Modern Librarianship, 1874-1922

Library Daylight

Tracings of Modern Librarianship, 1874-1922

Edited by Rory Litwin

With an introduction by Dr. Suzanne Stauffer

Library Juice Press, LLC
Duluth, Minnesota

All items published herein are in the public domain, with the exception of the Introduction. The copyright to the Introduction is held by Dr. Suzanne Stauffer (2006).

Published by Library Juice Press, 2006

Library Juice Press
PO Box 3320
Duluth, MN 55803

http://libraryjuicepress.com/

ISBN 13: 978-0-9778617-4-3
ISBN 10: 0-9778617-4-0

Printed on acid-free paper.

For Ruth Hafter

Contents

Contents — vii.

Editor's Preface — xiii.

Introduction — 1.

1874	**Germantown Quakers Check the Spread of Novel Reading** From the 1874 annual report of a small public library established by Quakers in Germantown, Pennsylvania. Published in *The Nation*.	15.
1876	**A Librarian's Work, By John Fiske** *The Atlantic Monthly* (Vol 38, Iss 228), October 1876.	17.
1878	**Boston Medical Library Dedicatory Address** From *Medical Essays—1842-1882*, by Oliver Wendell Holmes, Sr. (The physician and poet, not the jurist O. W. Holmes, Jr.) Dedicatory Address at the opening of the Medical Library in Boston, December 3, 1878.	35.
1880	**Brief item in *The Nation* on copyright in Germany** From *The Nation*, Vol. XXX—No. 766 (March 4, 1880), p.177.	51.
1883	**The Father of the American Libraries** By Bunford Samuel *The Century; a popular quarterly*. Volume 26, Issue 1 (May 1883).	53.
1886	**Women in Libraries: How They are Handicapped** By Melvil Dewey. Excerpts from a March 13, 1886 address before the Association of College Alumni, originally published in *Library Notes* 1 (October 1886).	59.
1887	**Columbia Library School** By Melvil Dewey. Published in *Library Notes*, v.1 No.4, March 1887.	63.

1892	**Proceedings of the Fourteenth American Library Association Conference, Lakewood: The Woman's Meeting** Published in *Library Journal* 17 (August 1892).	71.
1894	**Librarianship as a Profession for Women** By Miss Richardson. Originally published in *The Library* 6 (1894).	79.
1895	**Improper Books** A paper delivered at the 1895 ALA Conference in Denver, Colorado. By George T. Clark, Librarian, San Francisco Free Public Library.	85.
1896	*Hear the Other Side*—**1896 ALA President's Address** The address of ALA President John Cotton Dana, Librarian of the Denver Public Library. The conference was in Cleveland and Mackinaw, Ohio, September 1-4 and 8, 1896.	89.
1899	**The Telegraph in the Library** By Richard Garnett, in *Essays in Librarianship and Bibliography* (New York: Harper, 1899).	97.
1901	**Library Cooperation** By Lodilla Ambrose. *The Dial; a Semi-monthly Journal of Literary Criticism, Discussion, and Information.* July 16, 1901. Vol. 31, No. 362.	101.
1903	**On George Iles' plea for a headquarters for ALA** "A Library of Libraries." *The Nation*, July 30, 1903, p. 89.	105.
1904	**Wild Flower Show at the Free Library** Sixty Varieties Gathered in and About Oakland Exhibited in the Children's Room. From *The San Francisco Call*, March 27, 1904.	109.
	The Library: Its Past and Future By Guido Biagi, Director, Royal Laurentian Library, Florence, Italy. A talk given at the ALA Annual Conference, St. Louis, Missouri, 1904.	111.

1905	**The Library as Social Centre** The opening address at the Red Wing Meeting of the Minnesota Library Association, October 12, 1905, by Miss Gratia Alta Countryman.	125.
1912	**Phones Installed in Free Library** Patrons Now May Save Themselves Needless Trips for Books That Are "Out." *San Francisco Call* (daily newspaper), April 7, 1912, p. 64.	129.
	Letter to the Editor of *The Nation* on "The librarian who reads is dead" Published Nov. 7, 1912.	131.
1913	**The Heyday of Librarians** *The Nation,* July 3, 1913.	133.
	Note on 1913 ALA Annual Conference in *The Dial* *The Dial: Semi-monthly Journal of Literary Criticism, Discussion, and Information.* July 16, 1913. Vol. 55, No. 650.	137.
	The Region of the Unromantic *The Dial: a Semi-monthly Journal of Literary Criticism, Discussion and Information.* December 1, 1913, p. 465.	139.
1914	**First Aid to the Enquiring Reader** *The Dial; a Semi-monthly Journal of Literary Criticism, Discussion and Information.* June 1, 1914; Vol. 56, No. 671.	141.
	Some Old-Time Old-World Librarians By Theodore W. Koch *The North American Review*, Aug 1914. vol. 200, no. 705, p. 244.	143.
1915	**The People's Share in the Public Library** By Arthur E. Bostwick, Librarian, St. Louis Public Library. Read before the Chicago Woman's Club, Jan. 6, 1915 Published in *Library Journal*, April, 1915.	157.
	Women Assistants and the War Published in *Library World* 17 (January 1915) By M.F.	167.

How Far Should the Library Aid the Peace Movement and Similar Propaganda? 173.
By George F. Bowerman, Librarian, The Public Library of the District of Columbia. An address at the American Library Association National Conference in Berkeley, California, 1915.

The Libary's Primary Duty 181.
President's Address, ALA Annual Conference, Berkeley, CA, June 3-9, 1915. By Hiller C. Wellman, Librarian, City Library, Springfield, Massachussetts.

Some Tendencies of American Thought 189.
By Dr. Arthur E. Bostwick, Librarian, St. Louis Public Library. Read before the New York Library Association at Squirrel Inn, Haines Falls, Sept. 28, 1915, and before the Missouri Library Association at Joplin, Missouri, Oct. 21, 1915.

1916 **Librarianship: A Profession** 199.
W. E. Henry, Librarian, University of Washington, Seattle.

The Larger Publicity of the Library 209.
By Joseph L. Wheeler, Librarian, Youngstown Public Library. Presented at the ALA Annual Conference in Asbury Park, New Jersey, 1916.

1917 **"Human Interest" in the Public Library** 219.
By Marilla Waite Freeman, Librarian, Goodwyn Institute, Memphis, Tennessee. *Library Journal*, January, 1917.

Great Reasons to Go to the New SF Main Library 223.
"Library Offers Wisdom to Knowledge Seekers. There Isn't Any Subject One Can't Get Facts About Among Books." *San Francisco Examiner*, Feb 18, 1917.

1920 **Libraries Should Provide for the Reader Who Smokes** 227.
San Francisco Examiner, February 20, 1919. p. 20.

Ankles of Library Girls Seized as They Stack Books 229.
San Francisco Examiner, December 5, 1920, p. 90.

x

1922	**Copyright and the Publishers: A Review of Thirty Years (and Reply)** By M. L. Raney, Librarian, Johns Hopkins University, and Frederic G. Melcher, Executive Secretary, National Association of Book Publishers. Baltimore, Maryland. ALA Annual Conference, Detroit, Michigan, 1922.	231.
	Index	243.

Editor's Preface

The thirty-six articles in this collection are all in the public domain, but a few of them originally reached my attention because they were discovered and republished by other compilers. Those compilations warrant mention.

In 1921, The H.W. Wilson Company published a compilation of articles edited by Arthur Bostwick entitled *The Library and Society: Reprints of Papers and Addresses*. This book was reprinted in 1968 by Books for Libraries Press of Freeport, New York, and is readily obtainable on the used market today and found in many libraries supporting library and information science programs. Through this source I discovered one of the articles that appears in this book: Gratia Countryman's "The Library as Social Centre" (1906). If you like *Library Daylight* I recommend getting your hands on a copy of Bostwick's compilation. Its forty-eight articles offer inspiration and interesting insights about the early days of American public libraries.

Another source of discovery was a compilation edited by Kathleen Weibel and Kathleen Heim (now de la Peña McCook): the 1979 Oryx Press publication, *The Role of Women in Librarianship: 1876-1976*. Through this source I found four of the articles that appear here: Melvil Dewey's "Women in Libraries: How they are Handicapped" (1886); "Proceedings of the Fourteenth American Library Association Conference, Lakewood: The Woman's Meeting" (1892); Miss Richardson's "Librarianship as a Profession for Women" (1894); and "Women Assistants and the War," by M.F. (1915). This is definitely a book worth seeking out if you are interested in the place of women in librarianship and the history of librarianship as a female intensive profession.

Other sources of discovery included *Poole's Index*, bound volumes of *Library Journal*, newspaper indices in microform, the historical database of *The Nation*, and the published proceedings of ALA's annual conferences. In addition, some of the articles were discovered by pure serendipity, while I was doing other research.

I hope readers enjoy this collection. I find it amazing to discover what has changed and what has remained the same over the last century.

Introduction

By Suzanne Stauffer. Ph.D.

The selections collected here provide a view of issues and challenges faced by the American public library throughout its two hundred year history. They remind us of the words of the Preacher in Ecclesiates, "There is nothing new under the sun" and of Alphonse Karr that "the more things change, the more they remain the same." Reading them, we see that the idea of the public library as a community center dates back to at least 1905, while the 1912 installation of telephones in the Oakland free library placed that system at the cutting edge of information technology. The tools and techniques—and hair styles—may have changed, but, as these selections demonstrate, librarians have always struggled with providing for the informational, recreational, and educational needs of the community which they serve.

Although library history can easily be traced back 5000 years to the Sumerians in Mesopotamia, the history of the free tax-supported public library in the United States, while notable, is not nearly as venerable. It has its roots in private collections and libraries established in the Northeast and Middle Atlantic region during the mid-17th century. These collections were formed around a core of religious and theological literature. As the size of the collection increased, it was likely to contain books on history, travel, political science, literary classics, and practical materials on agriculture and vocational topics. Although the larger collections were owned by the professional elite, such as ministers, doctors, lawyers, and government officials, many merchants, tradesmen, and others of the working class owned a few books, one of which was usually the Bible. The primary motive for the development of literacy and libraries during the Colonial Period was the ability to read and study the Bible and religious tracts on a daily basis, with professional needs a secondary force.

In addition to individual collections, groups banded together to form social libraries for purposes of personal, intellectual, professional, and moral improvement. All required payment for use. These libraries provided carefully selected, but limited, collections of materials designed to foster both individual and social improvement and reform. Circulating libraries, which rented popular fiction at a small fee to the casual reader, were decried by social reformers as an unhealthy influence on the young people, especially young women. Other predecessors of the public library established at this time were the school district library, private school and academy libraries, and Sunday School libraries. All eventually failed due to inadequate collections, lack of funds, and poor management.[1] As Bunford Samuel reminds us in his 1883 historical sketch, Benjamin Franklin was among those who founded one such library in Philadelphia in 1731. Whether it was indeed "the first of all lending libraries" is a matter of debate, but that it was certainly one of the longest-lasting, continuing today as the Library Company of Philadelphia.

The inadequacies and unreliability of voluntary support for establishing universal public library service soon became evident, particularly during years of economic crisis, when members withdrew their support and the social libraries collapsed.[2] In addition, the growing acceptance of society's responsibility for providing funding for basic educational services in order to establish and secure a stable social and economic order soon extended to the provision of public library services. The founding of the Boston Public Library in 1854, scarcely more than 150 years ago, signaled the beginning of the national public library movement. The Trustees of the Library articulated the rationale for the free tax-supported public library in language which resonated with the country's mood of self-improvement and social reform, "...it is of paramount importance that the means of general information should be so diffused that the largest possible number of persons should be induced to read and understand questions going down to the very foundations of social order..."[3] Many public libraries were founded when an existing social or private library was donated to the city for that use; in other cases, individual philanthropists donated money for buildings

---

[1] Jesse Hauk Shera, Foundations of the Public Library (Chicago: University of Chicago Press, 1949), 54-155; Michael H. Harris, History of Libraries in the Western World, 4th ed. (Lanham, MD: Scarecrow Press, 1999), 183-91.

[2] Shera, Foundations of the Public Library, 75-85; Harris, Libraries in the Western World, 186-7.

[3] Shera, Foundations of the Public Library, 156-99; Harris, Libraries in the Western World, 243-4.

INTRODUCTION 3

and collections. The single most influential donor was Andrew Carnegie, who provided funds for 1,679 library buildings in the United States between 1881 and 1920.[4]

Increasing industrialization, rapid urbanization, and a massive influx of immigrants to the cities, which resumed and escalated in the years following the Civil War, led to widespread poverty, political corruption, unsanitary conditions, and other "social ills" such as prostitution, gambling, and alcoholism. Many believed that all of society was threatened by this moral and social degeneration and the accompanying eclipse of democratic institutions. Progressivism as a movement arose from the post-Civil War social reform efforts to combat these evils and achieve social purity and unity through social, municipal, and economic reform, with the objective of restoring economic individualism and political democracy, promoting social welfare, and reforming labor practices, though the application of scientific knowledge and reason.[5]

This emphasis on alleviating society's moral afflictions allowed women to secure and enlarge their positions in public life. Nursing became a profession as many women built on their war experiences in that field. Others entered public education and social work, with the objective of infusing Protestant morality into the community as well as transmitting American culture to the new immigrant. Women's responsibilities continued to extend beyond the boundaries of the individual home to encompass their entire community at an accelerated and energetic pace. As one woman expressed it:

> Home is not contained within the four walls of an individual home. Home is the community. The city full of people is the Family. The public school is the real

---

[4]George Bobinski, Carnegie Libraries: Their History and Impact on American Public Library Development (Chicago: American Library Association, 1969).

[5]Ellen Carol DuBois, United States after 1865, ed. Bonnie Smith, Women's and Gender History in Global Perspective (Washington, D.C.: American Historical Association, 2000), 13-4; Richard Hofstadter, The Age of Reform: From Bryan to F. D. R. (New York: Random House, 1955), 3-11, 133; Robert H. Wiebe, The Search for Order, 1877-1920, Making of America (New York: Hill and Wang, 1967), 44-75.

> Nursery. And badly do the Home and the Family and the Nursery need their mother.[6]

This period also witnessed the entry of a select group of educated, dedicated, single, middle-class women into public affairs through the cause of female suffrage, and organizations such as the settlement house movement, the Women's Christian Temperance Union, the YWCA, and voluntary social clubs, all under the rubric of "domestic feminism" or, as it was more commonly called, "municipal housekeeping."[7] This metaphor not only permitted respectable women to enter public life by incorporating these activities into their accepted domestic sphere, it also elevated and ennobled them in the Victorian mind by associating them with the sacred duties of motherhood and "True Womanhood."

One of the means through which they hoped to achieve their goals for social reform and civic improvement was voluntary social clubs, in particular, women's clubs. Following the Civil War, when the social reform movements that would culminate in Progressivism were on the rise, women began to form literary and other secular societies with the express purpose of self-improvement and self-education through group study.[8] Although black women did organize at this time, it hardly needs to be said that membership of the clubs was strictly segregated, and that most consisted of educated middle- and upper-class white women.

---

[6]Rheta C. Dorr, What Eight Million Women Want (Boston : Small, Maynard, 1910), 237 quoted in Theodora Penny Martin, The Sound of Our Own Voices: Women's Study Clubs, 1860-1910 (Boston: Beacon Press, 1987), 174.

[7]Richard White, "It's Your Misfortune and None of My Own": A History of the American West, 1st ed. (Norman: University of Oklahoma Press, 1991), 311-9, 420; Karen J. Blair, The Clubwoman as Feminist: True Womanhood Redefined, 1868-1914 (New York: Holmes & Meier Publishers, 1980); Glenna Matthews, The Rise of Public Woman: Woman's Power and Woman's Place in the United States, 1630-1970 (New York: Oxford University Press, 1992), 155-8, 98; Anne Firor Scott, Natural Allies: Women's Associations in American History, ed. Mary Jo Buhle, et al., Women in American History (Urbana; Chicago: University of Illinois Press, 1992), 86-174; Wiebe, Search for Order, 44-75, 122-3.

[8] Scott, Natural Allies, 111; Anne Firor Scott, "Women and Libraries," Journal of Library History, Philosophy & Comparative Librarianship 21, no. Spring (1986); Blair, Clubwoman as Feminist, 57-60.

INTRODUCTION 5

By the last decade of the nineteenth century, these clubs had joined in the General Federation of Women's Clubs, and had extended their field of improvement from their members and their families to their communities, particularly in the areas of libraries, education, public health, and civic improvement.[9] The clubs were so ubiquitous that Sinclair Lewis endowed Gopher Prairie with the Thanatopsis Club, which "does do a good social work—they've made the city plant ever so many trees, and they run the rest-room for farmers' wives. And they do take such an interest in refinement and culture."[10]

Many of these clubs created their own "traveling libraries," sharing the reading materials necessary for self-improvement with sister clubs in their own state or region, especially in the poorer and more rural areas. Consequently, one of the first civic projects in which many of these clubs became actively involved was the establishment of a free public library, with the club's library serving as the nucleus of the collection.[11] In 1933, the

---

[9]Scott, Natural Allies, 141-2; Scott, "Women and Libraries."; Martin, Sound of Our Own Voices, 171-6; Abigail A. Van Slyck, Free to All: Carnegie Libraries & American Culture, 1890-1920 (Chicago: University of Chicago Press, 1995), 125-6, 35-6; Sophonisba P. Breckinridge, Women in the Twentieth Century: A Study of Their Political, Social and Economic Activities, American Woman: Images and Realities, Monographs. Recent Social Trends in the United States (New York: Arno Press, 1933), 14-23; Victoria Kline Musmann, "Women and the Founding of Social Libraries in California, 1859-1910" (Ph. D. diss., University of Southern California, 1982), 191-2; Marilyn J. Martin, "From Altruism to Activism: The Contributions of Women's Organizations to Arkansas Public Libraries" (Ph.D. diss., Texas Woman's University, 1993), 195-209; Paul John Ostendorf, "The History of the Public Library Movement in Minnesota from 1849 to 1916" (1984), 356; Patricia Dawn Robinson, "From Pedestal to Platform: The American Women's Club Movement, 1800-1920" (Ph.D., University of California, Davis, 1993), 360-4; Sally A. Myers, "Northwest Ohio Women's Literary Clubs as Arbiters of Culture: 1880-1918" (Ph. D. diss., Bowling Green State University, 1995); Paula Baker, "The Domestication of Politics: Women and American Political Society, 1780-1920," American Historical Review 89 (1984); June O. Underwood, "Civilizing Kansas: Women's Organizations, 1880-1920," Kansas History 7, no. Winter (1984/85); Barbara Welter, "The Cult of True Womanhood, 1820-1860," American Quarterly 18, no. Summer (1966).

[10]Sinclair Lewis, Main Street (New York: Prometheus Books, 1920, c1996), 65.

[11]Blair, Clubwoman as Feminist, 68; Scott, "Women and Libraries."; Musmann, "Women and Social Libraries", 192; Martin, "From Altruism to

American Library Association estimated that seventy-five percent of all public libraries then in existence had been started by women or women's clubs.¹² While this may have been an overestimation, nevertheless, as a recent history of Carnegie Libraries in the United States declares, "[t]hese clubs became crucial to the success of a library campaign in hundreds of communities because women were unflaggingly convinced of the benefits of a free public library and often sustained interest in the project long after others became disenchanted or frustrated."¹³

Although the post Civil War period meant increased poverty for some, the economic benefits of increasing industrialization meant increased affluence and access to education and accompanying heightened social status for others. Accompanied by the popular acceptance of science and rationalism rather than faith and authority as a means of knowing, this wider access to education resulted in the rise of the professional middle class in the United States. The 1860 census listed only 750,000 in this category. By 1890 that number had increased nearly threefold, to 2,160,000, and by 1910 that number had almost doubled, with 4,420,000 now declaring themselves to be "professionals." As their numbers and power increased, members of this new class founded professional associations, lobbied for state licensure, and established schools and training centers in order to preserve their status and prestige, facilitate communication, and maintain standards.¹⁴

Women as well as men benefitted from this access to education and professional training. By 1900, forty percent of college graduates were

---

Activism"; Paula D. Watson, "Founding Mothers: The Contribution of Women's Organizations to Public Library Development in the United States," Library Quarterly 64 (1994); Scott, Natural Allies, 149; Breckinridge, Women in the Twentieth Century, 29, 93; Ostendorf, "Public Library Movement in Minnesota", 361.

¹²Van Slyck, Free to All, 127.

¹³Theodore Jones, Carnegie Libraries across America: A Public Legacy (New York: John Wiley, 1997), 42.

¹⁴Thomas J. Schlereth, Victorian America: Transformations in Everyday Life, 1876-1915, ed. Richard Balkin, Everyday Life in America (New York: HarperCollins, 1991), 29; Hofstadter, Age of Reform, 148-73; Wiebe, Search for Order, 111-32.

women who, as newly minted alumnae, sought a more active, public arena for their skills and interests. They quickly dominated the fields of teaching, nursing, social work, home economics and librarianship, all of which were viewed as natural extensions of the domestic sphere. By 1910, eighty percent of teachers, ninety-three percent of nurses, and seventy-nine percent of librarians were women.[15] The universal gender hierarchy in pay and power meant that the majority of professional women could hope for a lower-level managerial position at best, while most had to be content with a career with little or no potential for professional development, if they chose a career rather than marriage and motherhood. Until the early years of the 20th century, however, librarianship offered more opportunities for advancement and professional development than did many other careers open to women.

Modern librarianship developed within this social and cultural environment. It was no coincidence that the American Library Association was organized in Philadelphia in the fall of 1876, a few months after the Centennial Exhibition had closed and the same year that the *American Library Journal*, the first professional journal of librarianship, began publication. As with other professional organizations, the purpose of the Association was toward "promoting the library interests of the country, and of increasing reciprocity of intelligence and goodwill among librarians..."[16] In true social reform fashion, the new Association espoused public service and the effect of socially beneficial and culturally substantive knowledge rather than the mere acquisition and preservation of such sources of information, as exemplified in George T. Clark's 1895 address to the Annual Conference in Denver. Reading good books would result in individual improvement and lead inevitably to an informed, orderly, moral society.[17] The American Library Association was not alone in this belief, as the selection below from the Germantown Quakers annual report of 1874 demonstrates.

The specialized knowledge and training necessary for professional practice were given institutional recognition with the opening of the first

---

[15] Steven J. Diner, A Very Different Age: Americans of the Progressive Era (New York: Hill and Wang, 1998), 195; DuBois, United States after 1865, 6-7.

[16] Wayne A. Wiegand, The Politics of an Emerging Profession: The American Library Association, 1876-1917, Contributions in Librarianship and Information Science, No. 56 (New York: Greenwood Press, 1986), 3.

[17] Ibid., 12.

school of library science at Columbia College in 1887. This collection includes Melvil Dewey's first annual report on the progress of the school, which presents a very different picture of a library school than we see today, yet with all of the changes in tools and techniques, we still look forward to the time "when a man or woman seeking the place of a librarian without training for its duties will be thought as much a quack or charlatan as the physician seeking patients without having attended a medical school or served an apprenticeship with an accomplished practitioner."

Women were drawn to the profession by this emphasis on the moral and cultural aspects of librarianship, which were in accord with their socially accepted roles as guardians of morality and disseminators of culture. The field became increasingly attractive to college-educated women committed to social reform ideals who desired to use their education for the betterment of society before they became wives and mothers. They believed in the importance of efficiency as a moral force, of the physical environment in promoting social and moral health, and of education as a means of achieving social unity.[18]

Library work was promoted as a form of educational and public service analogous to teaching, with all of the moral and social benefits, but none of the "nervous strain and the wear and tear of the classroom."[19] Simultaneous with the founding of the first kindergartens, public libraries were opened to children for the first time, as librarians and teachers focused on educating and integrating working class and immigrant children, seen as more malleable and tractable than adults.[20] The field became even more acceptable for women with this concentration on nurturing the young.

In addition, Melvil Dewey, founder and director of the School of Library Economy at Columbia, actively recruited women as inherently

---

[18]Joanne E. Passet, Cultural Crusaders: Women Librarians in the American West, 1900-1917 (Albuquerque: University of New Mexico Press, 1994), 1-2; Van Slyck, Free to All, 162, 74-5; Suzanne Hildenbrand, "Revision Versus Reality: Women in the History of the Public Library Movement, 1876-1920," in The Status of Women in Librarianship : Historical, Sociological, and Economic Issues, ed. Kathleen M. Heim (New York: Neil-Schuman, 1983).

[19]Van Slyck, Free to All, 163.

[20]Schlereth, Victorian America, 247; Diner, Very Different Age, 198; Passet, Cultural Crusaders, 2, 111-3; Norman Brosterman, Inventing Kindergarten (New York: Abrams, 1997); Hildenbrand, "Revision Versus Reality."

INTRODUCTION

suited to the work. "The natural qualities most important in library work are accuracy, order (or what we call the housekeeping instinct), executive ability, and above all earnestness and enthusiasm."[21] Women responded to these arguments, making up approximately ninety-four percent of the forty-five hundred graduates from all library schools from 1888-1921, and ninety percent of librarians by 1920.[22]

Although Victorians valued libraries, along with art galleries and museum, as "citadels of self-culture" dedicated to education and civilization, and librarians as guardians of that culture and civilization, librarianship was among the lowest paid of all the female professions during that period, and many female librarians were poorly paid functionaries with little autonomy, status, or training. Male librarians who initially opposed the admission of women to the profession were soon forced to accept them, as taxpayers and library boards consistently refused to offer salaries comparable to professions such as law or medicine. Consequently, few men were attracted to the profession at the same time that demand was increasing, leaving the field open to women, who were willing to work for approximately half of what a man would make.[23]

Library boards in many small communities viewed the position as an honorable means of assisting needy men and women in the community, particularly widows and spinsters with no other means of support. Many also preferred to employ local women, believing that they would be more amenable to local pressure, and justifying the lower salaries with the excuse that they lived at home and had no traveling expenses.[24]

Nevertheless, under the leadership of such men as John Cotton Dana, librarians actively promoted their profession, their institution, and the Progressive ideals on which both were founded. They read and contributed

---

[21] Van Slyck, Free to All, 163.

[22] Diner, Very Different Age, 197; Passet, Cultural Crusaders, 2.

[23] Van Slyck, Free to All, 164; Diner, Very Different Age, 178, 97-8; Schlereth, Victorian America, 68; Joanne E. Passet, ""You Do Not Have to Pay Librarians:" Women, Salaries, and Status in the Early 20th Century," in Reclaiming the American Library Past: Writing The Women In, ed. Suzanne Hildenbrand, Information Management, Policies, and Services (New Jersey: Ablex, 1996).

[24] Passet, Cultural Crusaders, 5; Passet, "Women, Salaries, and Status."

to professional journals and participated in professional conferences, interacted with other reform-minded women, such as settlement workers, school teachers, and club women, and developed specialties within their field. Urban librarians developed children's librarianship from their work with immigrant children, while rural librarians created the county library system to serve farming families. Experienced, established librarians served as mentors and teachers to those new to the field through both formal and informal networks.[25] The need for such professionalization and the difficulties faced in achieving it are the topic of several of the selected works, most written by library leaders and library educators.

The years immediately preceding and following World War One witnessed the continuing rise of the middle class and the growth of urban centers, with a concomitant rise in consumerism and conformity to social norms, as exemplified in the works of Sinclair Lewis, Edith Wharton and F. Scott Fitzgerald. As public institutions, libraries supported and promoted these social developments, particularly the "Americanization" of the immigrants who flooded the country in the War's aftermath, as the selections from this period demonstrate.[26] In 1915, George F. Bowerman asked the question, "How Far Should the Library Aid the Peace Movement and Similar Propaganda?," while the San Francisco Examiner called for libraries to be "made especially comfortable for all the plain people who might be induced to use them if they were made more inviting to them in particular" by the introduction of designated reading rooms for smokers.

Librarians shifted their focus from collection development to reader services, and, as Joseph L. Wheeler shows, began to publicize the library to the community. Much of their efforts were aimed at further developing

---

[25] Laurel A. Grotzinger, "Invisible, Indestructible Network: Women and the Diffusion of Librarianship at the Turn of the Century," in Women's Work : Vision and Change in Librarianship, ed. Laurel A. Grotzinger, James V. Carmichael, and Mary Niles Maack, Occasional Papers, Graduate School of Library and Information Science, University of Illinois (Chicago: University of Illinois Press, 1994); Van Slyck, Free to All, 174; Mary Niles Maack, "Women as Visionaries, Mentors, and Agents of Change," in Women's Work : Vision and Change in Librarianship, ed. Laurel A. Grotzinger, James V. Carmichael, and Mary Niles Maack, Occasional Papers, Graduate School of Library and Information Science, University of Illinois (Chicago: University of Illinois Press, 1994).

[26] Lowell Arthur Martin, Enrichment: A History of the Public Library in the United States in the Twentieth Century (Lanham, Md.: Scarecrow Press, 1998).

INTRODUCTION

children's collection and services and targeting teenagers, although with notably less success, and reaching out to community groups. Adult reference and reader's advisory became staples of library service in nearly all public libraries, while some also experimented with providing service to the public schools and to the needs of small business owners. Education for librarianship continued to expand, with libraries in larger cities establishing training classes along the apprenticeship model and the opening of the profession school at Columbia University in accordance with the recommendations of the Williamson Report of 1920.[27] This period of growth and innovation ended with the stock market crash of 1929 and the subsequent Great Depression. This affected the public library as much as other public institutions, and so makes a logical place to end this brief overview of American public library history.

---

[27]Ibid.

The Essays

Germantown Quakers Check the Spread of Novel Reading

From the 1874 annual report of a small public library established by Quakers in Germantown, Pennsylvania. Published in *The Nation*.

In watching the use of our library as it is more and more resorted to by the younger readers of our community, I have been much interested in its influence in weaning them from a desire for works of fiction. On first joining the library, the new-comers often ask for such books; but failing to procure them, and having their attention turned to works of interest and instruction, in almost every instance they settle down to good reading, and cease asking for novels. I am persuaded that much of this vitiated taste is cultivated by the purveyors of the reading classes, and that they are responsible for an appetite they often profess to deplore, but continue to cater to under the plausible excuse that the public will have such works. This furnishing of unwholesome mental food or poison is gradually pervading our literature to an alarming extent, from the fictitious Sabbath-school little story-book, through our serials, to the more pretentious novel, vitiating the taste and giving false ideas of the life wherever found. Could the directors of our public libraries but see the evil and aid in checking its spread, they would be conferring a great benefit on the young people. Our library is doing a good work in that direction.

A Librarian's Work

By John Fiske
The Atlantic Monthly (Vol 38, Iss 228), October 1876.

I am frequently asked what in the world a librarian can find to do with his time, or am perhaps congratulated on my connection with Harvard College Library, on the ground that "being virtually a sinecure office (!) it must leave so much leisure for private study and work of a literary sort." Those who put such questions, or offer such congratulations, are naturally astonished when told that the library affords enough work to employ all my own time, as well as that of twenty assistants; and astonishment is apt to rise to bewilderment when it is added that seventeen of these assistants are occupied chiefly with "cataloguing;" for generally, I find, a library catalogue is assumed to be a thing that is somehow "made" at a single stroke, as Aladdin's palace was built, at intervals of ten or a dozen years, or whenever a "new catalogue" is thought to be needed. "How often do you make a catalogue?" or "When will your catalogue be completed?" are questions revealing such transcendent misapprehension of the case that little but further mystification can be got from the mere answer, "We are always making a catalogue, and it will never be finished." The "doctrine of special creations" does not work any better in the bibliographical than in the zoological world. A catalogue, in the modern sense of the word, is not something that is "made" all at once, to last until the time has come for it to be superseded by a new edition, but it is something that "grows," by slow increments, and supersedes itself only through gradual evolution from a lower degree of fullness and definiteness into a higher one. It is perhaps worth while to give some general explanation of this process of catalogue-making, thus answering once for all the question as to what may be a librarian's work. There is no better way than to describe, in the case of our own library, the career of a book from the time of its delivery by the express-man to the time when it is ready for public use.

New American books, whether bought or presented, generally come along in driblets, two or three at a time, throughout the year; large boxes of pamphlets, newspapers, broadsides, trade-catalogues, and all manner of woeful rubbish (the refuse of private libraries and households) are sent in from time to time; and books from Europe arrive every few weeks in lots of from fifty to three or four hundred. It is in the case of foreign books that our process is most thoroughly systematized, and here let us take our illustrative example.

When a box containing three or four hundred foreign books has been unpacked, the volumes are placed, backs uppermost, on large tables, and are then looked over by the principal assistant, with two or three subordinates, to ascertain if the books at hand correspond with those charged in the invoice. As the titles are read from the invoice, the volumes are hunted out and arranged side by side in the order in which their titles are read, while the entry on the invoice is checked in the margin with a pencil. These pencil-checks are afterwards copied into the margins of the book in which our lists of foreign orders are registered, so that we may always be able to determine, by a reference to this book, whether any particular work has been received or not. This order-book, with its marginal checks, is the only immediate specific register of accessions kept by us, as our peculiar system entails considerable delay in bringing up the "accessions catalogue."

After this preliminary examination and registry, the books are ready to be looked over by the "assistant librarian," who must first decide to what "fund" each book entered on the invoice must be charged. The university never buys books with its general funds, but uses for this purpose the income of a dozen or more small funds, given, bequeathed, or subscribed expressly for the purchase of books. Sometimes the donors of such funds allow us to get whatever books we like with the money, but more often they show an inclination to favor the growth of departments in which they feel a personal interest. Thus the munificent bequest of the late Mr. Charles Sumner is appropriated to the purchase of works on politics and the fine arts, while Dr. Walker's bequest provides more especially for theology and philosophy, and the estate of Professor Farrar still guards the interests of mathematics and physics. Under such circumstances, it is of course necessary to keep a separate account of each fund, and the data for such an account are provided by charging every new book as it arrives. On the margin of the invoice the names of the different funds are written in pencil against the entries, while the assistants separate the books into groups according to the funds to which they are charged. Five or six more assistants now arriving on the scene, the work of "collating" begins.[1]

Properly speaking, to "collate" is to compare two things with each

---

[1] We have lately found it convenient to make the collating precede the assignment of funds, but the change is so trivial that I have not thought it worth while to alter the text.

other, in order to estimate or judge the one by a reference to the other taken as a standard. In our library usage, the word has very nearly this sense when duplicate copies of the same work are collated, to see whether they coincide page for page. Bust as we currently use the word, to collate a book is simply to examine it carefully from beginning to end, to see whether every page is in its proper place and properly numbered, whether any maps or plates are missing or misplaced, whether the back is correctly lettered, or whether any leaves are so badly torn or defaced as to need replacing. In English cloth-bound books this scrutiny involves the cutting of the leaves—a tedious job which in half-bound books from the Continent is seldom required. En revanche, however, the collating of an English book hardly ever brings to light any serious defect, while in the make-up of French and German books the grossest blunders are only too common. Figures are unaccountably skipped in numbering the pages; plates are either omitted or are so bunglingly numbered that it is hard to discover whether the quota is complete or not; title-pages are inserted in the wrong places; sheets are wrongly folded, bringing the succession of pages into dire confusion; sometimes two or three sheets are left out, and sometimes where a work in ten volumes is bound in five, you will find that the first of these contains two duplicate copies of Vol. I., while for any signs of a Vol. II. You may seek in vain. In all bungling of this kind, the Germans are worse than the French; but both are bad enough when contrasted with the English, either of the Old World or of the New. This work of collating is in general of lower grade than the work of cataloguing, and can be entrusted to the less experienced or less accomplished assistants; but to some extent it is shared by all, and where difficulties arise, or where some book with Arabic or Sanskrit numbering turns up, an appeal to headquarters becomes necessary. When a book has been collated, the date of its reception and the name of the fund to which it has been charged are written in pencil on the back of the title-page, and at the bottom of the title-page, to the left of the imprint, is written some modification of the letter C, C', C.,Cv, etc., which is the equivalent to the signature of the assistant who has done the collating and is responsible for its accuracy.

After this is all over, the books, still remaining grouped according to their "funds," are ready to have the "seals" put in. The seal is the label of ownership, bearing the seal of the university and the name of the fund or other source from which the book has been procured, and is pasted on the inside of the front cover. Above it, in the left corner, is pasted a little blank corner-piece, on which is to be marked in pencil the number of the alcove and shelf where the book is to be placed, or "set up."

To set up a book on a shelf is no doubt a very simple matter, yet it involves something more than the mere placing of the volume on the shelf. Each alcove in the library has a "shelf-catalogue," or list of all the books in the alcove arranged by shelves. Such a catalogue is indispensable in determining whether each shelf has its proper complement of volumes, and whether, at the end of the year, all the books are in their proper places. When the book is duly entered on this shelf-catalogue, and has its corner-piece marked, it is at last ready to be "catalogued." After our lot of three or four hundred books have been treated in this way, they are delivered to the principal assistant, who parcels them out among various subordinate assistants, for cataloguing.

Here we enter upon a very wide subject, and one that is not altogether easy to expound to the uninitiated. A brief historical note is needed, to begin with. In 1830 Harvard University published a printed catalogue (in two volumes, octavo) of all the works contained in its library at that date. In 1833 a supplement was published, containing all the accessions since 1830, and these made a moderate-sized volume. Here is the essential vice of printed catalogues. Where the number of books is fixed once for all—as in the case of a private library, the owner of which has just died, and which is to be sold at auction—nothing is easier than to make a perfect catalogue, whether of authors or of subjects. It is very different when your library is continually growing. By the time your printed catalogue is completed and published, it is already somewhat antiquated. Several hundred books have come in which are not comprised in it, and among these new books is very likely to be the one you wish to consult, concerning which the printed catalogue can give you no information. If you publish an annual supplement, as the Library of Congress does, then your catalogue will become desperately cumbrous within five or six years. When you are in a hurry to consult a book, it is very disheartening to have to look through half a dozen alphabets, besides depending after all on the ready memory of some library official as to the books which have come in since the last supplement was published. This inconvenience is so great that printed catalogues have gone into discredit in all the principal libraries of Europe. Catalogues are indeed printed, from time to time, by way of publishing the treasures of the library, and as bibliographical helps to other institutions; but for the use of those who daily consult the library, manuscript titles have quite superseded the printed catalogue. In European libraries this is done in what seems to us a rather crude way. Their catalogues are enormous brown paper blank-books or scrap-books, on the leaves of which are pasted thin paper slips bearing the titles of the books in the library. Large spaces are left for the insertion of subsequent titles in their alphabetical order; and as a result of this method, the admirable catalogue of the library of the British Museum fills more than a thousand elephant folios! An athletic man, who has served his time at base-ball and rowing, may think little of lifting these gigantic tomes, but for a lady who wishes to look up some subject on would think it desirable to employ a pair of oxen and a windlass. All the libraries of Western Europe which I have visited seem to have taken their cue from the British Museum. But in this country we have hit upon a less ponderous method. To accomplish this end of keeping our titles in their proper alphabetical order, we write them on separate cards, of stiff paper, and arrange these cards in little drawers, in such a way that any one, by opening the drawer and tilting the cards therein, can easily find the title for which he is seeking. Our new catalogue is a marvel of practical convenience in this respect. At each end the row of stiff cards is supported by beveled blocks, in such a way that some title lies always open to view; and by simply tilting the cards with the forefinger, any given title is quickly found, without raising the card from its place in the drawer.

In September, 1833, our library began its second supplement, consisting of two alphabetical manuscript catalogues. Volumes received after that date were catalogued upon stiff cards arranged in drawers, while pamphlets were catalogued, after the European fashion, on slips of paper pasted into the great folio scrap-books. This distinction between pamphlets and volumes was a most unhappy one. To a librarian the only practical difference between these two kinds of book is that the latter can generally be made to stand on a shelf, while the former generally tumbles down when unsupported. This physical fact makes it necessary to keep pamphlets in files by themselves until it is thought worth while to bind them. But for the purposes of cataloguing it makes no difference whether a book consists of twenty pages between paper covers or of five hundred pages bound in full calf. If you wish to find M.Léon de Rosny's Aperçu general des langues sémitiques, you do not care, and very likely do not know, whether it is a "pamphlet" of fifty pages or a "volume" of three hundred, and you naturally grumble at a system which sends you to a second alphabet in order to maintain a purely arbitrary and useless distinction. In practice this double catalogue was found to be so inconvenient that in 1850, after the pamphlet titles had come to fill eight cumbrous volumes, it was abandoned, and henceforth pamphlets, as well as maps and engravings, were placed on the same alphabet with bound volumes.

Before long, however, it began to be felt necessary to reform this whole cumbrous system. To ascertain whether a given work was contained in the library, one had now to consult four different alphabets—the old printed catalogue, the first or printed supplement, the second or card supplement, and the eight ugly folios of pamphlet titles. These later supplements, moreover, being accessible only to the librarian and his assistants, were of no use to the general public, who, for the 135,000 titles added since 1833, were obliged to get their information from some of the officials. To remedy this state of things, a new card catalogue, freely accessible to the public, and destined to embrace in a single alphabet all the titles in the library without distinction, was begun in 1861 by my predecessor, Prof. Ezra Abbot. This catalogue was not intended to supersede the private card supplement begun in 1833, which for many reasons it is found desirable to keep up. But for the use of the public it will, when finished, supersede everything else and become the sole authoritative catalogue of the library. Since 1861 all new accessions have been put into this catalogue, while the work of adding to it older titles has gone on with varying speed: in 1869 it came nearly to a stand-still, but was resumed in 1874, and is now proceeding with great rapidity. About fifty thousand titles of volumes, and as many more of pamphlets, still remain to be added before this new catalogue can become the index to all the treasures of the library.[2]

Another great undertaking was begun simultaneously in 1861. The object of an alphabetical catalogue like those above described is "to enable a person to determine readily whether any particular work belongs to the library, and, if it does, where it is placed." If you are in search of Lloyd's Lectures on the Wave-Theory of Light, you will look in the alphabetical catalogue under "LLOYD, Humphrey." Now this alphabetical arrangement is the only one practicable in a public library, because it is the only one on which all catalogue can be made to agree, and it is the only one sufficiently simple to be generally understood. For the purpose here required, of finding a particular work, an arrangement according to subject-matter would be entirely chimerical. Nothing short of omniscience could ever be sure of finding a given title amid such a heterogeneous multitude. Every man who can read knows the order of the alphabet, but not one in a thousand can be expected to master all the points that determine the arrangement of a catalogue of subjects—as, for example, why one of three kindred treatises should be classed under the rubric of Philosophy, another

---

[2] About seven thousand of these old titles were added during the year ending in July, 1876.

under Natural Religion, and a third under Dogmatic Theology.[3] But while it would thus be impracticable to place our final reliance on any other arrangement than an alphabetical one, it by no means follows that a subsidiary subject-catalogue is not extremely useful. He who knows that he wants Lloyd's book on the undulatory theory is somewhat more learned in the literature of optics than the majority of those who consult libraries. For one who knows as much as this, there are twenty who know only that they want to get some book about undulatory theory. Now a subject-catalogue is preeminently useful in instructing such people in the literature of the subject they are studying. They have only to open a drawer that is labeled "OPTICS," and run along the cards until they come to a division marked "OPTICS—Wave-Theory," and there they will find perhaps a dozen or fifty titles of books, pamphlets, review articles, and memoirs of learned societies, all bearing on their subject, and enabling them to look it up with a minimum of bibliographical trouble. Such a classified catalogue immeasurably increases the usefulness of a library to the general public. At the same time, the skillful classification of books presents so many difficulties and requires so much scientific and literary training that it adds greatly to the labor of catalogue-making. For this reason great libraries rarely attempt to make subject-catalogues. At every library which I visited in England, France, Germany, and Italy, I received the same answer: "We do not keep any subject-catalogue, for we shrink from so formidable an undertaking." With a boldness justified by the result, however, Professor Abbot began such a catalogue of the Harvard library in 1861, and carried out the work with the success that might have been expected from his prodigious knowledge and consummate ingenuity.

It is sometimes urged that, in deference to the feebleness of human memory, an ideal library should have yet a third catalogue, arranged alphabetically, not according to authors, but according to titles. This is to accommodate the man who knows that he wants Lectures on the Wave-Theory of Light, but has forgotten the author's name. In an "ideal" library this might perhaps be well. But in a real library, subject to the ordinary laws of nature, it is to be remembered that any serious addition to the amount of catalogue-room or to the labor of the librarian and assistants is an expense which can be justified only by the prospect of very decided advantages. In most cases, the subject-catalogue answers the purposes of those who

---

[3] See the excellent remarks of Professor Jevons, in his Principles of Science, ii. 401.

remember the title of a work but have forgotten the author. In the very heterogeneous classes of Drama and Fiction, where this is not so likely to be the case, the exigency is provided for in Professor Abbot's system by a full set of cross-references from titles to authors. From this account it will be seen that any new book received to-day by our library must be entered on three catalogues—first on the card supplement which continues the old printed catalogue, secondly on the new all-comprehensive alphabet of authors, thirdly on the classified index of subjects. In our technical slang the first of these catalogues is known under the collective name of "the long cards," the second as "the red cards," the third as "the blue cards"—names referring to the shape of the cards and to certain peculiarities of the lines with which they are ruled. When our lot of three or four hundred books is portioned out among half a dozen assistants to be catalogued, the first thing in order is to write the "long cards." Each book must have at least one long card; but most books need more than one, and some books need a great many. Suppose you have to catalogue Mr. Stuart-Glennie's newly published Pilgrim Memories. This is an exceedingly easy book for the cataloguer, but it requires two cards, because of the author's compound name. The book must be entered under "Stuart-Glennie," because that is the form in which the name appears on the title-page, and which the author is therefore supposed to prefer. It is very important, however, that a reference should be made from "Glennie" to "Stuart-Glennie," else some one, remembering only the last half of the name, would look in vain for "Glennie," and conclude that the book was not in the library. Suppose, again, that your book is Jevons on Money and the Mechanism of Exchange. This belongs to the International Scientific Series, and therefore needs to be entered under "Jevons," and again on the general card which bears the superscription "International Scientific Series." Without such a general entry, books are liable to be ordered and bought under one heading when they are already in the library and catalogued under the other heading. The risk of such a mishap is small in the case of the new and well-known series just mentioned, but it is considerable in the case of the different series of British State Papers, or the Scelta di Curiosita Italian; and of course one rule must be followed for all such cases. Suppose, again, that your book is Grimm's Deutsches Woerterbuch, begun by the illustrious Grimm, but continued by several other hands. Here you must obviously have a distinct entry for each collaborator, and each of these entries requires a card. In writing the long card, the first great point is to ascertain every jot and tittle of the author's name; and, as a general rule, title-pages are very poor helps toward settling this distressing question. For instance, you see from the title-pages of Money and Pilgrim Memories that the authors are "W. Stanley Jevons," and "John S. Stuart-Glennie;" but your duty as an accurate cataloguer is not fulfilled until you have ascertained what names the W. and S. stand for in these cases. In the alphabetical catalogue of a great library, it is a matter of the first practical importance that every name should be given the utmost completeness that the most extreme pedantry could suggest. No one who has not had experience in these matters can duly realize that the number of published books is so enormous as to occasion serious difficulty in keeping apart the titles of works by authors of the same name. "Stanley Jevons" and "Stuart-Glennie" are very uncommon combinations of names; yet the occurrence of two or three different authors in an alphabetical catalogue, bearing this uncommon combination of names, would not be at all surprising. Indeed—to say nothing of the immense number of accidental coincidences—I think we may lay it down as a large comprehensive sort of rule, that any man who has published a volume or pamphlet us sure to have relatives of the same name who have published volumes or pamphlets. Such a fact may have some value to people like Mr. Galton, who are interested in the subject of hereditary talent, and who have besides a keen eye for statistics. I have never tabulated the statistics of this matter, and am stating only a general impression, gathered from miscellaneous experience, when I say that the occurrence of almost any name in a list of authors affords a considerable probability of its re-occurrence, associated with some fact of blood-relationship. One would not be likely to realize this fact in collecting a large private library, because private libraries, however large, are apt to contain only the classical works of quite exceptional mean and less important works which happen to be specially interesting or useful to the owner. But in a public library the treasures and the rubbish of the literary world are alike hoarded; and the works of exceptional men whom everybody remembers are lumped in with the works of all their less distinguished cousins and great-uncles, whose names the world of readers has forgotten. A librarian has the opportunity for observing many curious facts of this sort, but he will seldom have leisure to speculate about them. For while a great library is an excellent place for study and reflection, for everybody except the librarian, his position is rather a tantalizing one. In the midst of the great ocean of books, it is "water, water, everywhere, and not a drop to drink." To make up for the extreme vagueness with which authors customarily designate themselves on their title-pages is the work of assistants who write the long cards, and it is apt to be a very tedious and troublesome undertaking. Biographical and bibliographical dictionaries, the catalogues of our own and other libraries, university—catalogues, army-lists, clerical directories, genealogies of the British peerage, almanacs, "conversations-lexicons," literary histories, and volumes of memoirs—all these aids have to be consulted, and too often are consulted in vain, or give conflicting testimony which serves to raise the most curious and perplexing questions. To the outside world such anxious minuteness seems useless pedantry; but any skeptic who should serve six months in a library would become convinced that without it an alphabetical catalogue would soon prove unmanageable. "Imagine the heading 'SMITH, J.,' in such a catalogue!" says Professor Abbott. Where a name very common, we are fain to add whatever distinctive epithet we can lay hold of; as in the case of six entries of "WILSON, William," which are differenced by the addition of "Scotch Covenanter," "poet, of London," "M.A., of Musselburgh," "of Poughkeepsie," "Vicar of Walthamstow," "Pres. Of the Warrington Nat. Hist. Soc."

New difficulties arise when the title-page leaves it doubtful whether the name upon it is that of the author, or that of an editor or compiler. The names of editors and translators are often omitted and must be sought in bibliographical dictionaries. Dedicatory epistles, biographical sketches, or introductory notices are often prefixed, signed with exasperating initials, for a clew to which you may perhaps spend an hour or two in fruitless inquiry. In accurate cataloguing, all such adjuncts to a book must be noticed, and often require distinct reference-cards. Curious difficulties are sometimes presented by the phenomena of compound or complex authorship, as in works like the Bollandist Acta Sanctorum, conducted by a group of men, some of whom are removed by death, while their places are supplied by new collaborators. Some other immense work, like Migne's Patrologiae Cursus Completus, will give rise to nice questions owing to the indefiniteness with which its various parts are demarcated from each other. Many German books, on the other hand, are troublesome from the excessive explicitness with which they are divided, with subtitles and sub—sub—titles innumerable, in accordance with some subtle principle not always to be detected at the first glance. The proper mode of entry for reports of legal cases and trials, periodicals, and publications of learned societies, governments, and boards of commissioners, is sure to call for more or less technical skill and practical determination. Anonymous and pseudonymous works are very common, and even the best bibliographical dictionaries cannot keep pace with the issue of them. Were we can find, by hook or by crook, the real name of the author of a pseudonymous work, it is entered under the real name, with a cross-reference from the pseudonym. Otherwise it is entered provisionally under the fictitious name, as, for example,

"VERITAS, pseudon." Anonymous works are entered under the first word of the title, neglecting particles; and the head-line is left blank, so that is the author is ever discovered, his name may be inserted there, enclosed within brackets. In former times it was customary for the cataloguer to enter such works under what he deemed to be the most important word of the title, or the word most likely to be remembered; but in practice this rule has been found to cause great confusion, since people are by no means sure to agree as to the most important word. To some it may seem absurd to enter an anonymous Treatise on the Best Methods of preparing Adhesive Mucilage under the word "Treatise" rather than under "Mucilage;" but it should be remembered that he who consults an alphabetical catalogue is supposed to know the tile for which he is looking. And, in our own library at least, any one who remembers only the subject of the work he is seeking can always refer to the catalogue of subjects.

To treat more extensively of such points as these, in which none but cataloguers are likely to feel a strong interest, would not be consistent with the purpose of this article. For those who wonder what a librarian can find to do with his time, enough hints have been given to show that the task of "just cataloguing a book" is not, perhaps, quite so simple as they may have supposed. These hints have nevertheless been chosen with reference to the easier portions of a librarian's work, for a description of the more intricate problems of cataloguing could hardly fail to be both tedious and unintelligible to the uninitiated reader.

Enough has been said to show that a cataloguer's work requires at the outset considerable judgment and discrimination, and a great deal of slow, plodding research. The facts which we take such pains to ascertain may seem petty when contrasted with the dazzling facts which are elicited by scientific researches. But in reality the grandest scientific truths are reached only after the minute scrutiny of facts which often seem very trivial. And though the little details which encumber a librarian's mind do not minister to grand or striking generalizations, though their destiny is in the main an obscure one, yet if they were not duly taken care of, the usefulness of libraries as aids to high culture and profound investigation would be fatally impaired. To the student's unaided faculties a great library is simply a trackless wilderness; the catalogue of such a library is itself a kind of wilderness; albeit much more readily penetrated and explored; but unless a book be entered with extreme accuracy and fullness on the catalogue, it is practically lost to the investigator who needs it, and might almost as well not be in the library at all.

In the task of entering a book properly on the alphabetical catalogue, the needful researchers are for the most part made by the assistants; but the questionable points are so numerous, and so unlike each other, that none of them can be considered as finally settled until approved at head-quarters. After the proper entry has been decided on, the work of transcribing the title is comparatively simple in most cases. The general rule is to copy the whole of the title with strict accuracy, in its own language and without translation, including even abbreviations and mistakes or oddities in spelling. Mottos and other really superfluous matters on the title-page are usually omitted, the omission being scrupulously indicated by points. As regards the use of capital letters, title-pages do not afford any consistent guidance, being usually printed in capitals throughout. Our own practice is to follow in capitalizing the usage of the language in which the title is written; but many libraries adopt the much simpler rule of rejecting capitals altogether except in the case of proper names, and this I believe to be practically the better because the easier method,[4] though the result may not seem quite so elegant. After the transcription of the entire title, the number of volumes, or other divisions of the book, is set down; and next in order follows the "imprint," or designation of the place and date of publication. Finally, the size of the books (whether folio, or quarto, octavo, etc.) is designated, after an examination of the "signature marks;" the number of pages (if less than one hundred or more than six hundred) is stated;[5] plates, wood-cuts, maps, plans, diagrams, photographs, etc. are counted and described in general terms. Any peculiarities relating not to the edition, but to the particular copy catalogued, are added below in a note; such as the fact that the book is one of fifty copies on large paper, or has the author's autograph on the fly-leaf. In many cases it is found desirable to add a list of the contents of the work; and if it be a book of miscellaneous essays, each essay often has an additional entry on a card of its own.[6]

These details make up the sum of what is entered on the body of the long card; but in addition to all this, the left-hand margin contains the date of reception of the book, the fund to which it is charged, or the name of the

---

[4] Since this article was written, I have adopted the simpler rule, applying the French system of capitalization to all languages, with the sole concession to our English prejudice of capitalizing proper adjectives in English titles. Much time is thereby saved, and much utterly useless vexation avoided.

[5] In order to point out books of exceptionally large or small size. I believe it would be better to state the number of pages in every case.

[6] Where the essays are by different authors, a separate entry for each is of course necessary, though this is not always made on the long cards.

donor, and the all-important "shelf-mark," which shows where the book is to be found; while on the right-hand margin is written a concise description of the appearance of the book (i.e., "5 vol., green cloth"), and a note of its price. When all this is finished, the book is regarded as catalogued, and is sent, with its card in it, to the principal assistant for revision. From the principal assistant it is passed on to me, and it is the business of both of us to see that all details of the work have been done correctly. A pencil-note on the margin of the card shows the class and sub-class to which the book is to be assigned in the catalogue of subjects; and then the card is separated from the book. The book goes on to its shelf, to be used by the public; the card goes back to some one of the assistants, to be "indexed." In our library-slang, "indexing" means the writing pf the "red" and "blue" cards which answer to the "long" card; in other words, the entry of the title[7] on the new alphabetical and subject catalogues begun in 1861. For the most part this is merely a matter of accurate transcription, requiring no research. When these "red" and "blue" cards have been submitted to a special assistant for proof-reading, they are returned to me, and after due inspection are ready to be distributed into their catalogues. But for the original "long card" one further preliminary is required before it can be put into its catalogue.

Besides the various catalogues above described, our library keeps a "record-book" or catalogue of accessions arranged according to dates of reception. This accessions-catalogue was begun October 1, 1827, and records an accession for that year of one volume, price ten shillings and sixpence! In 1828, according to this record, the library received twenty-one volumes, of which eighteen were gifts, while three were bought at a total cost of $14.50! But either these were exceptionally unfruitful years, or—what is more likely—the record was not carefully kept, for the ordinary rate of increase in those days was by no means so small as this, though small enough when compared with the present rate. The accessions-catalogue has grown until it now fills twenty-one large folio volumes. The entries in it are made with considerable fullness by transcription from the long cards. Usually a month's accessions are entered at once, and when this has been done the long card is ready to take its place in the catalogue.

In this account of the career of a book, from its reception to the time when it is duly entered on all the catalogues, we find some explanation of the way in which a librarian employs his time. For while the work of cataloguing is done almost entirely by assistants, yet unless every detail passes under the librarian's eye, there is no adequate security for systematic

---

[7] The marginal portions of the long card are not transcribed in indexing.

unity in the results. The librarian must not indeed spend his time in proof-reading or in verifying authors' names; it is essential that there should be some assistants who can be depended upon for absolute accuracy in such matters. Nevertheless, the complexity of the questions involved requires that appeal should often be made to him, and that he should always review the work for the correctness of which he is ultimately responsible. As for the designation of the proper entry on the subject-catalogue, the cases are rare in which this can be entrusted to any assistant.

To classify the subject-matter of a book is not always in itself easy, even when the reference is only to general principles of classification; but a subject-catalogue, once in existence, affords a vast mass of precedents which, while they may lighten the problem to one who has mastered the theory on which the catalogue is constructed, at the same time make it the more unmanageable to any one who has not done so. To assign to any title its proper position, you must not merely know what the book is about, but you must understand the reasons, philosophical and practical, which have determined the place to which such titles have already been assigned. It is a case in which no mere mechanical following of tradition is of any avail. No general rules can be laid down which a corps of assistants can follow; for in general each case presents new features of its own, so that to follow any rule securely would require a mental training almost as great as that needed for making the rule. Hence when different people work independently at a classified catalogue, they are sure to get into a muddle.

Suppose, for example, you have to classify a book on the constitution of Massachusetts. I put such books under the heading "LAW—Mass.—Const.," but another person would prefer "LAW—Const.—Mass.," a third would rank them under "LAW—U.S.—Const. § Mass.," a fourth under "LAW—U.S. (Separate States), § Mass.—Const.," a fifth under "LAW—Const. § U.S.—Mass.," and so on, through all the permutations and combinations of which these terms are susceptible. Yet each of these arrangements would bring the title into a different part of the catalogue, so that it would be quite impossible to discover, by simple inspection, what the library contained on the subject of constitutional law in Massachusetts; and to this extent the catalogue would become useless. Many such defects are now to be found in our subject-catalogue, greatly to the impairment of its usefulness; and they prove conclusively that the work of classifying must always be left to a single superintendent who knows well the idiosyncrasies of the catalogue. This work consumes no little time. The titles of books are by no means a safe index to their subject-matter. To treat one properly you must first peer into its contents; and then no matter how excellent your memory, you will often have to run to the catalogue for precedents. As a rule, comparatively few cards are written by the librarian or principal assistant. Only the most difficult books, which no one else can catalogue, are brought to the superintendent's desk. Under this class come old manuscripts, early printed books without title-pages, books with Greek titles, and books in Slavonic, or Oriental, or barbarous languages. Early printed books require special and varying kinds of treatment, and need to be carefully described with the aid of such dictionaries as those of Hain, Panzer, and Graesse. One such book may afford work for a whole day. An old manuscript is likely to give even more trouble. There is nothing especially difficult in Greek titles, save for the fact that our assistants are all women, who for the most part know little or nothing of the language.[8] In general these assistants are acquainted with French, and with practice can make their way through titles in Latin and German. There are some who can deal with any Romanic or Teutonic language, though more or less advice is usually needed for this. But all languages east of the Roman-German boundary require the eye of a practiced linguist. To decipher a title, or part of a preface, in a strange language, it is necessary that one should understand the character in which it is printed, and should be able to consult some dictionary either of the language in question or of some closely related dialect. One day I had to catalogue a book of Croatian ballads, and, not finding any Croatian dictionary in the library, set up a cross-fire on it with the help of a Servian and a Slovenian dictionary.

This served the purpose admirably, for where a cognate word did not happen to occur in the one language it was pretty sure to turn up in the other. Sometimes—in the case, say, of a hundred Finnish pamphlets the labor is greater than it is worth while to undertake; or somebody may give us a volume in Chinese or Tamil, which is practically undecipherable. In such cases we consider discretion the better part of valor, and under the heading "FINNISH" or "CHINESE" write "One hundred Finnish pamphlets," or "A Chinese book," trusting to the future for better information. Sometimes a polyglot visitor from Asia happens in, and is kind enough to settle a dozen such knotty questions at once.

Another part of a librarian's work is the ordering of new books, and this is something which cannot be done carelessly. Once a year a council of professors, after learning the amount of money that can be expended during the year, decides upon the amounts that may be severally appropriated to

---

[8] We have since, I am glad to say, found an exception to this rule, and Greek titles are now disposed of in regular course.

the various departments of literature. Long lists of desiderata are then prepared by different professors, and handed in to the library. Besides this a considerable sum is placed under the control of the librarian, for miscellaneous purchases, and any one who wishes a book bought at any time is expected to leave a written request for it at my desk. As often as we get materials for a list of two or three hundred titles, the list is given, before it is sent off, to one of our most trustworthy assistants, to be compared with the various catalogues as well as with the record of outstanding orders. To ascertain whether a particular work is in the library, or on its way thither, may seem to be a very simple matter; but it requires careful and intelligent research, and on such a point no one's opinion is worth a groat, who is not versed in all the dark and crooked ways of cataloguing. The fact that a card-title is not to be found in the catalogue proves nothing of itself, for very likely the card may be "out" in the hands of some assistant. Nothing is more common than for a professor to order some well-known work in his own department of study which has been in the library for several years, and so long as the art of cataloguing is as complicated as it now is, such misunderstandings cannot be altogether avoided. Very often this is due to the variety of ways in which one and the same book may be described, and cannot be ascribed to any special cumbrousness or complexity of our system. All this necessitates a thorough scrutiny of every title that is ordered, for to waste the library's money in buying duplicates is a blunder of the first magnitude. Yet in spite of the utmost vigilance, it is seldom that a case of two or three hundred books arrives which does not contain two or three duplicates. One per cent. Is perhaps not an extravagant allowance to make for human perversity, in any of the affairs of life in which the ideal standard is that of complete intelligence and efficiency.

The danger of buying a duplicate because a card-title does not happen to be in its place is one illustration of the practical inconvenience of card-catalogues. The experience of the past fifty years has shown that on the whole such catalogues are far better than the old ones which they have superseded; but they have their short-comings, nevertheless, and here we have incidentally hit upon one of them. Besides this, a card-catalogue, even when constructed with all the ingenuity that is displayed in our own, is very much harder to consult than a catalogue that is printed in a volume. On a printed page you can glance at twenty titles at once, whereas is a drawer of cards you must plod through the titles one by one. Moreover, a card-catalogue occupies an enormous space. Professor Abbot's twin catalogue of authors and subjects, begun fourteen years ago, is already fifty-one feet in length, and contains three hundred and thirty-six drawers! During the past six weeks some four thousand cards have been added to it. What will its dimensions be a century hence, when our books will probably have begun to be numbered by millions instead of thousands? Gore Hall is to-day too small to contain our books: will it then be large enough to hold the catalogue? Suppose, again, that our library were to be burned; it is disheartening to think of the quantity of bibliographic work that would in such an event be forever obliterated. For we should remember that while a catalogue like ours is primarily useful in enabling persons to consult our books, it would still be of great value, as a bibliographical aid to other libraries, even if all our own books were to be destroyed.[9] This part of its function, moreover, it cannot properly fulfill even now, so long as it can be consulted only in Gore Hall. Our subject-catalogue, if printed to-day, would afford a noble conspectus of the literature of many great departments of human knowledge, and would have no small value to many special inquirers. Much of this usefulness is lost so long as it remains in manuscript, confined to a single locality.

For such reasons as these, I believe that the card-system is but a temporary or transitional expedient, upon which we cannot always continue to rely exclusively. By the time Professor Abbot's great catalogue is finished (i.e., brought up to date) and thoroughly revised, it will be on all accounts desirable to print it. The huge mass of cards up to that date will then be superseded, and might be destroyed without detriment to any one. But the card-catalogue, kept in accordance with the present system, would continue as a supplement to the printed catalogue. The cumbrousness of consulting a number of alphabets would be reduced to a minimum, for there would be only two to consult" the printed catalogue and its card-supplement. Then, instead of issuing numberless printed supplements, there might be published, at stated intervals (say of ten years), a new edition of the main catalogue, with all the added titles inserted in their proper place. On this plan there would never be more than two alphabets to consult; and of these the more voluminous one would be contained in easily manageable printed volumes, while the smaller supplement only would remain in card-form.

It is an obvious objection that the frequent printing of new editions of the catalogue, according to this plan, would be attended with enormous expense. This objection would at first sight seem to be removed if we were to adopt Professor Jewett's suggestion, and stereotype each title on a

---

[9] Thus I often find valuable information in the printed catalogue of the Bodleian Library, and wish that the splendid catalogue of the million books in the British Museum were as readily accessible.

separate plate. Let there be a separate stereotype-plate for each card, so that in every new edition new plates may be inserted for the added titles; and then the ruinous expense of fresh composition for every new edition would seem to be avoided. It is to be feared, however, that this show of having solved the difficulty is illusory. For to keep such a quantity of printer's metal lying idle year after year would of itself entail great trouble and expense. The plates would take up a great deal of room and would need to be kept in a fireproof building; and the interest lost each year on the value of the metal would by and by amount to a formidable sum. It is perhaps doubtful whether, in the long run, anything would be saved by this cumbrous method. Possibly—unless some future heliographical invention should turn to our profit—the least expensive way, after all, may be to print at long intervals, without stereotyping, and to depend throughout the intervals on card-supplements. But this question, like many others suggested by the formidable modern growth of literature, is easier to ask than to answer.

In this hasty sketch many points connected with a librarian's work remain unmentioned. But in a brief article like this, one cannot expect to give a complete account of a subject embracing so many details. As it is, I hope I have not wearied the reader in the attempt to show what a librarian finds to do with his time.

John Fiske.

Boston Medical Library Dedicatory Address

From *Medical Essays*—1842-1882, by Oliver Wendell Holmes, Sr. (The physician and poet, not the jurist O. W. Holmes, Jr.).

Dedicatory Address at the opening of the Medical Library in Boston, December 3, 1878.

It is my appointed task, my honorable privilege, this evening, to speak of what has been done by others. No one can bring his tribute of words into the presence of great deeds, or try with them to embellish the memory of any inspiring achievement, without feeling and leaving with others a sense of their insufficiency. So felt Alexander when he compared even his adored Homer with the hero the poet had sung. So felt Webster when he contrasted the phrases of rhetoric with the eloquence of patriotism and of self-devotion. So felt Lincoln when on the field of Gettysburg he spoke those immortal words which Pericles could not nave bettered, which Aristotle could not have criticised. So felt he who wrote the epitaph of the builder of the dome which looks down on the crosses and weathercocks that glitter over London. We are not met upon a battle-field, except so far as every laborious achievement means a victory over opposition, indifference, selfishness, fainheartedness, and that great property of mind as well as matter—inertia. We are not met in a cathedral, except so far as every building whose walls are lined with the products of useful and ennobling thought is a temple of the Almighty, whose inspiration has given us understanding. But we have gathered within walls which bear testimony to the self-sacrificing, persevering efforts of a few young men, to whom we owe the origin and development of all that excites our admiration in this completed enterprise; and I might consider my task as finished if I contented myself with borrowing the last word of the architect's epitaph and only saying, Look around you!

The reports of the librarian have told or will tell you, in some detail, what has been accomplished since the 21st of December, 1874, when six gentlemen met at the house of Dr. Henry Ingersoll Bowditch to discuss different projects for a medical library. In less than four years from that time, by the liberality of associations and of individuals, this collection of nearly ten thousand volumes, of five thousand pamphlets, and of one hundred and twenty-five journals, regularly received—all worthily sheltered beneath this lofty roof—has come into being under our eyes. It has sprung up, as it were; in the night like a mushroom; it stands before us in full daylight as lusty as an oak, and promising to grow and flourish in the perennial freshness of an evergreen.

To whom does our profession owe this already large collection of books, exceeded in numbers only by four or five of the most extensive medical libraries in the country, and lodged in a building so well adapted to its present needs? We will not point out individually all those younger members of the profession who have accomplished what their fathers and elder brethren had attempted and partially achieved. We need not write their names on these walls, after the fashion of those civic dignitaries who immortalize themselves on tablets of marble and gates of iron. But their contemporaries know them well, and their descendants will not forget them—the men who first met together, the men who have given their time and their money, the faithful workers, worthy associates of the strenuous agitator who gave no sleep to his eyes, no slumber to his eyelids, until he had gained his ends; the untiring, imperturbable, tenacious, irrepressible, all-subduing agitator who neither rested nor let others rest until the success of the project was assured. If, against his injunctions, I name Dr. James Read Chadwick, it is only my revenge for his having kept me awake so often and so long while he was urging on the undertaking in which he has been preeminently active and triumphantly successful. We must not forget the various medical libraries which preceded this: that of an earlier period, when Boston contained about seventy regular practitioners, the collection afterwards transferred to the Boston Athenaeum; the two collections belonging to the University; the Treadwell Library at the Massachusetts General Hospital; the collections of the two societies, that for Medical Improvement and that for Medical Observation; and more especially the ten thousand volumes relating to medicine belonging to our noble public city library—too many blossoms on the tree of knowledge, perhaps, for the best fruit to ripen. But the Massachusetts Medical Society now numbers nearly four hundred members in the city of Boston. The time had arrived for a new and larger movement. There was needed a place to which every respectable member of the medical profession could obtain easy access; where, under one roof, all might find the special information they were seeking; where the latest medical intelligence should be spread out daily as the shipping news is posted on the bulletins of the exchange; where men engaged in a common pursuit could meet, surrounded by the mute oracles of science and art; where the whole atmosphere should be as full of professional knowledge as the apothecary's shop is of the odor of his medicaments. This was what the old men longed for—the prophets and kings of the profession, who

> "Desired it long,
> But died without the sight."

This is what the young men and those who worked under their guidance undertook to give us. And now such a library, such a reading-room, such an exchange, such an intellectual and social meeting place, we be hold a fact, plain before us. The medical profession of our city, and, let us add, of all those neighboring places which it can reach with its iron arms, is united as never before by the commune vinculum, the common bond of a large, enduring, ennobling, unselfish interest. It breathes a new air of awakened intelligence. It marches abreast of the other learned professions, which have long had their extensive and valuable centralized libraries; abreast of them, but not promising to be content with that position. What glorifies a town like a cathedral? What dignifies a province like a university? What illuminates a country like its scholarship, and what is the nest that hatches scholars but a library? The physician, some may say, is a practical man and has little use for all this book-learning. Every student has heard Sydenham's reply to Sir Richard Blackmore's question as to what books he should read—meaning medical books. "Read Don Quixote," was his famous answer. But Sydenham himself made medical books and may be presumed to have thought those at least worth reading. Descartes was asked where was his library, and in reply held up the dissected body of an animal. But Descartes made books, great books, and a great many of them. A physician of common sense without erudition is better than a learned one without common sense, but the thorough master of his profession must have learning added to his natural gifts.

It is not necessary to maintain the direct practical utility of all kinds of learning. Our shelves contain many books which only a certain class of medical scholars will be likely to consult. There is a dead medical literature, and there is a live one. The dead is not all ancient, the live is not all modern. There is none, modern or ancient, which, if it has no living value for the student, will not teach him something by its autopsy. But it is with the live literature of his profession that the medical practitioner is first of all concerned. Now there has come a great change in our time over the form in which living thought presents itself. The first printed books—the incunabula—were inclosed in boards of solid oak, with brazen clasps and corners; the boards by and by were replaced by pasteboard covered with calf or sheepskin; then cloth came in and took the place of leather; then the pasteboard was covered with paper instead of cloth; and at this day the quarterly, the monthly, the weekly periodical in its flimsy unsupported dress of paper, and the daily journal, naked as it came from the womb of the press, hold the larger part of the fresh reading we live upon. We must have the latest thought in its latest expression; the page must be newly turned like the morning bannock; the pamphlet must be newly opened like the anteprandial oyster.

Thus a library, to meet the need of our time, must take, and must spread out in a convenient form, a great array of periodicals. Our active practitioners read these by preference over almost everything else. Our specialists, more particularly, depend on the month's product, on the yearly crop of new facts, new suggestions, new contrivances, as much as the farmer on the annual yield of his acres. One of the first wants, then, of the profession is supplied by our library in its great array of periodicals from many lands, in many languages. Such a number of medical periodicals no private library would have room for, no private person would pay for, or flood his tables with if they were sent him for nothing. These, I think, with the reports of medical societies and the papers contributed to them, will form the most attractive part of our accumulated medical treasures. They will be also one of our chief expenses, for these journals must be bound in volumes and they require a great amount of shelf-room; all this, in addition to the cost of subscription for those which are not furnished us gratuitously.

It is true that the value of old scientific periodicals is, other things being equal, in the inverse ratio of their age, for the obvious reason that what is most valuable in the earlier volumes of a series is drained off into the standard works with which the intelligent practitioner is supposed to be familiar. But no extended record of facts grows too old to be useful, provided only that we have a ready and sure way of getting at the particular fact or facts we are in search of. And this leads me to speak of what I conceive to be one of the principal tasks to be performed by the present and the coming generation of scholars, not only in the medical, but in every department of knowledge. I mean the formation of indexes, and more especially of indexes to periodical literature.

This idea has long been working in the minds of scholars, and all who have had occasion to follow out any special subject. I have a right to speak of it, for I long ago attempted to supply the want of indexes in some small measure for my own need. I had a very complete set of the "American Journal of the Medical Sciences;" an entire set of the "North American Review," and many volumes of the reprints of the three leading British quarterlies. Of what use were they to me without general indexes? I looked them all through carefully and made classified lists of all the articles I thought I should most care to read. But they soon outgrew my lists. The "North American Review" kept filling up shelf after shelf, rich in articles which I often wanted to consult, but what a labor to find them, until the index of Mr. Gushing, published a few months since, made the contents of these hundred and twenty volumes as easily accessible as the words in a dictionary! I had a, copy of good Dr. Abraham Rees's Cyclopaedia, a treasure-house to my boyhood which has not lost its value for me in later years. But where to look for what I wanted? I wished to know, for instance, what Dr. Burney had to say about singing. Who would have looked for it under the Italian word cantare? I was curious to learn something of the etchings of Rembrandt, and where should I find it but under the head "Low Countries, Engravers of the," an elaborate and most valuable article of a hundred double-columned close-printed quarto pages, to which no reference, even, is made under the title Rembrandt. There was nothing to be done, if I wanted to know where that which I specially cared for was to be found in my Rees's Cyclopaedia, but to look over every page of its forty-one quarto volumes and make out a brief list of matters of interest which I could not find by their titles, and this I did, at no small expense of time and trouble.

Nothing, therefore, could be more pleasing to me than to see the attention which has been given of late years to the great work of indexing. It is a quarter of a century since Mr. Poole published his "Index to Periodical Literature," which it is much to be hoped is soon to appear in a new edition, grown as it must be to formidable dimensions by the additions of so long a period. The "British and Foreign Medical Review," edited by the late Sir John Forties, contributed to by Huxley, Carpenter, Laycock, and others of the most distinguished scientific men of Great Britain, has an index to its twenty-four volumes, and by its aid I find this valuable series as manageable as a lexicon. The last edition of the "Encyclopaedia Britannica" had a complete index in a separate volume, and the publishers of Appletons' "American Cyclopaedia" have recently issued an index to their useful work, which must greatly add to its value. I have already referred to the index to the "North American Review," which to an American, and especially to a New Englander, is the most interesting and most valuable addition of its kind to our literary apparatus since the publication of Mr. Allibone's "Dictionary of Authors." I might almost dare to parody Mr. Webster's words in speaking of Hamilton, to describe what Mr. Gushing did for the solemn rows of back volumes of our honored old Review which had been long fossilizing on our shelves: "He touched the dead corpse of the 'North

American,' and it sprang to its feet." A library of the best thought of the best American scholars during the greater portion of the century was brought to light by the work of the indexmaker as truly as were the Assyrian tablets by the labors of Layard. A great portion of the best writing and reading literary, scientific, professional, miscellaneous, comes to us now, at stated intervals, in paper covers. The writer appears, as it were, in his shirt-sleeves. As soon as he has delivered his message the book-binder puts a coat on his back, and he joins the forlorn brotherhood of "back volumes," than which, so long as they are unindexed, nothing can be more exasperating. Who wants a lock without a key, a ship without a rudder, a binnacle without a compass, a check without a signature, a greenback without a goldback behind it?

I have referred chiefly to the medical journals, but I would include with these the reports of medical associations, and those separate publications which, coming in the form of pamphlets, heap themselves into chaotic piles and bundles which are worse than useless, taking up a great deal of room, and frightening everything away but mice and mousing antiquarians, or possibly at long intervals some terebrating specialist. Arranged, bound, indexed, all these at once become accessible and valuable. I will take the first instance which happens to suggest itself. How many who know all about osteoblasts and the experiments of Ollier, and all that has grown out of them, know where to go for a paper by the late Dr. A. L. Peirson of Salem, published in the year 1840, under the modest title, Remarks on Fractures? And if any practitioner who has to deal with broken bones does not know that most excellent and practical essay, it is a great pity, for it answers very numerous questions which will be sure to suggest themselves to the surgeon and the patient as no one of the recent treatises, on my own shelves, at least, can do.

But if indexing is the special need of our time in medical literature, as in every department of knowledge, it must be remembered that it is not only an immense labor, but one that never ends. It requires, therefore, the cooperation of a large number of individuals to do the work, and a large amount of money to pay for making its results public through the press. When it is remembered that the catalogue of the library of the British Museum is contained in nearly three thousand large folios of manuscript, and not all its books are yet included, the task of indexing any considerable branch of science or literature looks as if it were well nigh impossible. But many hands make light work. An "Index Society" has been formed in England, already numbering about one hundred and seventy members. It aims at "supplying thorough indexes to valuable works and collections which have hitherto lacked them; at issuing indexes to the literature of special subjects; and at gathering materials for a general reference index." This society has published a little treatise setting forth the history and the art of indexing, which I trust is in the hands of some of our members, if not upon our shelves. Something has been done in the same direction by individuals in our own country, as we have already seen. The need of it in the department of medicine is beginning to be clearly felt. Our library has already an admirable catalogue with cross references, the work of a number of its younger members cooperating in the task. A very intelligent medical student, Mr. William D. Chapin, whose excellent project is indorsed by well-known New York physicians and professors, proposes to publish a yearly index to original communications in the medical journals of the United States, classified by authors and subjects. But it is from the National Medical Library at Washington that we have the best promise and the largest expectations. That great and growing collection of fifty thousand volumes is under the eye and hand of a librarian who knows books and how to manage them. For libraries are the standing armies of civilization, and an army is but a mob without a general who can organize and marshal it so as to make it effective. The "Specimen Fasciculus of a Catalogue of the National Medical Library," prepared under the direction of Dr. Billings, the librarian, would have excited the admiration of Haller, the master scholar in medical science of the last century, or rather of the profession in all centuries, and if carried out as it is begun will be to the nineteenth all and more than all that the three Bibliothecae—Anatomica, Chirurgica, and Medicinae-Practicae—were to the eighteenth century. I cannot forget the story that Agassiz was so fond of telling of the king of Prussia and Fichte. It was after the humiliation and spoliation of the kingdom by Napoleon that the monarch asked the philosopher what could be done to regain the lost position of the nation. "Found a great university, Sire," was the answer, and so it was that in the year 1810 the world-renowned University of Berlin came into being. I believe that we in this country can do better than found a national university, whose professors shall be nominated in caucuses, go in and out, perhaps, like postmasters, with every change of administration, and deal with science in the face of their constituency as the courtier did with time when his sovereign asked him what o'clock it was: "Whatever hour your majesty pleases." But when we have a noble library like that at Washington, and a librarian of exceptional qualifications like the gentleman who now holds that office, I believe that a liberal appropriation by Congress to carry out a conscientious work for the advancement of sound knowledge and the bettering of human conditions, like this which Dr. Billings has so well begun, would redound greatly to the honor of the nation. It ought to be willing to be at some charge to make its treasures useful to its citizens, and, for its own sake, especially to that class which has charge of health, public and private. This country abounds in what are called "self-made men," and is justly proud of many whom it thus designates. In one sense no man is self-made who breathes the air of a civilized community. In another sense every man who is anything other than a phonograph on legs is self-made. But if we award his just praise to the man who has attained any kind of excellence without having had the same advantages as others whom, nevertheless, he has equalled or surpassed, let us not be betrayed into undervaluing the mechanic's careful training to his business, the thorough and laborious education of the scholar and the professional man.

Our American atmosphere is vocal with the flippant loquacity of half knowledge. We must accept whatever good can be got out of it, and keep it under as we do sorrel and mullein and witchgrass, by enriching the soil, and sowing good seed in plenty; by good teaching and good books, rather than by wasting our time in talking against it. Half knowledge dreads nothing but whole knowledge.

I have spoken of the importance and the predominance of periodical literature, and have attempted to do justice to its value. But the almost exclusive reading of it is not without its dangers. The journals contain much that is crude and unsound; the presumption; it might be maintained, is against their novelties, unless they come from observers of established credit. Yet I have known a practitioner—perhaps more than one—who was as much under the dominant influence of the last article he had read in his favorite medical journal as a milliner under the sway of the last fashion plate. The difference between green and seasoned knowledge is very great, and such practitioners never hold long enough to any of their knowledge to have it get seasoned.

It is needless to say, then, that all the substantial and permanent literature of the profession should be represented upon our shelves. Much of it is there already, and as one private library after another falls into this by the natural law of gravitation, it will gradually acquire all that is most valuable almost without effort. A scholar should not be in a hurry to part with his books. They are probably more valuable to him than they can be to any other individual. What Swedenborg called "correspondence" has established itself between his intelligence and the volumes which wall him within their sacred enclosure. Napoleon said that his mind was as if furnished with drawers—he drew out each as he wanted its contents, and closed it at will when done with them. The scholar's mind, to use a similar comparison, is furnished with shelves, like his library. Each book knows its place in the brain as well as against the wall or in the alcove. His consciousness is doubled by the books which encircle him, as the trees that surround a lake repeat themselves in its unruffled waters. Men talk of the nerve that runs to the pocket, but one who loves his books, and has lived long with them, has a nervous filament which runs from his sensorium to every one of them. Or, if I may still let my fancy draw its pictures, a scholar's library is to him what a temple is to the worshipper who frequents it. There is the altar sacred to his holiest experiences. There is the font where his new-born thought was baptized and first had a name in his consciousness. There is the monumental tablet of a dead belief, sacred still in the memory of what it was while yet alive. No visitor can read all this on the lettered backs of the books that have gathered around the scholar, but for him, from the Aldus on the lowest shelf to the Elzevir on the highest, every volume has a language which none but be can interpret. Be patient with the book collector who loves his companions too well to let them go. Books are not buried with their owners, and the veriest book-miser that ever lived was probably doing far more for his successors than his more liberal neighbor who despised his learned or unlearned avarice. Let the fruit fall with the leaves still clinging round it. Who would have stripped Southey's walls of the books that filled them, when, his mind no longer capable of taking in their meaning, he would still pat and fondle them with the vague loving sense of what they had once been to him—to him, the great scholar, now like a little child among his playthings?

We need in this country not only the scholar, but the virtuoso, who hoards the treasures which he loves, it may be chiefly for their rarity and because others who know more than he does of their value set a high price upon them. As the wine of old vintages is gently decanted out of its cobwebbed bottles with their rotten corks into clean new receptacles, so the wealth of the New World is quietly emptying many of the libraries and galleries of the Old World into its newly formed collections and newly raised edifices. And this process must go on in an accelerating ratio. No Englishman will be offended if I say that before the New Zealander takes his stand on a broken arch of London Bridge to sketch the ruins of St. Paul's in the midst of a vast solitude, the treasures of the British Museum will have found a new shelter in the halls of New York or Boston. No Catholic will think hardly of my saying that before the Coliseum falls, and with it the imperial city, whose doom prophecy has linked with that of the almost eternal amphitheatre, the marbles, the bronzes, the paintings, the manuscripts of the Vatican will have left the shores of the Tiber for those of the Potomac, the Hudson, the Mississippi, or the Sacramento. And what a delight in the pursuit of the rarities which the eager book-hunter follows with the scent of a beagle! Shall I ever forget that rainy day in Lyons, that dingy bookshop, where I found the Aetius, long missing from my Artis bledicae Principes, and where I bought for a small pecuniary consideration, though it was marked rare, and was really tres rare, the Aphorisms of Hippocrates, edited by and with a preface from the hand of Francis Rabelais? And the vellum-bound Tulpius, which I came upon in Venice, afterwards my only reading when imprisoned in quarantine at Marseilles, so that the two hundred and twenty-eight cases he has recorded are, many of them, to this day still fresh in my memory. And the Schenckius—the folio filled with casus rariores, which had strayed in among the rubbish of the bookstall on the boulevard—and the noble old Vesalius with its grand frontispiece not unworthy of Titian, and the fine old Ambroise Pare, long waited for even in Paris and long ago, and the colossal Spigelius with his eviscerated beauties, and Dutch Bidloo with its miracles of fine engraving and bad dissection, and Italian Mascagni, the despair of all would-be imitators, and pre-Adamite John de Ketam, and antediluvian Berengarius Carpensis—but why multiply names, every one of which brings back the accession of a book which was an event almost like the birth of an infant? A library like ours must exercise the largest hospitality. A great many books may be found in every large collection which remind us of those apostolic looking old men who figure on the platform at our political and other assemblages. Some of them have spoken words of wisdom in their day, but they have ceased to be oracles; some of them never had any particularly important message for humanity, but they add dignity to the meeting by their presence; they look wise, whether they are so or not, and no one grudges them their places of honor. Venerable figure-heads, what would our platforms be without you?

Just so with our libraries. Without their rows of folios in creamy vellum, or showing their black backs with antique lettering of tarnished gold, our shelves would look as insufficient and unbalanced as a column without its base, as a statue without its pedestal. And do not think they are kept only to be spanked and dusted during that dreadful period when their owner is but too thankful to become an exile and a wanderer from the scene of single combats between dead authors and living housemaids. Men were not all cowards before Agamemnon or all fools before the days of Virchow and Billroth. And apart from any practical use to be derived from the older medical authors, is there not a true pleasure in reading the accounts of great discoverers in their own words? I do not pretend to hoist up the Bibliotheca

Anatomica of Mangetus and spread it on my table every day. I do not get out my great Albinus before every lecture on the muscles, nor disturb the majestic repose of Vesalius every time I speak of the bones he has so admirably described and figured. But it does please me to read the first descriptions of parts to which the names of their discoverers or those who have first described them have become so joined that not even modern science can part them; to listen to the talk of my old volume as Willis describes his circle and Fallopius his aqueduct and Varolius his bridge and Eustachius his tube and Monro his foramen—all so well known to us in the human body; it does please me to know the very words in which Winslow described the opening which bears his name, and Glisson his capsule and De Graaf his vesicle; I am not content until I know in what language Harvey announced his discovery of the circulation, and how Spigelius made the liver his perpetual memorial, and Malpighi found a monument more enduring than brass in the corpuscles of the spleen and the kidney.

But after all, the readers who care most for the early records of medical science and art are the specialists who are dividing up the practice of medicine and surgery as they were parcelled out, according to Herodotus, by the Egyptians. For them nothing is too old, nothing is too new, for to their books of ail others is applicable the saying of D'Alembert that the author kills himself in lengthening out what the reader kills himself in trying to shorten.

There are practical books among these ancient volumes which can never grow old. Would you know how to recognize "male hysteria" and to treat it, take down your Sydenham; would you read the experience of a physician who was himself the subject of asthma, and who, notwithstanding that, in the words of Dr. Johnson, "panted on till ninety," you will find it in the venerable treatise of Sir John Floyer; would you listen to the story of the King's Evil cured by the royal touch, as told by a famous chirurgeon who fully believed in it, go to Wiseman; would you get at first hand the description of the spinal disease which long bore his name, do not be startled if I tell you to go to Pott—to Percival Pott, the great surgeon of the last century.

There comes a time for every book in a library when it is wanted by somebody. It is but a few weeks since one of the most celebrated physicians in the country wrote to me from a great centre of medical education to know if I had the works of Sanctorius, which he had tried in vain to find. I could have lent him the "Medicina Statica," with its frontispiece showing Sanctorius with his dinner on the table before him, in his balanced chair which sunk with him below the level of his banquet-board when he had swallowed a certain number of ounces—an early foreshadowing of Pettenkofer's chamber and quantitative physiology—but the "Opera Omnia" of Sanctorius I had never met with, and I fear he had to do without it.

I would extend the hospitality of these shelves to a class of works which we are in the habit of considering as being outside of the pale of medical science, properly so called, and sometimes of coupling with a disrespectful name. Such has always been my own practice. I have welcomed Culpeper and Salmon to my bookcase as willingly as Dioscorides or Quincy, or Paris or Wood and Bache. I have found a place for St. John Long, and read the story of his trial for manslaughter with as much interest as the laurel-water case in which John Hunter figured as a witness. I would give Samuel Hahnemann a place by the side of Samuel Thomson. Am I not afraid that some student of imaginative turn and not provided with the needful cerebral strainers without which all the refuse of gimcrack intelligences gets into the mental drains and chokes them up—am I not afraid that some such student will get hold of the "Organon" or the "Maladies Chroniques" and be won over by their delusions, and so be lost to those that love him as a man of common sense and a brother in their high calling? Not in the least. If he showed any symptoms of infection I would for once have recourse to the principle of similia similibus. To cure him of Hahnemann I would prescribe my favorite homoeopathic antidote, Okie's Bonninghausen. If that failed, I would order Grauvogl as a heroic remedy, and if he survived that uncured, I would give him my blessing, if I thought him honest, and bid him depart in peace. For me he is no longer an individual. He belongs to a class of minds which we are bound to be patient with if their Maker sees fit to indulge them with existence. We must accept the conjuring ultra-ritualist, the dreamy second adventist, the erratic spiritualist, the fantastic homoeopathist, as not unworthy of philosophic study; not more unworthy of it than the squarers of the circle and the inventors of perpetual motion, and the other whimsical visionaries to whom De Morgan has devoted his most instructive and entertaining "Budget of Paradoxes." I hope, therefore, that our library will admit the works of the so-called Eclectics, of the Thomsonians, if any are in existence, of the Clairvoyants, if they have a literature, and especially of the Homoeopathists. This country seems to be the place for such collection, which will by and by be curious and of more value than at present, for Homoeopathy seems to be following the pathological law of erysipelas, fading out where it originated as it spreads to new regions. At least I judge so by the following translated extract from a criticism of an American work in the "Homoeopatische Rundschau" of

Leipzig for October, 1878, which I find in the "Homoeopathic Bulletin" for the month of November just passed: "While we feel proud of the spread and rise of Homoeopathy across the ocean, and while the Homoeopathic works reaching us from there, and published in a style such as is unknown in Germany, bear eloquent testimony to the eminent activity of our transatlantic colleagues, we are overcome by sorrowful regrets at the position Homoeopathy occupies in Germany. Such a work [as the American one referred to] with us would be impossible; it would lack the necessary support."

By all means let our library secure a good representation of the literature of Homoeopathy before it leaves us its "sorrowful regrets" and migrates with its sugar of milk pellets, which have taken the place of the old pilulae micae panis, to Alaska, to "Nova Zembla, or the Lord knows where."

What shall I say in this presence of the duties of a Librarian? Where have they ever been better performed than in our own public city library, where the late Mr. Jewett and the living Mr. Winsor have shown us what a librarian ought to be—the organizing head, the vigilant guardian, the seeker's index, the scholar's counsellor? His work is not merely that of administration, manifold and laborious as its duties are. He must have a quick intelligence and a retentive memory. He is a public carrier of knowledge in its germs. His office is like that which naturalists attribute to the bumble-bee—he lays up little honey for himself, but he conveys the fertilizing pollen from flower to flower.

Our undertaking, just completed—and just begun—has come at the right time, not a day too soon. Our practitioners need a library like this, for with all their skill and devotion there is too little genuine erudition, such as a liberal profession ought to be able to claim for many of its members. In reading the recent obituary notices of the late Dr. Geddings of South Carolina, I recalled what our lamented friend Dr. Coale used to tell me of his learning and accomplishments, and I could not help reflecting how few such medical scholars we had to show in Boston or New England. We must clear up this unilluminated atmosphere, and here—here is the true electric light which will irradiate its darkness.

The public will catch the rays reflected from the same source of light, and it needs instruction on the great subjects of health and disease—needs it sadly. It is preyed upon by every kind of imposition almost without hindrance. Its ignorance and prejudices react upon the profession to the great injury of both. The jealous feeling, for instance, with regard to such provisions for the study of anatomy as are sanctioned by the laws in this

State and carried out with strict regard to those laws, threatens the welfare, if not the existence of institutions for medical instruction wherever it is not held in check by enlightened intelligence. And on the other hand the profession has just been startled by a verdict against a physician, ruinous in its amount—enough to drive many a hardworking young practitioner out of house and home—a verdict which leads to the fear that suits for malpractice may take the place of the panel game and child-stealing as a means of extorting money. If the profession in this State, which claims a high standard of civilization, is to be crushed and ground beneath the upper millstone of the dearth of educational advantages and the lower millstone of ruinous penalties for what the ignorant ignorantly shall decide to be ignorance, all I can say is

God save the Commonhealth of Massachusetts!

Once more, we cannot fail to see that just as astrology has given place to astronomy, so theology, the science of Him whom by searching no man can find out, is fast being replaced by what we may not improperly call theonomy, or the science of the laws according to which the Creator acts. And since these laws find their fullest manifestations for us, at least, in rational human natures, the study of anthropology is largely replacing that of scholastic divinity. We must contemplate our Maker indirectly in human attributes as we talk of Him in human parts of speech. And this gives a sacredness to the study of man in his physical, mental, moral, social, and religious nature which elevates the faithful students of anthropology to the dignity of a priesthood, and sheds a holy light on the recorded results of their labors, brought together as they are in such a collection as this which is now spread out before us.

Thus, then, our library is a temple as truly as the dome-crowned cathedral hallowed by the breath of prayer and praise, where the dead repose and the living worship. May it, with all its treasures, be consecrated like that to the glory of God, through the contributions it shall make to the advancement of sound knowledge, to the relief of human suffering, to the promotion of harmonious relations between the members of the two noble professions which deal with the diseases of the soul and with those of the body, and to the common cause in which all good men are working, the furtherance of the well-being of their fellow-creatures!

NOTE. As an illustration of the statement in the last paragraph but one, I take the following notice from the "Boston Daily Advertiser," of December 4th, the day after the delivery of the address: "Prince Lucien Bonaparte is now living in London, and is devoting himself to the work of collecting the creeds of all religions and sects, with a view to their classification—his object being simply scientific or anthropological."

Since delivering the address, also, I find a leading article in the "Cincinnati Lancet and Clinic" of November 30th, headed "The Decadence of Homoeopathy," abundantly illustrated by extracts from the "Homoeopathic Times," the leading American organ of that sect.

In the New York "Medical Record" of the same date, which I had not seen before the delivery of my address, is an account of the action of the Homoeopathic Medical Society of Northern New York, in which Hahnemann's theory of "dynamization" is characterized in a formal resolve as "unworthy the confidence of the Homoeopathic profession."

It will be a disappointment to the German Homoeopathists to read in the "Homoeopathic Times" such a statement as the following: "Whatever the influences have been which have checked the outward development of Homoeopathy, it is plainly evident that the Homoeopathic school, as regards the number of its openly avowed representatives, has attained its majority, and has begun to decline both in this country and in England."

All which is an additional reason for making a collection of the incredibly curious literature of Homoeopathy before that pseudological inanity has faded out like so many other delusions.

Brief item in *The Nation* on copyright in Germany

From *The Nation*, Vol. XXX—No. 766 (March 4, 1880), p.177.

An original and amusing contribution to the copyright discussion has been made by Mr. Eduard Quaas in a book-trade-journal article, which we find reprinted in the *Literarische Correspondenz*, the organ of the German authors' union. Much has been said, of late years, about the unfortunate state of the German literary man, as compared with his brothers of France and England, and three causes have been assigned for it: namely, the enormous number of translations of novels, travels, histories, etc.; the extensive reading of English books; and the popularity of works which are beneath criticism, and hence unknown. These evils are not ignored by Mr. Quaas, but they seem to him of little importance compared with the harm done by circulating libraries. The circulation of a book in one of these institutions is, he says, in principle, the same thing as its dramatization upon the stage; that is, a large number of persons have the benefit of the author's conception, without any profit accruing there from to him. By statute, however, the theatre-manager is obliged to make a bargain with his author, while the latter has no protection against the owner of a library. Every library copy of a book by a popular author represents, say, fifty readers, and of these it is presumable that at least ten would buy the book if it were otherwise inaccessible. This assumption is substantiated by the statistics of the book-trade in France, where there are very few circulating libraries, and these used only by the poor. Mr. Quaas therefore proposes an addition to the copyright law, by which the announcement of All Rights Reserved would make a library liable to an action for damages. Under "circulating" libraries should be understood only those in which compensation is received for the loan of books. Under the new system those libraries would still exist, and would still do the literary class an important service, for until an author had acquired a reputation he would wish to further it by means of them.

The Father of the American Libraries

By Bunford Samuel
The Century; a popular quarterly. Volume 26, Issue 1 (May 1883).

It was in the year 1731, the fourth of King George the Second's reign, that the Philadelphia, the oldest American library, and, so far as is known, the first of all lending libraries, took its beginning. Fifty young men, artisans and gentlemen of that town, joined themselves into a literary association, and subscribed a hundred pounds for the purchase of books, agreeing also to pay each ten shillings annually during fifty years for the same purpose. It has lasted through changes of government and fashion, and possesses an interest beyond its mere local importance, from the historic associations which gather around it. Polished granite and enameled brick might tower around, but its dark old red brick front maintained an unshaken dignity as did Franklin's statue—"with a gown for his dress, and a Roman head," as the Doctor, when asked his wishes, quaintly expressed them. Banks might chink their money; courts, post-office, and custom-house disgorge their bustling crowds next door—but as you passed through its vestibule, embellished with old leathern firebuckets, and the door swung noiselessly behind you, all became quiet. You might have been miles from the life outside, for any information coming through your ears. A repose fell on you insensibly. Old pictures looked down on you, and soberly bound books. The wired cases, and the old green tables in the alcoves, seemed to have been there always. Its habitués all knew one another, as well as all about one another's great-great-grandfathers. They laughed decorously over old jokes—a new joke would have seemed hardly in other. Everything breathed quiet and long-continued good understanding. The epithet "old" came naturally to one's lips. "That good old library," Thackeray calls it, writing to Mr. William B. Reed.

The little fiction of the English law, that the king can never die, might almost be applied in the same sense to many members of the library whose shares, like the English throne, have never been vacant, one of the family always inheriting it. Out of a beadroll as long as that of Homer's ships a few instances may be given of this curious persistency of shares in families. Colonel William Bradford became a shareholder in 1769. His son, William Bradford, Attorney-General of the United States under Washington, next held the share, which is still in the family. Dr. Thomas Cadwalader, lieutenant-governor of the province, and father of two Revolutionary officers, General John and Colonel Lambert Cadwalader, was one of the original directors in 1731, and his descendants are still shareholders. Governor Thomas McKean, one of the signers of the Declaration, acquired in 1777 a share, which his family still holds.

In fact, it might have been thought that as it had existed, so it would always exist. With its ease, its long existence, and connection with men whose names belong to the history of their age, it had become a sort of conservative social influence. It was unagitated by questions of cataloguing, undisturbed by debates whether a library should be merely a reservoir, or should also assume the function of a filter. In brief, its periods of existence were unmarked by any of those interrogations with which, nowadays, we see fit to punctuate every experience of life. Nevertheless, the Library Company underwent, as shall presently be told, an entire change of scene. The old building has been abandoned to the Philistines and now flaunts a large gilded sign—a sign of the times—on its astonished front. And a void exists in the breasts of many ancient Philadelphians, unsatisfied by the knowledge that the cultured Bostonian or the scornful New Yorker, as he emerges from the railroad station on Broad street, is confronted by the finest building wholly devoted to library uses in America, and one which has few, if any, equals in Europe.

The library was well sponsored, being Franklin's "first project of a public nature." John Dickinson, Godfrey the mathematician, Benjamin Rush, Charles Thomson, Secretary of Congress, and Franklin himself—who was also at one time librarian—were among its early directors, and it was cradled in buildings whose names now form part of our fund of national recollections. Franklin says:

> "At the time I established myself in Philadelphia there was not a good bookstore in any of the colonies southward of Boston. In New York and Philadelphia, the printers were indeed stationers; they sold only paper, etc., almanacs, ballads, and a few common school-books. Those who loved reading were obliged to send for their books from England; the members of the Junto (his club) had each a few. We had hired a room to hold our club in. I proposed that we should each of us bring our books to that room, where they would not only be ready to consult in our conferences, but become a common benefit, each of us being at liberty to borrow such as he wished to read at home.***This was accordingly done, and for some time contented us.***Yet some inconveniences occurring, each

took his books home again. And now I set on foot my first project of a public nature, that for a subscription library. The institution soon manifested its ability, was imitated in other towns and in other provinces.***Reading became fashionable, and our people having no amusements to divert their attention from study, became better acquainted with books, and in a few years were observed by strangers to be better instructed and more intelligent than people of the same rank in other countries."

That the leaven did indeed work as Franklin said we may infer from the fact that in a few years Philadelphia took a decided lead in the art of printing, in amount as well as execution, and that it had a larger number of newspapers. From direct testimony, including that of the Rev. Jacob Duche, who, though of foreign extraction, became himself a director of the Library, and afterward made himself notorious by an attempt to persuade Washington to forsake the American cause, we would infer that the character of the society was decidedly literary. He writes, in 1774:

"There is less distinction among citizens of Philadelphia than among those of any other city in the world.***Literary accomplishments here meet with deserved applause. But such is the taste for books, that almost every man is a reader."

The Company, in its first choice of reading matter, took the advice of James Logan, the confidential friend of Penn, "esteeming him to be a gentleman of universal learning and the best judge of books in these parts." It is noticeable that, in their list of about fifty authors, the only ones which may be said to belong to light literature are the "Guardian," "Tatler," "Spectator," and Addison's works. The books were imported from England, and with them came the first gift to the Library. Peter Collinson, a London mercer, wrote:

"Gentlemen, I am a stranger to most of you, but not to your laudable intention to erect a public library. I beg your acceptance of my mite, 'Sir Isaac Newton's Philosophy' and 'Philip Miller's Gardener's Dictionary.' It will be an instance of your candour to accept the intention and good-will of the giver and not regard the meanness of the gift."

The books were at first kept in the house of Robert Grace, whom Franklin characterizes as "a young gentlemen of some fortune, generous, lively, and witty, a lover of punning and of his friends." Afterward they were allotted a room in the State-House; and, in 1742, a charter was obtained from the Proprietaries. In 1790, having in the interval absorbed several other associations and sustained a removal to Carpenter's Hall, where its apartment had been used as a hospital for wounded American soldiers, the Library was at last housed in a building especially erected for it at Fifth and Chestnut streets, where it remained until within the last few years.

It brought only about eight thousand volumes into its new quarters, for it had languished somewhat during the Revolution and the war of words which attended our political birth. But it had received no injury. Two meetings had been called to consider measures of removal to a safe place, but whether its members were engaged in taking care of their country or of themselves, they did not attend the meetings, and the red-coats marching in on the little visit they paid us after Germantown, found the books, and red them, too. But the red-coats behaved, in this instance, at least, peaceably, paying loyally for their use and not damaging nor confiscating nor carrying away a single volume.

Many relics of the Revolutionary time are stored in the Library, among them a colossal bust of Minerva, which stood behind the chair of the Speaker of the first Congress that met in Philadelphia. The writer of this paper is at Logan's library-table, sitting in a chair used by Washington, while Dickinson's writing-desk holds some books on the right, West's portrait of Franklin looks from overhead, and a lock of Washington's hair hangs near his left hand. Penn's and Cromwell's clocks, too, keep remembrance of other times, and go on ticking, as if reckless of a balance. Besides memories, however, the library gathered little during those sads days of the Revolution. But when the scene changed, and the weeping women who tended the wounded in churches and on door-steps after the defeat at Germantown were replaced by the triumphing cavalry who rode through the shouting streets to the State-House to lay at the feet of Congress the captured standards of Cornwallis, our Company felt the reaction, and in a little while sent an order to London for books—its first importation in nine years.

Two years after removal to its quarters on Fifth street, the Library received the most valuable gift of books it has as yet had. James Logan, friend and adviser of Penn and of the celebrated Colonial Governor, Thomas Lloyd, President of Council, and holding other high trusts in the Province, had gathered a most important collection of books. Mr. Logan was translator of Cicero's "Cato Major," the first classic published in America, beside being versed in natural science. His library comprised, as he tells us, "over one hundred volumes of authors, all in Greek, with mostly their version; all the Roman classics without exception; all the Greek mathematicians. Besides, there are many of the most valuable Latin authors, and a great number of modern mathematicians." These, at first bequeathed as a public library to the city, became a branch of the Philadelphia Library under certain conditions, one of which was that, barring contingencies, one of the donor's descendants should always hold the office of trustee. And today his direct descendant fills the position, and is perhaps the only example in this country of an hereditary office-holder.

The Library lost a few books by its one experience of fire, in 1831, and nearer our own times gained an important addition by a courtesy it was enabled to do the British Government. The story takes us back to the Revolution of 1688. On the flight of James II, from his throne, his lord high chancellor of Ireland converted the state papers of which he had custody into family papers; in other words, he kept them. His grandson, on leaving America about the beginning of this century, presented them to the Library of Philadelphia. This gift, containing the private correspondence of James I. with the Privy Council of Ireland, the Diary of the Marquis of Clanricarde, a letter of Queen Elizabeth, and other manuscripts, the Company—being bound by no reservation to its giver—took an opportunity of restoring to the British Government. This courtesy was responded to by the gift, on the part of the English, of a large and valuable series of Government publications.

In 1869 died Dr. James Rush, son of Benjamin Rush, and himself well known as the author of a work on the human voice, and as husband of a lady who almost succeeded in naturalizing the salon in this country. By his will about one million dollars were devoted to the erection and maintenance of an isolated and fire-proof library-building, which was to be named the Ridgway Library, in memory of his wife. This building was offered to the Philadelphia Company, and the bequest was accepted. That institution had by this time accumulated about one hundred thousand volumes, containing many of those rarities for which there is an eternal struggle between the bookhunter and fire, rats, plate-hunters, worms, and kindred vermin. It owns some fine specimens of illuminated manuscripts, exemplars of Caxton, Fust, and Shoeffer, the inventors, or at least sharers in the invention, of printing; of Pynson, Wynkyn de Worde, Sweynheym, and Pannartz; a work of Jenson, believed to be unique; of Koburger, and other works irreplaceable if lost. It is therefore gratifying to those who are aware of the heavy toll fire has levied on knowledge to know that the collection has been, in so far as may be, placed out of reach of a danger which the original "twelve leathern fire buckets and a ladder," procured by the directors, might not have averted.

A building of the Doric order was erected, which with its grounds covers an entire square or block, and is calculated to contain four hundred thousand volumes, or three times as many as the Library at present has, and to this building the more valuable books of the Library were removed in 1878; the fiction and more modern works being placed in another designed in imitation of the old edifice, and nearer the center of the city.

When it is added that Dr. Rush's bequest included also the correspondence and papers of his father—which contain among many others letters from distinguished persons, letters from Washington, Franklin, Hamilton, Kosciuszko, etc., and that mysterious diary of Benjamin Rush which John Adams alludes to, and which played an important part in the controversy between Mr. Bancroft and Mr. William B. Reed, but which nobody seems to have viewed—it will be seen that few more valuable gifts have been made to the public. To the public, it may be said, for although this library is in its origin and maintenance entirely a private institution, the use of its books is freely given to any respectable reader. I have tried briefly to show that this oldest American library has had an honorable career, and exerted an appreciable and wholly good influence; while illustrating something of that peculiar character of quietness which Philadelphia has retained since Penn directed that the people should so build their houses "that there may be ground on each side for gardens, or orchards, or fields, that it may be a green country town, which will never be burnt and always wholesome." Indeed, few institutions have been more naturally the growth of a community, or better illustrate the good effects of such unstimulated growth, than the old Philadelphia Library.

Women in Libraries: How They are Handicapped

By Melvil Dewey

Excerpts from a March 13, 1886 address before the Association of College Alumni, originally published in *Library Notes* 1 (October 1886).

There is a large field of work for college-bred women in promoting the founding of new libraries, infusing new life into old ones, or serving on committees or boards of trustees where their education and training will tell powerfully for the common good. Active interest of this kind may fairly be expected of every college graduate.

In the more direct work for which salaries are paid, there is an unusually promising field for college girls and in few lines of work have women so nearly an equal chance with men. There is almost nothing in the higher branches which she cannot do quite as well as a man of equal training and experience; and in much of library work women's quick mind and deft fingers do many things with a neatness and dispatch seldom equaled by her brothers.

My experience is that an increasing number of libraries are willing to pay for given work the same price, whether done by men or women. Yet why are the salaries of women lower? In all my business and professional life I have tried to give women more than a fair chance at all work which I had to offer. Experience has taught me why the fairest employers, in simple justice, usually pay men more for what seems at first sight the same work. Perhaps these reasons may help you to avoid some of the difficulties.

1. Women have usually poorer health and as a result lose more time from illness and are more crippled by physical weakness when on duty. The difficulty is most common to women, as are bright ribbons and thin shoes and long hair, but it is a question of health, not of sex. A strong, healthy woman is worth more than a feeble man for the same reason that a strong man gets more than a weak woman.

2. Usually women lack business and executive training. Her brothers have been about the shops and stores and in the streets or on the farm hearing business matters discussed and seeing business transacted from earliest childhood. The boys have been trading jack knives and developing the business bumps while the girls were absorbed with their

dolls. It would be a miracle at present if girls were not greatly inferior in this respect and it is this fact which accounts for so few prominent chief librarianships being held by women. But this is the fault of circumstances, not necessarily of sex, and women who have somehow got the business ideas and training and have executive force are getting the salaries that such work commands. When girls have as good a chance to learn these things, I doubt not that they will quite equal their brothers and will keep cash and bank accounts and double entry books for their private affairs. A man brought up girl-fashion, as not a few are, proves just as helpless on trial and as a result gets only a "woman's salary."

3. Lack of permanence in her plans is one of the gravest difficulties with women. A young man who enters library work and later thinks of a home of his own, is stimulated to fresh endeavors to make his services more valuable. Many a young man's success in life dates from the new earnestness which took possession of him on his engagement. But with women the probability or even the possibility that her position is only temporary and that she will soon leave it for home life does more than anything else to keep her value down. Neither man or woman can do the best work except when it is felt to be the life work. This lack of permanence in the plans of women is more serious than you are apt to realize. If woman wishes to be as valuable as man she must contrive to feel that she has chosen a profession for life and work accordingly. Then she will do the best that is in her to do as long as she is in the service and if at any time it seems best to change her state, the work already done has not been crippled by this "temporary" evil.

4. With equal health, business training and permanence of plans, women will still usually have to accept something less than men because of the consideration which she exacts and deserves on account of her sex. If a man can do all the other work just as well as the woman and in addition can, in an emergency, lift a heavy case, or climb a ladder to the roof or in case of accident or disorder can act as fireman or do police duty, he adds something to his direct value; just as a saddle horse that is safe in harness and not afraid of the cars, will bring more in nine markets out of ten, than the equally good horse that can be used only in the saddle. So in justice to those who wish to be fair to women, remember that she almost always receives, whether she exacts it or not, much more waiting on and minor assistance than a man in the same place and therefore,

with sentiment aside, hard business judgment cannot award her quite as much salary. There are many uses for which a stout corduroy is really worth more than the finest silk...

We greatly prefer college-bred women in selecting new librarians: 1. Because they are a picked class selected from the best material throughout the country. 2. Because the college training has given them a wider culture and broader view with a considerable fund of information all of which will be valuable working material in a library as almost nowhere else. 3. Because a four years' course successfully completed is the strongest voucher for persistent purpose and mental and physical capacity for protracted intellectual work. 4. Chiefly because we find that the training of the course enables mind to work with a quick precision and steady application rarely found in one who has not had this thorough college drill. Therefore we find it pays to give higher salaries for college women...

The salary to women for the first year is seldom more than $500 and at present few have grown to over $1000, though here and there $1200 to $1500 are paid to women of experience. But there is no reason why a woman cannot do the same work for which our leading librarians receive $3000 to $5000 and I have no doubt that as women of education, with thorough technical training and experience come forward, the salaries will rapidly increase. For this highest grade work the demand exceeds the supply and will grow steadily the new development of the library system. If one finds many more well paid positions for teachers, there are vastly more competitors for each of these places than for that of the trained librarian. After careful study it seems to me that to an earnest woman of superior ability the library field already offers in its present period of rapid growth as good and opening financially as teaching.

Columbia Library School

By Melvil Dewey. Published in *Library Notes*, v.1 No.4, March 1887.

(Ed. note: Dewey's famous "simplified spelling" can be seen throughout this article.)

The first year is proving more of a success than its best friends dared to hope. We have space only for brief notes. Full information, as on all historical matters, will be found in the *Library Journal*, where the records of all the various library organizations must be sought. Having admitted a class of 20, instead of the ten to which it was to be limited, a change of quarters was necessary; but the entire old library (90x40 feet), now assigned to the school, gives ample room. To this class-room has been transferred the old A.L.A. Bibliothecal Museum, which has been lately doubled in value by large additions. As fast as the needs are recognized, new provisions are made for the school which will each year find added conveniences and facilities for profitable study.

Most of the students have been so persistent in their study and practice that they have seemed to live in the library. Lunch is brought up to those wishing it by the school page assigned to wait on the class, and for 14 hours daily there is opportunity for work. The fair criticism on the four months' course was that too much was crowded into it. The strain was very great, but the interest and enthusiasm of the class seemed equal to anything; and a census of the score of earnest workers showed a uniform improvement in health during the term, most gratifying to those who feared a general breakdown.

With all this work time has been found for many enjoyable extras. Many courtesies have been extended, including complimentary tickets for the entire class for various entertainments and lectures. As the guest of Mr. George Hannah, librarian of the Long Island Historical Society, the class and teachers enjoyed a delightful lunch as part of their Brooklyn visit. Alternate Friday evenings have been spent socially at the home of the director of the school, where music, simple refreshments, and general good fellowship helpt to develop the esprit du corps evident in the pioneer class.

The significant fact about the first year is the rapid development. This class came for three months, most of them having made positiv arrangements to leave at that time. After six weeks they petitioned for an extra month, which was granted, and later most of the class determined to take the full two years' course. The College has met these demands for something broader and more satisfactory than it had dared to offer in the experimental year. The first annual *Register of the School* has been issued, and the fourth *Circular of Information* now printing, shows how large an advance has been made on the plans for the coming year.

The gifts of samples were so generous that each student now owns a very fair bibliografical museum of his own, some of the class reporting that an extra trunk was necessary to transport home their acquisitions. Many favors have been shown by the Library Bureau, R. R. Bowker, publisher of the *Library Journal, Publisher's Weekly, Literary News,* and the *American Catalogue* and by the Harpers, Appletons, Putnams, and others.

A large number of librarians and others interested attended now and then a lecture to sample the school's good things, and in several cases visitors spent from a few days to two or three weeks.

The practice problems, many of them being real cases under discussion in well-known libraries, and the visits each week to study some library, book house, or bindery in operation, proved exceedingly practical, and concentrated much library experience into a very short time.

The faculty feel about this class as do most mothers about an only child—that it is of very exceptionable merit. The fine large class picture of students and teachers by Pach Bros. seems to strengthen this opinion so far as appearances can be trusted.

Their services seem in demand midway in their course. The president of the class, Mr. George Watson Cole, late of the Fitchburg library, is now librarian of the Pratt Institute, Brooklyn. Mr Patten, Miss Stott, and Miss Bonnell are engaged in the N. Y. Free Circulating Library; Miss Miller is first assistant at Lafayette (Ind.); Misses Seymour and Woodworth go to the new Osterhout Free Library in Wilkes-Barre, Pa.; Miss Fernald is cataloging the new library at Saugus, Mass.; Misses Griswold and Chapman are librarian and assistant at the Y. W. C. A., N. Y.; Miss Talcott is assistant at the Hartford library, and six of the rest are busily at work in the Columbia library, some of them having declined offers from other libraries.

CHANGES IN THE LIBRARY SCHOOL FOR THE SECOND YEAR.

Careful comparison of the new Circular of Information with last year's announcements shows a markt development of the plans. We note some of the points, advising those interested to read the details for themselves, as the pamphlet can be had free by applying to the Library School, Columbia College, N. Y.

The first year's experience has shown a greater demand than was realized from both students and employers for thoro preparation. Evidently the time is not far distant when a man or woman seeking the place of a librarian without training for its duties will be thought as much a quack or charlatan as the physician seeking patients without having attended a medical school or served an apprenticeship with an accomplished practitioner. The college hesitated to offer more than it was sure was now wanted, and the three months' course was as far as it went for the first year. The second year shows a long stride toward a professional school with as full a two years' course as is given in the law and medical schools. One term per year has become three—short, but of solid work without vacations—thus giving as many exercises in the year as any department of the college. Beside the three months' course of the first year, a preparatory term, beginning eight weeks before the first Thursday in January, fits all students who have not been engaged in a library, for intelligent and profitable work in the crowded lecture term. The third term of the junior year is also eight weeks, up to the college commencement. Those who take also their apprenticeship work in the Columbia library may work as much of the rest of the year as they choose, but this completes the regular class exercises. A senior year corresponding in terms is provided, and a third year of advanced work for those who can give the time is now in preparation. The faculty have submitted to the trustees a proposition to confer on college graduates who complete satisfactorily the two years' course, the degree B. L. S., Bachelor of Library Science, and the Master's degree, M. L. S., for the three years' course. For this year, however, only diplomas or certificates of proficiency are offered.

These degrees will not be given as a matter of course to all who spend two years in the School, but only on rigid examination, it being the purpose of the School to set its standard so high that its degree shall be a voucher of nativ ability and thoro preparation for entering the profession. A college degree is not yet absolutely required for admission to the School, but more strict examinations are to be passed by non-graduates. The age limit for entrance is raised to 20 years, and applications are required to be made on a blank provided, which calls, among other things, for full information as to previous education and experience. The plan is to admit only ten to the regular class, and there are already 20 applicants for next year, with good promise of 50 before the term opens. The School prefers a small class carefully selected from a large number as those promising to do the best work in the profession. There is already an overstock at mediocre librarians, assistants, and catalogers, and the influence of the School is intended to diminish rather than to increase their number.

In the School itself women have exactly the same privileges as men and also in the College, except that women are not admitted to the class exercises of the men in other departments. The College degrees have however been opened to women who pass the required examinations. A circular explaining this fully will be mailed on application.

The fees are $50 per year or $20 for all the lectures of any single month.

The proportionate fee for a single course of lectures is given on application for each course. Tho the advantages are so greatly increast, it will be noted that the fee remains at $50.

A Fellowship of $500 per year is offered to the most successful student of each class, together with several scholarships yielding from $100 to $300 each per year; those winning these honors being required to discharge certain duties in the college library as part of their training. It is hoped in this way to encourage the best students to spend more time on their preparation and increase the number of those who will take the three years' course, which will include considerable work in languages and comparativ literature, as well as the advanced work in bibliografy and library economy. One of the markt successes of the last year has been the bibliografical lectures by various professors of the university. This feature is to be very largely extended hereafter, so that bibliografy will receive as full treatment as library economy, and perhaps justify a change of name from the limited Library Economy to the generic name Library Science, covering bibliografy, cataloging, classification, and the group of topics connected with library management known as library economy. When the school was named it was thought best to begin with only the technical part and wait till the demand of the public justified broadening the scope to cover library science.

There has been introduced for next year a course, by proficient scholars, on the various great literatures of the world treated from the librarian's standpoint, and also a short course, which will doubtless be fully developed later, on the leading languages as the librarian's tools.

The faculty has been organized, five non-resident lecturers appointed, and in many ways there is evidence that the School is to take on more of the scholastic form with its second year.

Several hundred books have been bought specially for the School, and a selection of those most wanted for study is placed in the classroom for more convenient use, while duplicates of the most needed works are provided to be taken home by those who cannot afford to buy them. Provision has been made for places of meeting for clubs for mutual improvement formed among the students; rapid additions are also being made to the illustrativ collections, and every effort is put forth to make the School as practically useful as possible to its students. Each succeeding class will of course enjoy all the advantages of its predecessors with whatever has been added since, but no higher standard of appreciation could be asked by the faculty than has been shown by the pioneer class.

Students are warned not to hope to make up for lack of preparation or to take extra studies while at the School, for the required work is so heavy as to require all their energies. For those who take only a partial course abundant and attractiv opportunities are offered for other work.

While the standard of admission has been so much raised and the course lengthened, full opportunity is still given to those engaged in libraries to come for such time as they can spare and get such help as they can from the School. The enlarged rooms make it possible to receive more students, but the regular class is limited to ten, in order not to offer more well-trained candidates than there is a ready demand for. Those who have already secured positions and do not ask the School to become responsible for their acquirements or to assist them to places will be received as during the first year, with only examination enuf to satisfy the facillty that they can profit by the School.

In the same way private book owners not intending to enter the profession, but wishing to take any part of the course, are allowed to do so on payment of the moderate fee.

PREPARATION FOR THE LIBRARY SCHOOL.

Constant inquiries are made as to the best use of the time till the opening of the preparatory term. Much can wisely be done before, for there will be enough left to do after getting to the School to keep all occupied.

In technical matters comparativly little can be done to advantage till after the first term. We note:

Handwriting. One of the details that should be attended to is the library handwriting, which takes not a little time from some who ought not to spare it from their studies. In this number we give full advice about this. Those who enter the School can have brief criticisms and suggestions from a teacher if they send samples of their handwriting. By acquiring a suitable hand, students can earlier be allowed to do catalog work of great value as practice.

Visiting libraries. This should be done as far as convenient, since each library seen broadens somewhat one's ideas. The methods of work, catalogs, etc., should be specially examined. It is hardly wise to spend extra time or money on such visits; for, after the School, pupils will have learned how to get much more good from them. The same remark applies to binderies, printing-offices, book stores, etc.

Reading. The first thing needed is a set of *LIBRARY NOTES*, of which a complete indext volume costs only $1. In each number is something specially written for students. The rules for card catalogs (20 pages in No. 2) require no little time from the novice, and the sample cards printed after them serve as models. In succeeding numbers matter prepared specially for the class will be given, and it is the assumption in all lectures and class exercises that each student has a set of the *NOTES* for reference to the many rules, tables, and illustrations.

Much more extensive than *Library Notes* and therefore more important if it can be afforded, is a set of the *Library Journal*, in which is more important matter for the young librarian than he will find in all the rest of the language together. We cannot too strongly urge the importance of access to the *Library Journal*, but its considerable cost may deter many. All the prominent libraries have full sets, and many can read it in their home libraries. If necessary it is worth some sacrifice to secure at least the most important of the II V. now completed and to subscribe for the current numbers. Liberal concessions in cost can be had by those coming to the School. If all cannot be afforded, the most useful material will be found in v. 5, 4, 3, and in that now printing, and we recommend that they be bought in that order. An article pointing out how the Journal is worth in cash much more than its cost to any earnest young librarian will appear, we hope, in the next *NOTES*. From time to time we shall give reading lists which will assume that the student has access to the Journal.

The U. S. Bureau of Education Report on Public Libraries publisht in 1876 is the most important single volume, but it was written before the Association was founded or the *Journal* started, and few of the articles would be written today by their authors as they are printed there. This should be secured if a copy can be pickt up second hand, as sometimes happens. The Library Bureau is able occasionally to buy a copy, and application could wisely be made there. It is doubtful if it is well for students to spend time or money on other books in this field before they lay the foundation for their wisest use in the short course at the School.

Bibliografy. Anything and everything that increases his knowledge of books will be directly valuable to the librarian, but the time can be much better spent after some instruction, and the list of the best books to read in this field is deferred.

General education. While everything counts in preparation, the most important is a knowledge of the German, French, and Latin languages, not as philosophy but as working tools. The pupil that can read German and French readily has an immense advantage. Next in order come Italian, Spanish, and Greek, or some of the Scandinavian tungs, but these are much less often needed, and can be acquired later. German and French, if known, will be in daily use.

After the first term every student has work enuf laid out to last him for years. Before that, more than enuf has been suggested above. We prefer to have the preceding summer largely devoted to laying in an estra stock of strength and good helth for the activ work of the School. It is better to spend such time as can wisely be given, on German and French, the library hand, and general reviews of literature and history rather than to try to anticipate the instruction of the School in bibliografy and library economy.

Proceedings of the Fourteenth American Library Association Conference, Lakewood: The Woman's Meeting

Published in *Library Journal* 17 (August 1892).

The Woman's Meeting was called to order may 19 at 2:30 P.M. by Miss Mary S. Cutler, who briefly explained that the call for the meeting had come from the Secretary of the Association, and called on the members to nominate a chairman. Miss E. M. Coes, of the New York Free Circulation Libraries, was elected chairman, and Mrs. Melvil Dewey, Secretary. Miss Cutler presented by title a paper on

What A Woman Librarian Earns

The work of the modern librarian is so little understood that an outline of what it covers may not only prove interesting reading, but also throw light on the question of what should be a fair financial return for this service to the reading public.

The librarian must be both a good business woman and an educator in the highest sense of the word. First, she must build up the library. Her problem is as follows: Given a multitude of books and a limited fund, to select those best suited to the needs and tastes of her particular readers. She must take an inventory of stock once a year. She must present to the trustees both a monthly and annual report on work and finances. She must be familiar with recent thought in library architecture, as she is often called on to suggest plans for a new building or for the enlargement of an old one.

She must make the resources of the library available by a wise classification of books; by a catalog which indicates clearly to the reader if the book he seeks is in the library, also what books on a subject are most valuable for his purpose; by individual help, being ready at any moment to drop other work and spend an hour or two if need be in hunting up answers to questions from all sorts and conditions of readers. She must also devise and carry on a system of charging books which shall secure their safety, at a minimum of work and waiting for both borrowers and attendants.

She must inspire her assistants, even those of the lowest grade, with her own ideals, so that the spirit of courtesy and of helpfulness shall pervade the place like an atmosphere.

She is not content to satisfy the demands made on the library; she creates a demand.

She establishes a close connection between the library and the public schools, gaining the cooperation of the teachers in bringing up a generation of readers with pure tastes and a genuine love of good reading. She grants special privileges to reading and art clubs, buying with reference to their needs. The librarian is one of the most efficient promoters of university extension, as the library is its natural centre. She prints lists of books and articles on topics of current interest, buys books for the mechanic and the foreigner, talks with the foreigner in his own language, cooperates with the church and press in local forms. The librarian must be in touch with the latest and best thought of the time and with the growth of her own community, making the library an active, aggressive, educational force.

All this and more is being done by the modern librarians, both men and women.

How much money does the woman-librarian receive, and how much is received by women who fill subordinate library positions?

An official statement has been secured of salaries paid to all the women employed in 25 of the most prominent libraries in the country, prominent from their size, wise administration, and efficiency. They represent 15 States, two Eastern, three Middle, eight Western, and two Southern, and several types of libraries, free public, subscription, state, and college. Other statistics which follow are also official.

Three hundred and ninety-six women are employed in 25 prominent libraries, receiving from $240 to $1500, an average salary of $570. This includes work of all grades, and the average is greatly reduced by the large number required to do mechanical work in comparison with the few needed for supervisory and independent work.

Fifteen women of recognized ability, trained as apprentices in large libraries or in the school of experience, receive from $550 to $2000, an average salary of $1150; 38 women, trained in the Library School which was opened in 1887, receive from $600 to $1500, an average salary of $900. The 15 highest salaries paid to library school women average $100. Seven women as librarians of State libraries receive from $625 to $1200, an average salary of $1000. The 24 men filling similar positions receive an average salary of $1450.

From all of the preceding lists have been selected 37 women who have made a decided success of the work. Their salaries, tabulated as follows, are effected by local conditions, and are in many cases not in proportion to the value of services rendered:

One at $2000; one at $1800; one at $1740; four at $1500; one at $1320; one at $1300 six at $1200; one at $1100; two at $1080; six at $1000; five at $900; four at $800; three at $700; one at $550.

From these figures and a general estimate based on a large acquaintance with librarians, I conclude that a woman occupying a subordinate position in a library, where faithfulness, accuracy, and a fair knowledge of books are the only essentials, can expect from $300 to $500. A good cataloger, or a librarian with average ability and training, can expect to receive from $600 to $900. A woman with good natural ability and fitness for the work, with a liberal education and special training, can expect $1000 at the head of a library, or of a department in a large library, with a possible increase to $1500 or $2000. Women rarely receive the same pay for the same work as men.

Salaries are lowered: (1) By political influence in certain libraries supported by the city and state, which discourages good work by making the tenure of office uncertain. (2) By the fact that working among books is considered an attractive and "genteel" employment, without the severe strain of teaching. (3) Because many library trustees have not the modern conception of a library and are content with inferior work. (4) Because many other library trustees take advantage of a woman's willingness to work for less than she earns when she knows her work is useful. The women in one well-known library accept, year after year, for high-grade service the pitiful dole of twenty cents an hour.

Salaries tend to increase and are increasing steadily because there are so few men or women able to meet the growing demand for trained librarians.

A woman's fitness for library work is proved. She has already a recognized place in the profession. She has contributed somewhat to the literature of the subject and holds offices of honor in the American Library Association. This is due largely to the liberal spirit of the leaders in the library movement of the last twenty years.

In England she has no such place. At the last conference of the Library Association of the United Kingdom the President apologized to me for what he called the dullness of the sessions saying that of course there could be nothing in the discussions of a library association to interest ladies.

In America her position in the future will be what she has power to make it. She has a fair chance, and if she fails it will be her own fault. A genius for organization, executive ability, and business habits, a wide knowledge and love of books amounting to a book-instinct, and the gift of moving and inspiring other minds are absolutely essential to the highest success. The palm of honor and of opportunity waits for her who shall join a genius for organization to the power of a broad, rich, catholic, and sympathetic womanhood. The work is worth the best energies of the strongest minds, and in the long run will win appreciation and proper financial support.

Mrs. M.R. Sanders spoke on

Reading Rooms; What a Woman May Do In Them

The opportunities for influencing readers, specially boys; the firmness and tact often required to preserve order and discipline; what a woman may accomplish in cases where a man's physical strength is usually thought necessary.
Miss Middleton, Miss Green, and Miss James each gave bits of personal experience.
The chairman asked Miss Green to say something from her own experience as to "exactness in cataloging" and of women "as bookkeepers." She had found young women, on the whole, more exact, more willing to take pains. The balance, in her experience, was a little in favor of the girls. As to bookkeeping, she mentioned one case in a prominent public library, where a woman, without any assistant, had been bookkeeper for twenty years, and in all that time had never been known to make a mistake that could be criticized.

Time being limited, Miss M.E. Sargent read by title her paper on

Woman's Position in Library Service

In lieu of any opinions of my own I present for your consideration and for discussion what I have been able to gather as to a woman's possibilities and also her limitations in such service. I quote first from a librarian's views: "Some doubt has been expressed of the capacity of a woman to manage a city library. The objectors, I think, must be unacquainted with the recent library history of Massachusetts. Man of our large libraries are administered by women, and I have never heard that they did not give as much satisfaction to trustees and the public as men." The writer then speaks of the excellent work of Miss James of Wilkes-Barre, of Miss Thurston at Newton, of Miss Hayward at Cambridge, Miss Chandler of Lancaster, and some others. "Besides these there are 97 other women who are librarians of public libraries in this State and 51 who are librarians of libraries not public. That is to say, out of 427 libraries 156 are in charge of women... A woman may be imbued with all the modern ideas of librarianship—of assisting the public, of teaching the public, elevating the public." Referring to libraries outside of Massachusetts he cites the splendid work of Miss Coe, the head of the New York Free Circulating Library.

In quite an opposite strain are the following words from a trustee's standpoint: "My reason for preferring a man for the head of a library in a large city is not based on what may be called a library *per se*. It is connected with the business side of the librarian's position. Unfortunately women are hedged about with rules of decorum and courtesy which somewhat interfere with their usefulness in many relations in a municipal or a business community; with the trustees, for instance, who may change from time to time—may include conflicting elements—may comprise men of rough or at least of downright and positive character. A man's relations with such a board are freer and more likely to be influential than a woman's, because he can talk right *at* them and *with* them, without offense on either side. He is usually accustomed to hasty and unfair criticism and knows how to meet it effectively. With the city government—especially the council who make appropriations—a man can work far more efficiently than a woman can. He can go out among them at their offices and stores, or in the City Hall corridor; can learn what influences are brought to bear on them, and so benefit the library in a score of ways closed to a woman. With the rougher class of the community, with laborers and artisans, a man, for obvious reasons, can do more effective work. Women, more rarely, have the disciplinary power over a mixed force of men and women under them than men do; but that is rather a personal matter, to be tested in experience. Some women have it in a marked degree; many men are lacking in this direction. Now I am not bigoted; perhaps these views are wrong, but they are founded on wide business experience, and an observation of many libraries and librarians all over this country. My theory seems to be generally accepted in practice, at any rate; for men are the head of most if not all the libraries in large cities."

For myself, with Miss Willard, I feel that "we should study the largeness of life and not its limitations." We should be divine optimists, "who, rowing hard against the stream, see distant lights of Eden gleam, and know the dream is not a dream."

"We are hedged about the rules of decorum and courtesy." Max O'Rell has said that unsexing in America has been a blessed thing for us.

"The freedom enjoyed by American women has enabled them to mould themselves in their own fashion. They do not copy any other women; they are original. I can recognize an American woman without hearing her speak. You have only to see her enter a room or a car and you know her for Johnathan's daughter. Married or unmarried, her air is full of assurance, of a self-possession that never fails her, and when she looks at you or talks to you her eyes express the same calm consciousness of her worth. They say in France that Paris is the Paradise of women. If so, there is a more blissful place than Paradise; there is another word to invent to give an idea of the social position enjoyed by American ladies. If I had to be born again and I might choose my sex and my birthplace I would shout at the top of my voice, "Oh, make me an American woman."

And then again, in dealing with the rougher elements above alluded to, force does not always mean "bayonets and cannon balls." The silent and unseen are still the strongest powers of all. A scientific age is proving what faith has always taught, that "thought and will and love are the only forces that endure."

"Time is the greatest alembic in which all are tested." The work of Miss Mitchell in science, of Miss Edwards in Egyptology, may be cited as examples of what can be accomplished by women.

With the true love for the work, with a similar devotion and the needed inspiration and aspiration, why cannot a like result be accomplished in *our* service, and why may we not be able to prove that our possibilities outweigh our limitations. We can at least console ourselves with the thought expressed by Thoreau, "It is the business of mankind to polish the world, and ever one who works is scrubbing in some part."

"Where your heart is interested, let your life take part; where your life takes part, let your heart glow."

> "Some evils must be trampled down
> Beneath our feet, if we would gain,
> In the bright fields of fair renown,
> The right of eminent domain.

> "Standing on what too long we bore
>   With shoulders bent and downcast eyes,
> We may discern—unseen before—
>   A path to higher destinies."

In closing the chairman spoke of the interest, freedom of discussion, and special value to the young librarians of such meeting as this. Voted: That a committee be appointed to organize a Woman's Section of the A.L.A., to report at the next conference in Chicago. The Chair appointed Miss H.P. James, Mrs. Melvil Dewey, and Miss H.E. Green, with power to add to the committee. Adjourned.

Annie Dewey, *Secretary pro tem.*

Librarianship as a Profession for Women

By Miss Richardson
Originally published in *The Library* 6 (1894).

Now that women are entering as competitors in almost every field of labour formerly looked upon as belonging exclusively to the sterner sex, it may not be uninteresting to hear a little about library work as a profession for women.

In the first place, let us look for a moment at the mere routine work which goes on in every free library, and which is done for the most part by the assistants—I refer to the labeling, repairing and issuing of books. The first two will in all probability be done more quickly and neatly by a girl than a boy; and as regards the issuing of books, there is an advantage in having at least one female assistant, as many of the lady borrowers prefer to be attended to by one of their own sex. In those libraries which have separate reading-rooms for ladies, it is also essential that a female assistant should look after the room and attends to the renewal of the papers and periodicals placed there.

But to proceed to the real work of a librarian, that which is done for the most part behind the scenes, such as choosing new books, classifying and cataloguing them, attending to correspondence, and the numerous other duties which are comprised in a librarian's work. Here, too, a woman will be as much at home as a man, and will make the institution under her charge a success.

In America, women are taking their places in this ever-widening sphere of labour, and proving that they can do work of this kind quite as well as their brothers. There they have more opportunities of getting a fair trial than we in England possess, for library committees are convinced that librarianship is a profession eminently suited to earnest women of education and refinement, and give them every encouragement accordingly.

The Library School at Albany seems to be doing a good work in training and sending out women ready to labour for the uplifting of those in the towns where their lot is cast, and that good may be done amongst the readers, especially young readers, cannot be denied.

Now that so much more education is considered necessary for every station in life, libraries will soon be found in every town in the kingdom, and this will open up a vast field of labour for both men and women. It is only lately that librarianship has been included amongst the professions at all, and it depends mainly on librarians themselves whether their work is recognized by the outside public or not.

A paper was read at the second annual meeting of the Library Association, held in Manchester in 1879, by the late Alderman Thomas Baker, who was then chairman of the libraries' committee, on "The Employment of Young Women as Assistants in Free Public Libraries." [See page 7.] Mr. Baker said he believed the plan was first tried in the Manchester libraries, and had proved a success. At that time they were only employed as assistants; but since then ladies have held the position of librarians in the branches of the Manchester library, who have, doubtless, in the first place, served in the capacity of assistant in one of the libraries under the corporation.

A girl who enters a library as assistant, and intends to make the work her life-work, if we may so call it, neglects no opportunity of learning as much as possible of the technical part of librarianship, and at the same time tries to improve herself in general knowledge. There is not much time for very deep study of any subject, for the hours in a library are usually very long; but a librarian, male or female, who is always on the alert to find out the books which will be most useful to borrowers and persons who come to seek information of various kinds, will make the institution under his or her charge more popular and flourishing than one who is very learned in any one subject, and, perhaps, oblivious of the fact that the visitors to a library do not all incline to the same study as himself, but expect a little attention to their needs and wants from the librarian. At the same time once can never know enough, and must be ever ready for fresh ideas, and prepared to learn as much as possible.

Women are employed in many of the great American libraries, and even hold the post of chief librarian in some of them. There, however, they are specially trained at the Library School, and are put on an equality with men, and so obtain the same advantages. Some go in for cataloguing as a speciality; this is suited to the quiet, shy women, who, though fully qualified for the work, prefer to do that part of it which may be accomplished away from public view. Others, who do not shine in cataloguing, are well fitted to meet and aid those who come to consult the books under their charge. Some combine both qualities, and are fitted to take control of a library. In England women are not yet admitted into the old and large reference libraries which are scattered over the country, nor into the libraries connected with our colleges, but they are gradually making their way as librarians in the public libraries which are springing up in many of our provincial towns. In this position they must have an all-round knowledge of library work, and be able to help the readers and borrowers in their search for works on special subjects, or even to direct the reading of those who are unable to make a wise choice for themselves.

Here I may just mention that women have acquired rather a bad reputation for being slow in coming to a decision, and when asked to give an opinion on a disputed point or to recommend the best book on a certain subject, they hesitate, are not quite sure, and so on. This is a fault to which many women are prone, and one which must be cured if they are to work on the same level as men. If a woman means to get on in library work, she must learn to be self-reliant, and to make up her mind at once when a decision is to be made. It must be owned, however, that this reproach is not so much deserved as it was some years ago. Girls are now taught on the same principles as boys in many cases, and instead of being made *fine ladies* are taught business habits from childhood, and left to use their own judgement in various matters. This sort of education is bearing fruit already, and the girls who have had this advantage are readier to compete for the same work as their brothers than those who have been brought up in the old-fashioned way. A woman may have as sold an education as a man, and use it as means of earning a livelihood, and still be a womanly woman.

The wider the education possessed by a librarian the more successful the work is likely to prove, and now that librarianship is being found to be as well suited to the capacity of woman as man, there will be keen rivalry between the sexes, for our colleges. Girton and Newnham amongst the number are sending out year by year women who are well taught, self-reliant, and ready to work to the best of their ability in whatever calling they have chosen. That of librarianship will be, I think, one which will commend itself to many as a means of helping others in the search after knowledge, and will also be found an agreeable employment. Miss Black, who was one of the first two librarians at the People's Palace, London, formerly of Newnham College, Cambridge, passed the graduation examinations, and would have obtained the degree had she been a man. Miss James, the late librarian, had three ladies as assistants, two of whom studied at Newnham College, and the other at Lady Margaret Hall, Oxford. All these ladies have found the work most attractive, and, to quote their own expressed opinions, they think there is at present no occupation more suited to women who are fairly well educated, and possess a real love of books. It ought not to be taken up as a mere pastime however, for nothing can be done in this work without earnestness, interest and thoroughness, also devotion to books. At Blackpool, Bridgwater, Darlaston, Darwen, Glossop, Nantwich, Poole,

Fleetwood, Middleton, Northwich, Sittingbourne, Willenhall, Carnarvon, Galashiels, Hawick, Selkirk, and Widnes, ladies fill the office of librarian. At Peel Park Library and Regent Road, Salford, and at two or three of the branch libraries at Manchester, ladies are employed as librarians. In addition to the above named towns, the following libraries employ female assistants, viz.: Battersea, Clerkenwell, Westminster and Chelsea, London; Aberdeen, Derby, Doncaster, Edinburgh, Oldham, Nottingham, Paisley, Sheffield, Glasgow (Stirling's Library, Baillie Instituion), Bradford, Bristol, Manchester, Liverpool, and St. Helens, and the three lady librarians at Blackpool, Salford, and Widnes have female assistants.

But to be a successful librarian, a woman must have a a practical training in all the work connected with a library; and to get this it is necessary that she should become, in the first place, an assistant to some librarian, who will teach her the technicalities of his craft.

England has not as yet found it necessary to establish a special college for the training of librarians, such as in successful operation in the United States, but still something has been done, and the L.A.U.K. examination of library assistants is a step in the right direction; and, doubtless, before long, all applicants for the post of librarian will have to produce certificates from this body. As women prove their capability for this kind of work, better appointments than those they now fill will be thrown open to them; and they will be engaged in the higher positions in our great libraries, and will so work and use their talents that their influence will be felt by many in towns other than those in which their work lies. But that time has not yet come; they must, at present, be content to wield their sway over the libraries which are so quickly springing up around us, and let their work, by its quality and usefulness, prove them fit for still better things.

Another hindrance to the employment of women in libraries is, that many enter the filed, not with the view of making it a life-work, but merely as a means to an end. They think it a pleasant sort of work, but do not intend to remain at it. Now, the best work cannot be done, unless it is felt to be the work on which one's life is to be spent, and few or no women will remain in a library after marriage, for instance. But if their work is to be a real work, this must not be an obstacle. Let the work be done during the time they are engaged in it—be it long or short—in such a manner, that when they leave it, it has not to be done over again by the next comer, but is as perfect as it is possible to make it.

At present, the employment of women as librarians is in its infancy, but is sure to prove a success; for girls who make up their minds to embrace the library profession as their life-work will work patiently and well, and will lose no opportunity of learning all that will aid them in their duties, and will show that, given the same opportunities as boys, they will do equally as well in this as in many other professions, and may, perhaps, excel some of them.

In conclusion, I would just remark that we do not wish to supplant our male friends in this work, but only ask that fair opportunities may be given to those of our sex who are anxious and willing to become labourers in this field of public work.

Improper Books

A paper delivered at the 1895 ALA Conference in Denver, Colorado.
By George T. Clark, Librarian, San Francisco Free Public Library. *Papers and Proceedings of the Seventeenth General Meeting of the American Library Association,* pp. 33-35.

In thinking of this matter of improper books I have been reminded of the definition given by a certain professor, who asked his class in botany to tell him what a weed was. No one being ready to respond, he informed them that a weed was "the right thing in the wrong place." The wild flowers which in springtime clothe the hillsides in variegated hues add beauty to the landscape and afford the naturalist materials for interesting researches. Comparison of the flora of different countries at the same period, or of the same country during different epochs supplies important data in the life history of earth. But these same wild flowers spring up in the corn field, are regarded simply as weeds which must be eradicated without delay.

Similarly, there are many books which, in their proper places, may serve agood and useful purpose, but which under other conditions may exert a most baleful influence. In order, then, to determine what books are improper we must take into consideration the character and functions of the library for which they were intended, and the purpose they are supposed to serve. Is the institution a college, subscription, society, or free public library? Are the funds at its disposal sufficient to warrant buying liberally of all kinds of books, or are they in that not infrequent state which compels the exercising of a rigid selective process, and limits the purchases to absolute necessities? All these are questions which must be taken into consideration in fixing the standard which shall determine the fitness or unfitness of books.

What, then, shall be the standard for a public library maintained by revenues derived from taxation? To determine this, we must arrive at some definite idea as to the proper functions of public libraries. Why has the State enacted laws under which holders of property are compelled to pay taxes for the support of such institutions? It is expected that a public library will contribute to the general welfare of the people, and be an institution which shall exert an elevating influence on the community. In fact, that it shall assist in the education of the people and the making of good citizens. Unless it does exercize these functions, what justice is there in making it a burden on the taxpayers? What right has it to exist?

The theory that a library is primarily an educational institution is quite generally accepted. Being such, the books purchased for it must be of such a character that it shall be enabled to perform the functions of such an institution. In addition to the strictly educational features, however, it is conceded that a library may well provide the means for healthful recreation. In so doing, it promotes the welfare of the community and fulfils one of the objects of its being. The duties of those having the selection of books would seem, then, to be quite plainly outlined. The books should either be capable of adding to the general store of knowledge, of exercizing some beneficial influence upon the mind, or of providing wholesome amusement or recreation.

The establishment of such a standard would exclude many of the books now issuing in such a constant stream from the press. Some of these, for a short time, have great popularity, especially if they are sensational or contain between their covers matters that will not bear discussion in good society.

The librarian may find it difficult to resist the popular demand sure to follow for books widely advertised and much talked about. When the book is decidedly bad his course is clear, but more perplexing are those books having the negative merit of not being positively harmful, but which absorb the time and attention that might well be turned in a better direction.

It is claimed by some that it is the duty of the public library to supply the books the people want; but a little thought will show the fallacy of such claims. That would be a strangely governed household wherein the children had only to express a desire to have it gratified. It is also urged that books by such writers as Braeme, Southworth, and Stephens, have a place in the public library because of their drawing qualities; that they attract a certain class of readers which otherwise would remain away, and that after a time, these readers will have absorbed such literature to the point of saturation, and can then be induced to take something of a higher order. But it is doubtful whether better results could not be obtained by other methods without such a waste of means. By supplying such books, a library fosters the taste that craves them, and increases the demand.

Those administering a public library have a higher duty to perform than merely to follow in the wake of the passing fancies of the popular mind. It is much easier to follow than to lead, but they must bear in mind their responsibilities to future generations as well as the present. The value of the library, depending on the character of its contents, is lessened by every worthless book that goes upon the shelves. Its future value, therefore, depends largely on the wisdom of its management during the present. Now, having fixed a standard in our minds, how are we to decide as to what books come up to it? Life is too short and the books too numerous to permit a personal examination in all cases. Evidently we must rely upon the judgment of others to aid us in separating the wheat from the chaff.

I will briefly explain the method pursued in the institution with which I am associated. All purchases are under the supervision of a book committee consisting of five members of the Board of Trustees. It may be well to state that under the existing law the term of a trustee of this library is for life, and the composition of the committees remains practically unchanged year to year. The chairman of the book committee is a gentleman of broad culture and of great liberality in his views. He is a graduate of Harvard, and served for a brief term as president of our State University. Among the other members of the committee are a justice of the Supreme Court, a well-known writer, and the principal of one of our public schools.

At their monthly meetings these gentlemen consider the items recommended for purchase by the librarian, or in other ways brought to their attention. They are very discriminating, and consider carefully the merits of the books proposed, and the relative need for them. The order lists, as made up, include only the approved items. The librarian is expected to be informed on current publications, and to know something about a book before recommending it.

In addition to the formal orders made up in this manner, there are purchased each month books on what we term "the hundred-dollar list." The book committee has at its command the sum of $100 per month for the purchase of publications which it is desirable to obtain without unnecessary delay. The books on these lists are selected in the following manner: The librarian makes a monthly visit to the four leading book stores in the city, and after looking over the stock selects as many of the desirable books as can be purchased without exceeding the limit. With the breadth of a continent between us and the leading publishing centres, there are many books which never find their way to the counters of the local dealers unless specially ordered, and during dull seasons the supply from which to select is meagre. It may happen that one month not more than $50 worth can be purchased, but this is offset by buying $150 worth some month when there is a better stock to chose from.

The books thus selected are then sent to the library subject to the approval of the book committee. It sometimes happens that their judgment and the librarian's do not coincide, in which case the book goes back to the dealer. Buying in this manner, before the books have been on the market long enough for much to be known about them, and before the critics have had time to assign them to their proper places, there is a chance to go astray. We endeavor to keep on the safe side, however, by confining our selections to those of which we can feel sure, leaving doubtful books until more is known of them.

Of course, with a system like this, it is impossible to have the new books ready for circulation on the day of their publication, or on the following. We cannot accommodate those who consider it a duty to read all the latest novels. They must rely upon the subscription libraries and the book stores. But we do endeavor to add to our shelves each year, just as many books of permanent value as our funds allow, and to acquire them as expeditiously as circumstances permit, trying to build up a library that shall not be strong in some classes as the expense of weakness in others, but one that shall be symmetrical in all its parts, with possibly a special emphasis on some features which under existing conditions may be entitled to greater consideration. it is our aim to foster a desire for good literature, and we endeavor to make such literature available to all.

Hear the Other Side—1896 ALA President's Address

The address of ALA President John Cotton Dana, Librarian of the Denver Public Library. The conference was in Cleveland and Mackinaw, Ohio, September 1-4 and 8, 1896. *Papers and Proceedings of the Eighteenth General Meeting of the American Library Association,* pp. 1-5.

I sometimes fear my enthusiasm for the free public library is born more of contagion than of conviction. Consider the thing in some of its evident aspects. You have a building perhaps erected to perpetuate a good man's memory, a monument and of use only as a monument; or constructed in accordance with the views of an architect whose ideas of beauty are crude and whose thought of utility is naught; ill-adapted to the purpose for which it is intended; poorly lighted; badly ventilated. In it are stored a few thousand volumes, including, of course, the best books of all time—which no one reads—and a generous per cent. of fiction of the cheaper sort. To this place come in good proportion the idle and the lazy. Also the people who can't endure the burden of a thought, and who fancy they are improving their minds, while in fact they are simply letting the cool water of knowledge trickle through the sieve of an idle curiosity. The more persistent visitors are largely men who either have failed in a career, or never had a career, or do not wish a career. We all know our own indolents, our own idlers, our own "boarders." There is little that is inspiring, *per se*, in the sight of the men who gather in the newspaper reading room of any free public library. There is not much that is encouraging in a careful look at the people who are the more constant visitors to the shelves of the reference department. Who wear out our dictionaries, the students of language or the competitors in a word-building contest? Of those who come to the delivery counter, if our friends tell the truth, 60 to 80 per cent. rarely concern themselves, as far as the library knows them, with anything outside of fiction, and in that field concern themselves generally only with the latest novel, which they wish because it is the latest. And of this 60 to 80 per cent., a large proportion—probably at least half—prefer to get, and generally do get, a novel of the cheaper kind.

I am stating the case plainly. I share your enthusiasm; but that enthusiasm is not seldom to me—and I believe you—a cause for surprise. Has it not often come sharply home to every one of you—the hopelessness of the task we assume to set ourselves? the triviality of the great mass of the free public library's educational work? the discouraging nature of the field?

the pettiness, the awful pettiness of results?

Nor is this all. That we strive for great things and accomplish the infinitely little; that our output is by no means commensurate with the size of the plant and the cost of its maintenance, this is by no means the only fact which may rightly sober our enthusiasm.

Fathers and mothers love their children and look after their happiness. The more they do this, the more they concern themselves that the human beings they have brought into the world be self-reliant, self-supporting people, knowing how to live in harmony with their fellows, and wishing so to live, the more civilized they are. Parental responsibility is something the sense of which has never been too acute. That I may rightly scorn and despise my neighbor is his children are not decent, attractive, civilized; that my neighbor may rightly consider himself disgraced if his offspring grew not up in the fear of the admonition of the—good citizen; these things are not yet commonly received. The native manners and the education of the American child are looked upon, not so much as the result of parentage and home training, as the good gift of God and the public school.

A strong sense of parental responsibility—this is a prime essential in the growth of true culture—in the increase of social efficiency. And this feeling of obligation to train properly the souls of one's own creation; this sense that the parent can win public approval as a parent only when the result is an additional factor in the public's happiness and comfort; this rule of living would surely result, if rightly applied, in careful consideration of the child's education. But what have we done? We have turned the whole subject of education over to the community. We have made it depend very largely on the result of an annual counting of noses. We have let it slip gradually into the hands of those veritable and inevitable children of government—the politicians. The American parent is indifferent to the character of the education of his children. The interposition of the community in what should be his affairs has not only made him indifferent to those affairs, it has made others indifferent that he is so. He pays his taxes. If the schools are poor the fault is at the school-board's door, not his.

I am dwelling long on this point, for it is vital.

The free public library not only relieves the idle and incompetent and indifferent from the necessity—would he have books—of going to work to earn them; it not only checks the growth of the tendency of the private individual to collect a library of his own, adapted to his own needs, and suiting his own tastes and those of his children, just as the free public school may lead them to be indifferent to their formal education. Certainly, fathers and mothers whose children use public libraries seem to care very little what and how much their children read. They conceal their solicitude from librarian and assistants, if it exists. Yet, if a collection of books in a community is a good thing for the community—and we seem to think it is; and if it is a good thing particularly for the children of the community—as we seem to think it is, then it is a good thing, not in itself simply, not as an object of worship, not as an adequate excuse for the erection of a pleasing mortuary monument on the public street, but for its effect on young folks' manners and on young folks' brains. But to produce a maximum effect herein, to produce even a desirable effect, the right books must be put into the right hand at the right time. Can any do this rightly save the parents at least co-operate with them? But the public library is not an institution which the mother helps to support because she has come to believe in it; because it is her pleasure, because she can and does keep a watchful eye on its growth and methods. It is part of the machinery of the state. She confides her children to its tender mercies in the same spirit with which her forbears confided in their king! And she does no more.

Furthermore, the essence of government is force. This essence remains whether the visible form be king or majority. It is open to question—I put it mildly—whether it is expedient to touch with the "strong hand" the impulse of a people to train with earnest thought their young, or the impulse of a people to give light to their fellows. People wish, in the main, to educate their children. Without this wish a school system, public or private, would be impossible. This wish is the vital fact; that the system is public and tax-supported is the secondary fact; the result, not the cause. People wish also, in the main, to give their fellows and themselves the opportunity for self-improvement. This wish is the vital fact at the bottom of the free, compulsorily supported public library. It is on these vital facts we should keep our eyes and our thoughts, not on the feature of compulsion. Work, then, for the extension of the public library from the starting-point of human sympathy, from the universal desire for an increase of human happiness by an increase of knowledge of the conditions of human happiness, not from the starting point of law, compulsion, of enforcing on others our views of their duty.

I have said enough in this line. To the observant eye our libraries are not altogether halls of learning; they are also haunts of the lazy. They do not interest parents in their children; perhaps they lead parents to be indifferent to their children.

But really, you say, all this is not our concern. You have had this thought—what is all this to us?—already and many times in these few minutes. We find ourselves here; loving the companionship of books;

desirous of extending the joys they can give to our fellows; embarked in public service, and active—none are more so; honest—none are more so, in our work of making good use of books. Your modern librarian is in his daily life no disputatious economist, idly wavering, like the fabled donkey, between the loose hay of a crass individualism and the chopped feed of a perfectionist socialism. He is a worker. If there are things to be said which may add to the efficiency of his attempts to help his fellows to grow happier and wiser, let us hear them; and for this we have come together.

I have said these things, I am sure you will believe me, not with the wish to lessen the zeal of one of us in our chosen work. A moment's look at the case against us cannot anger us—that were childish; cannot discourage us—that were cowardly; it may lead us to look to the joints in our armor; it should lead us to renew our efforts. If the free public library movement be not absolutely and altogether a good thing—and he is a bold economist who vows that it is—how urgent is the call to us to make each our own library the corrective, as far as may be, of the possible harm of its existence. A collection of books gathered together at the public expense does not justify itself by the simple fact that it is. If it be not a live educational institution it were better never established. It is ours to justify to the world the literary warehouse. A library is good only as the librarian makes it so. Can we do more than we have done to justify our calling? Can we make ourselves of more importance to the world?—of more positive value to the world? Our calling is dignified in our own eyes, it is true; but we are not greatly dignified in the eyes of our fellows. The public does not ask our opinions. We are, like the teachers, students; and we strive, like them, to keep abreast of the times, and to have opinions on vital topics formed after much reading and some thought. But save on more trivial questions, on questions touching usually only the recreative side of life, like those of literature commonly so called, our opinions are not asked for. We are, to put it bluntly, of very little weight in the community. We are teachers; and who cares much for what the teacher says? I am not pausing now to note exceptions. We all know our masters and our exemplars; and I shall not pause to praise the men and women who have brought us where we are; who have lifted librarianship, in the estimation of the wise and good, to a profession, and have made it comparatively an easy thing for you and me to develop our libraries, if we can and will, into all that they should be, and to become ourselves, as librarians, men and women of weight and value in the community. I do not pause to praise them. They understand as well as I that approval and counsel cannot well come from me to them.

I have said that your library is perhaps injuring your community; that you are not of any importance among your own people. And these, you tell me, are hard sayings. In truth they are. I am not here to pass you any compliments. If for five minutes we can divest ourselves of every last shred of our trappings of self-satisfaction, and arouse in ourselves for a moment a keen sense of our sins of omission, of things left undone or not well done, I shall be content, and shall consider that we have wisely opened these Cleveland sessions. I would wish to leave you, here at the very beginning of our discussions, not, indeed, in the Slough of Despond, but climbing sturdily, and well aware that you are climbing, the Hill of Difficulty. Others, I can assure you, will, long before our conference ends, lead us again, and that joyfully, to our Delectable Mountains.

Pardon me, then, while I say over again a few of the things that cannot be too often said.

Look first to your own personal growth. Get in touch with the world. Let no one point to you as to an instance of the narrowing effects of too much of books. Broaden out. Be social. Impress yourself on your community; in a small way if not in a large. Be not superior and reserved. Remember that he who to the popular eye wears much the air of wisdom is never wise.

Coming to your chosen profession: Speak out freely on matters of library management; and especially, in these days, on matters of library constructions. In recent years millions of dollars have been spent on library buildings in this country, and we have not yet a half dozen in the land that do not disgrace us. If we have stood idly by and not made our opinions, our knowledge, our experience, felt by trustees and architects, then is ours the blame, and we are chief among the sufferers. Persuade architects and their associations, local and national—who ignore us because in our inconsequence they know they can—that they may wisely and without loss of dignity consult the professional librarian about the building he is to occupy. I say persuade them; I might better say compel them. To compel them will be easy when you have become of importance in the world. Even now it is not too soon to attempt to confer with them. You can at once make the beginning of friendly and helpful relations with the American Institute of Architects. But you must ask, not demand.

Advertise the A. L. A. and what it stands for. Help to broaden its field. support heartily measures which look to a greater degree of publicity for it. Interest your trustees in it. Interest your friends, and your patrons and constituents in it. Be ready and willing to do your share of the work—and there's no end of work—that each year must be done to keep it properly alive and well in the public eye. Call the attention of your trustees to the difference between the efficient library, such as the A. L. A. advocates and strives for, and the dead-and-alive collection of books, still altogether too common where the A. L. A. spirit has not yet penetrated. Consider the contrast between the possible public library and the public library that is. If the causes for that contrast lie at your door, face them frankly and bravely, and strive to remove them.

Do not forget the Library Department of the National Educational Association, recently established. It gives you excuse, and it gives you cause, to take an interest, more active even that heretofore, in the introduction of books and library methods into school work, and to concern yourselves more than ever before with the general reading of teachers and their pupils. Impress upon teachers the value to them of your library. Persuade them, if you can, that to do their best work they must know well and use freely the good books.

See that your local book and news man is heartily with you in the work of spreading knowledge of the right use of books and in encouraging ownership of books in your community. If you come in contact with the bookseller and the publisher of the great cities do what you can to persuade them that to join in the work of the A. L. A. is not only to benefit the community at large, but to help their own particular business as well.

Be not slow in giving hearty recognition to those who have, in the beginnings of library science, taken the first place and borne the burdens and made an easy way for us who follow. If, perhaps against some odds, a librarian, man or woman, is making an eminent success of some great city library, may you not properly send him, once and again, a word which shall signify that you, at least, are alive to the fact of this good work and are yourself encouraged and inspired thereby? Like words of approval you may well extend to the good men, outside of the profession proper, who have given their time and energy, a labor of love, to improve certain features of library work. I need not specify.

Interest in your work in your own community your local book-lovers and book-collectors and book-worms and private students and plodders and burners of the midnight oil. Get in touch with the teachers of literature in the colleges and schools of your neighborhood. Expound to such, and to the general reader as well, whenever you properly can, the difficulty and the possibilities of your calling, your conquests in classification and cataloging, and your advances in bibliography and indexing, and the progress in recent years of general library economy. Remember that all these things can be even better done in the small community, in the village library of a few hundred volumes, than in the large library of the great city.

Note the women's clubs, art associations, historical societies, scientific societies. Do not forget the private schools. In the small town you can gain without difficulty the good-will of the local newspaper. You can often assist the editor in his work, and lead him to help you in return. The clergymen in your town certainly care somewhat for the reading of their young people, and will co-operate with you in any intelligent effort to increase it and improve it. The Sunday-school libraries of your neighborhood are open to your suggestions, if you approach them properly. And the Y. M. C. and the Y. W. C. associations will gladly take from you advice and assistance in the management of their reading rooms and libraries.

None are so poor that they cannot give to others; and few libraries are so small that they cannot spare books and magazines enough to make a little library which may be sent out into a still smaller community and there do good service.

Do the business men and the business women, the active people, those who feed us and clothe us and transport us, those who have brought about in the last few decades the great increase in creature comforts for every one, do these business people take an active interest in your library? Do they care for you, or for your opinion? If not, is it their fault? is it that they are gross and dull and material and worldly; or is it that you, the wise librarian, know not yet how to bring your educational forces to bear on the life that now is? Our work is but begun so long as we are not in close touch with the man of affairs.

Remember that as you in your little town, or in your city, widen the sphere of your influence, grow to be a person of worth and dignity in the community, you thereby add so much to the dignity and the the effectiveness of the whole profession. If in a city or town near you there is a library which, in its general arrangement is not what it should be, which is but a dusty pile of printed pages or but a roosting-place for a flock of cheap novels, yours is in part the fault, and you are largely the loser. When a dweller in that town, one unacquainted with library affairs—and most are such—hears you alluded to as a "librarian," he thinks of you as a person akin to the bibliothecal pagan who fails to manage the library of his own town, the only library he knows by which he can measure your work. He is a "librarian"; you are a "librarian." We wear the livery of our coworkers as well as our own.

Keep these thoughts in mind and you will see how essential it is, would our profession reach the standing we wish it to reach, would we make it everywhere an honor to wear our name, that every smallest library be an effective educational machine, and that every humblest librarian be an active, enthusiastic, intelligent worker. Yet some people in charge of accumulations of books must even now be urged to join the A. L. A. See that your library is interesting to the people of the community, the people who own it, the people who maintain it. Deny your people nothing which the book-shop grants them. Make your library at least as attractive as the most attractive retain store in the community. Open your eyes to the cheapness of books at the present day, and to the unimportance, even to the small library, of the loss of an occasional volume; and open them also to the necessity of getting your constituency in actual contact with the books themselves. Remember always that taxation is compulsion; that taxation is government; that government, among present-day human creatures, is politics; that the end of an institution may not justify its means; that a free public library may be other than a helpful thing. See to it, therefore, the more carefully that your own public library at least is rationally administered, and promotes public helpfulness.

The Telegraph in the Library

By Richard Garnett, in *Essays in Librarianship and Bibliography* (New York: Harper, 1899).

Library administration, like all other departments of human activity in this age, must experience the results of the unexampled development of science in its application to the affairs of life. The most immediately obvious of these are the mechanical: so simple a device as the sliding-press, as will be shown in its place, has saved the nation thousands of pounds. The most promising field for such achievements has hitherto been the United States, where the application of scientific contrivances to ordinary purposes is more general than in Europe, and where the more important libraries are new structures, where improvements can form part of the original plan, with no fear of impediment from arrangements already existing. Next to mechanics photography and electricity may be named as the scientific agencies chiefly adapted for the promotion of library service. Photography has been sufficiently treated in another essay in this volume. The services of electricity will be most cordially acknowledged by those who best remember the paralysis of literary work, alike official and private, engendered by a fog at the British Museum, and in particular recall the appearance of the Reading Room, a Byzantine "tower of darkness," with a lantern dimly burning in the centre, the windows presenting the appearance of slate, and dubious figures gliding or stumbling through the gloom—attendants brought in from the library to take care that the handful of discontented readers did not profit by the opportunity to steal the books. All this nuisance has been abolished by the electric light, which not only renders the Reading Room available for the public on dark days, but allows the ordinary work of the Museum to be carried on in all departments; the same may be said of all other libraries. The beautiful, potent, and above all safe electric ray is an advantage to all, and in dark days a passage from death unto life for those libraries where, as in the Museum, gas has been proscribed on account of its danger and its injurious effects upon books.

The services of electricity to libraries, however, are by no means exhausted by the electric light. It is capable of rendering aid even more important, and the more so in proportion to the extent of the library. The need for rapid communication throughout large buildings has been in some measure met by the telephone, whose usefulness is impaired by its incapacity for transmitting and recording written messages. Recourse must be had to the telegraph—not, of course, that ordinary description of the instrument where the record is made in dots and dashes, intelligible solely to the expert—but the printing telegraph, where the message appears in clear type, or a facsimile of the transmitter's handwriting. The use of such telegraphs for various purposes, especially those of the Stock Exchange, is now very familiar, and there is perhaps no place where it could be introduced with more signal advantage than the Reading Room of the British Museum.

There is no great reason at present for complaint of delay in bringing books from the Museum library to the Reading Room; but the system is not, as so many other points of Museum administration are, one to challenge the administration and emulation of other libraries. It is impossible to observe its working without pronouncing it cumbrous and below the present level of civilised ingenuity. The reader writes his ticket at the catalogue desk, generally with a pen trying to his temper, and the captive of his bow and spear. He then walks some distance to deposit it in a basket on a counter, where it remains until a boy is at hand to carry it to the corridor outside the Reading Room, where it is put into a clip and drawn up to the gallery. All these operations are indispensable so long as recourse is solely had to human muscle, but they evidently involve great loss of time. The object to be aimed at should be the delivery of the ticket at the table of the attendants who procure the book in the library simultaneously with its being written in the Reading Room; and this seeming impossibility can be achieved by the employment of a writing telegraph by which, as fast as the message is written at one end of the wire, it is recorded in facsimile at the other. The present writer has experimented with the American Telautograph, and, so far as the experiments went, nothing could be more satisfactory. No knowledge of telegraphy whatever is required from the operator: he simply inscribes his message with a style on a piece of tissue-paper, and it reappears simultaneously at the other end of the wire. Nothing seems necessary but to furnish the catalogue desks with electrical transmitters (which occupy no great space) instead of inkstands, and to provide for the carrying of the wires out of the room. When the writer endeavoured to introduce electrical communication in 1894, he feared that this requisite would present difficulties, but was assured by experts that it really offered none. The ticket written by the reader might be retained by him as a memorandum: if it could be repeated in duplicate at the other end, one copy might be treated as now; the other, with any necessary correction, might be pasted at once into the register, saving all the time now occupied in registration.

It is of course perfectly possible that hitches and breakings down might at first occur from time to time, from the delicacy of the machine employed, or from other causes. The machines have not been properly tested, nor can they be, except by a continuous course of experiment. But whence this morbid fear of experiment? After Darwin's definition, the apprehension should surely be on the other side. A single machine, kept at work for a week, would be sufficient to test the principle. The first experiments with electric light at the Museum were anything but promising, but Sir Edward Bond persevered, and the result is what we see.

And how brilliant a result the establishment of telegraphic communication would be! The saving of time is no doubt the most practical consideration, but apart from this, how vast the improvement in the economy of the Reading Room! No more troops of boy attendents, with the inevitable noise and bustle; nothing but the invisible messenger speeding on his silent errand, and the quiet delivery of books at the desks: an unparalleled scene of perfect physical repose in the midst of intense mental activity. Of course the improvement would not stop with the Reading Room, and ere long all departments would be connected by the writing telegraph.

This paper, of course, is not written with any view of recommending the Telautograph. Instruments better adapted for the purpose may exist, although the writer has not met with them. He originally proposed the employment of a printing telegraph as a means of abridging delays in the Reading Room as long ago as 1876. The great improvements in administration introduced at that time, however, rendered the need less urgent; nor, perhaps, was electrical science itself then sufficiently developed. Acquaintance with the Telautograph led him to take the subject up again in 1893 and 1894, and he still hopes to find the electric force a match for *vis inertiae*.

Library Cooperation

By Lodilla Ambrose
The Dial; a Semi-monthly Journal of Literary Criticism, Discussion, and Information.
July 16, 1901. Vol. 31, No. 362.

The American Library Association has just held its twenty-third general meeting, at Waukesha, Wisconsin. At the first meeting of the association, in 1876, attention was directed to the possibilities of cooperation among librarians for the attainment of worthy ends not to be secured by individuals working singly. The early volumes of the *"Library Journal"* contain frequent contributions on this topic. In fact, the question has always been with the association.

This principle of cooperation was applied to indexing, and Poole's Index to Periodical Literature, with its multiple supplements, and the A. L. A. Index to General Literature, resulted. Its application to reciprocal relations between libraries led to inter-library loans. Now the professor in an isolated Kansas college may pursue his own advanced studies, because through his library he may borrow books from Harvard University Library. Another phase of the larger library's work for the smaller is seen in the many-sided developments of the traveling library idea as carried out by state libraries and library commissions. Prior to 1901, seventeen states had made provision for the aiding of very small libraries and communities with no libraries by the formation of state library commissions. The lessening of administrative expenses by printing and distributing catalogue cards to libraries through some central bureau was recognized as a desideratum at the outset. But obstacles were met in the varying sizes of cards used by libraries, and in difficulties of selection and distribution. Valuable annotated bibliographies of selected titles on various subjects have been possible only through cooperation and the generous financial support of such friends of libraries as Mr. George Iles of New York City. The bibliography American history is now half through the press.

A factor destined to be powerful in many future cooperative undertakings for libraries came to the front at this conference—the Library of Congress. Its coming was greeted with the enthusiasm its importance demands. At the public meeting of the association the chief address was by the Librarian of Congress, Mr. Herbert Putnam, on "What may be done for Libraries by the Nation." He defined his subject as what the nation as a unit acting through its central authority may do. He said, in brief:

"Only as assumed by central authority are some undertakings possible. The federal government is already aiding libraries in varied ways. It encourages the manufacture of good books, it exempts from duty foreign books for libraries, it establishes bureaus of scientific research, it is the largest publisher in the world, it uses a million pounds of paper stock a year and distributes over three hundred thousand of its own issues, it has a clearing-house for duplicate United States documents, it is indexing its own publications, it maintains a bureau in the interest of educational institutions, it maintains a bureau in the interest of educational institutions, and this bureau has brought out several valuable library publications. The government maintains its own great libraries; for example, that of the Surgeon-General's Office, whose elaborate catalogue has already cost more than $250,000. "But government activities in behalf of libraries naturally center in the Library of Congress. This was created as a legislative library, but it is now referred to as something more. Its building was paid for by the country at large, it is often alluded to as the national library of the United States, and such it may become. Its conditions differ from those of the British Museum. There a student need not go over five hundred miles to reach his national library, here he may have to go three thousand miles. It should serve students in Washington, it ought also to provide for scholars in the country at large by loaning books to them and by employing specialists to answer questions sent to Washington. To meet their needs, it should accumulate original sources, works of importance for occasional reference, the useless books that libraries in general cannot afford space for, and the general mass of books. All this involves the costly processes of cataloguing and classification. Cooperative undertakings should have headquarters in Washington. The Library of Congress may provide a national clearing-house for miscellaneous duplicates. Toward these things we are drifting. We have the building, the equipment, the books. The library contains seven hundred thousand volumes, and five hundred thousand other items. Its resources are not omnipotent, but they are comprehensive. It is strong in Americana, political and social science, jurisprudence, learned societies and serials in general. As far as deliberate purchase is concerned two extremes are to be abstained from, books merely popular and those merely curious. Books are to be bought that will aid in the establishment of fact. The library has the organization, having now a staff of 261 persons, not including caretakers, printers, or binders. It has a division of bibliography, a bindery, and a printing office. But it has also a large arrear of work, including the classification and shelf-list, and the author and subject catalogues. A library of reference books for Congress should be arranged, and the other libraries of the District of Columbia should be coordinated with the Library of Congress, and it should have a catalogue of all these libraries. In some respects the equipment is inadequate for these larger undertakings. Its authorities should consider what may be done in the distribution of printed cards to general libraries. it may become the bibliographic bureau of the United States and issue publications. If it is to be the national library, it should loan books to other libraries, serving the scholar through the local library."

No greater boon could come to American libraries than the realization of the plans projected by Mr. Putnam for the development of a national library, and outlined in the foregoing brief synopsis. This library is the natural centre for all great bibliographical undertakings in this country, and the natural point of contact with international enterprises.

During the conference, an agreement was reached between Mr. Putnam and the publishing board of the American Library Association, and as a result the Library of Congress is to furnish its printed cards for distribution to other libraries. The details of the plan are still to be worked out, but it will certainly be of the greatest benefit to the libraries of the country. It means reduced expense and drudgery, and increased inspiration as a consequence. One of the older librarians even said that he could now depart in peace for he had seen cooperative printed cards established at the national library.

Undoubtedly the general public cares very little about the details of library cataloguing and classification. If it gets prompt service, it asks no questions. But it must be a matter of deep interest to scholars to see the librarians giving an increasing amount of attention to the expert bibliographical aide of library matters. This tendency was very marked at this meeting. Two long sessions of one section were devoted to details of certain modifications in cataloguing rules, the standpoint of the libraries for scholars being chiefly considered. Still another session was occupied with bibliography in its strict sense. Another indication of the same trend is the organization within two years of the Bibliographic Society of Chicago. This society held an informal meeting at Waukesha, many of the non-resident members being present. The spirit there manifested will probably develop this into a national society in a few years. The full and frequent consideration of the problems of the small public library, with its abbreviated catalogue of books chiefly American, has been a necessity. The stress laid upon the books for children, and on children's rooms, is as it should be. But the lack of the scholarly element in American library affairs has been unfavorably commented on abroad, even while the American success in practical library technique is freely admitted. This new emphasis on the scholarly side of librarianship is a welcome development.

A period of library expansion is evidently at hand. The gifts to libraries from June 1, 1900, to July 1, 1901, include 405 separate gifts, amounting to $16,130,220.12; and of these gifts, 394 are for libraries in the United States. The chief donor to libraries is Mr. Andrew Carnegie, his benefactions amounting in this year to more than eleven millions. With princely gifts to libraries, with Dr. John S. Billings as the new president of the American Library Association, with cooperative cataloguing established on a basis never before possible, with scholarship receiving increasing recognition in library affairs, the outlook for American libraries is heartening in the highest degree.

On George Iles' plea for a headquarters for ALA

"A Library of Libraries"
The Nation, July 30, 1903, p. 89.

At the recent meeting of the American Library Association, Mr. George Iles, whose services to critical cataloguing have won him the gratitude of many readers, made a plea, now published in pamphlet form, for a headquarters for the Association. By gaining such a home the Association, which now conducts an occasional dress parade, would organize itself into a working staff to direct and promote library interests throughout the country all the year round. Such an institution as a repository of all kinds of information on preserving and circulating books would be a library of libraries. Its usefulness will appear as its various departments are enumerated.

At headquarters would naturally be collected all manner of information about library buildings—photographs, plans, and description of furnishings. Thus a great number of examples to follow or to avoid would be furnished to library committees; and in order that the profusion of material should not cause bewilderment, the central officials would appraise each building from the point of view of library economy, pointing out in detail its advantages and defects. In some of our greatest library buildings the architects have signally failed to grasp the practical needs of the situation. Clearly it would be well if, before putting pencil to paper, every architect with a library to build should first seek the fountain-head of modern library lore. Undoubtedly, the necessary materials would be sent on liberal conditions to those who could not make the pilgrimage in person.

In its department of administration the general staff would merely continue under more favorable circumstances the work already excellently begun by the American Library Association. Here one approaches mystery. The layman must be content to believe that the science of classification grows wider and deeper with the process of suns, and he must accept of faith, too, that gentle moral suasion by which communities are weaned from the novelette and put upon adult diet of poetry, history, and biography. Again, the competing claims of book-stack and open shelves may not be weighed by the inexpert. But there is doctrine for all these matters, and a central authority alone could hope to build up a set of dogmas sufficiently flexible and exact to have authoritative weight. It is certain that the broad lines of library polity might be established by such a body, and many defects due to inexperience and the absence of authorities done away with.

Naturally, Mr. Iles spoke in behalf of the work with which his name is particularly associated—that of appraisal of books. This means, in short, that beyond the usual indications, library catalogues should briefly characterize each book and estimate its value. A good beginning has been made in Mr. J. N. Larned's creditable work, "The Literature of American History," but Mr. Iles looks forward to a time when all "working books" shall be thus appraised. As things are to-day, the average reader is helpless before the list of hundreds of titles under each subject head. A note on each catalogue card giving the character of the book would yield the assistance now necessarily imperfectly supplied by the library attendants. But evidently the preparation of such critical notes requires expert skill and involves considerable expense. Probably no single library could afford to undertake it. A central library committee, however, could do this useful work for the country at large—issuing either the complete "appraisal" cards or pasters to be used on the present library cards. As literature accumulates upon all subjects, such evaluation becomes increasingly more imperative. It could be managed nowhere so economically as by a committee with specialist collaborators, which might reasonably hope to sell its cards and catalogues throughout the country.

Finally, the proposed general library staff might coordinate and control the work of library extension. "Travelling libraries" are already familiar to our readers. Circulating Art Exhibitions, composed of carefully selected reproductions of fine examples, have been inaugurated with success by several States. There is a comic suggestion about the "circulating lecture," but the thing itself is sensible enough. Carefully prepared lectures with the necessary lantern slides are sent about, and the lecture is read by a member of the local association. One might feel that it would be far better to select for illustration essays and printed lectures from standard literature; but as to the general practicability of the plan there is no doubt. At the central repository are kept slides and manuscripts, and the lectures are usually accompanied by a small collection of books on the subject of the course. Last winter, Professor Penhallow, from his headquarters at Montreal, thus conducted free lectures in fifty-one towns, villages, mining, and lumber camps throughout the Dominion. It is highly desirable that some skilled body should have the care of all such movements, for nowhere is half-culture more out of place than in popular education. The people fare ill when they exchange carelessness of the things of the mind for the sentimentality of the faddist of the vulgarity of the intellectual quack. In all these matters a committee of library extension might exercise a very tonic influence.

Mr. Iles saves to the last his estimate of the cost and condition of an effective Library of Libraries. Some great central library must give it, if not house room, at least the freedom of the premises; and some benefactor or benefactors must start it with an endowment of a million dollars. When the usefulness of such an institution is once fully understood, we do not anticipate any difficulty on either score.

Wild Flower Show at the Free Library

Sixty Varieties Gathered in and About Oakland Exhibited in the Children's Room

From *The San Francisco Call*, March 27, 1904.

Oakland, March 26.—A beautiful collection of wild flowers gathered in and about Oakland was exhibited today in the Children's room of the Oakland Free Library, about sixty varieties in all being on exhibition, nearly all of which came from the canyons and hills in Oakland and Berkeley.

The flower show was the idea of Librarian Greene and the flowers were secured and arranged by a committee of public school teachers of Oakland.

The members of the committee were Miss F. J. de Wolf, chairman; Miss J. K. Burrall; Miss C. J. Giamboni, Mrs. F. C. Preble, Miss M. Moore, Miss Margaret Fortler, Miss E. M. Sherman, Miss Montgomery, Miss Margaret Bradley, Miss Carolyn Reed, Miss Sally Hampton, Mrs. Van Duyne, Miss White, Miss Storrie, Miss Julia Smith, Miss Vandergaw, Miss Pierce and Miss Wythe.

After the close of the flower show the flowers were given to local churches.

The Library: Its Past and Future

By Guido Biagi, Director, Royal Laurentian Library, Florence, Italy. A talk given at the ALA Annual Conference, St. Louis, Missouri, 1904. *Papers and Proceedings of the Twenty-Sixth General Meeting of the American Library Association,* pp. 8-15.

The first founders of public libraries having been Italians, it will perhaps be neither strange nor unfitting that an Italian, the custodian of one of the most ancient and valued book-collections in the world, should speak to you of their past. He may, however, appear presumptuous in that he will speak to you also of their future, thus posing as an exponent of those anticipations which are now fashionable. It is in truth a curious desire that urges us and tempts us to guess at the future, to discover the signs of what it will bring us, in certain characteristics of the present moment. It answers to a want in human nature which knows not how to resign itself to limitations of the present, but would look beyond it into time and space.

This looking forward toward the future is no selfish sentiment; it springs from the desire not to dissipate our powers in vain attempts, but to prepare new and useful material for the work of the future, so that those who come after us may move forward without hindrance or perturbation, without being obliged to overturn and destroy, before they can build up anew. Thus does it happen in nature; huge secular trunks flourish and grow green by luxuriant offshoots which add new vigor of life to the old and glorious stock.

We may perhaps discover the secret of the future of the library by looking back over its past, by attentively studying the varying phases through which it has passed in its upward path towards a splendid goal of wisdom and civilization. By thus doing we may prepare precious material for its future development and trace with security the line of its onward movement. It is of supreme importance that humanity in general, as the individual in particular, know whither its efforts must be directed, that there may be no straying from the straight path. We are sailors on a vast sea bound toward a shore we known not of; when we approach it, it vanishes like a mirage from before our eyes. But we have as guides the stars which have already ruled our destinies, while before us flames, on the distant horizon, that light of the Idea towards which our ships and our hearts move eagerly. Let us stand firm at the helm and not despise the counsels of some old pilot who may perhaps seem faint-hearted to young and eager souls. He who is hurried along by the excitement of the course, by the impetuosity of the motion, finds neither time nor place to look back and to meditate, which is necessary that he may look foward with sharper and calmer gaze.

Modern life among the young and more venturesome peoples is a giddy race. They run, they annihilate the space before them, they press onward, ever onward, with irresistable impetus, but we cannot always say that this headlong course leads straight to the goal. We are not sure, even, that it may not sometimes be running in a circle, a retracing of their steps. In mechanics a free wheel turning upon itself and moving no machinery is so much lost power. Let us beware of free wheels which consume without producing, which give the illusion of movement whilst they still remain stationary. Modern civilization bears within itself a great danger: the endeavor which loses the end by a misuse of the means, and which though busy is ever idle—idle, yet never at rest. It may be, therefore, that a momentary return to the past with all that it can teach will be useful to all of us. Progress has rightly been compared to a continual ascent. Modern man sees before him ever vaster horizons; the eye of science discovers in the infinitely distant and in the infinitely small ever new worlds whether of suns or of bacteria. In the same way do conceptions and ideas ever widen and tend to a more comprehensive generalization. All the march of civilization, both material and moral, consists in rising from a single primordial idea to another more complex and so on to the highest scientific abstractions. Woe to science if it stops short in the course of this evolution; its reputation would be injured beyond repair. In material things, the fate of certain words shows us the great advance that that has been made: the words are the same but the things they represent are very different. We still give the name of Casa (Capsa, that is, hut) to our splendid dwellings, which have here among you reached their highest point of development in your sky-scrapers; we still give to the great trans-atlantic steamers, floating cities, the name of boats, which was once applied to the first rude canoes of the troglodites. The first function of the Casa and of the boat still remains, but how differently are the details carried out. So also, the book, the liber, whose etymology is preserved in the word library, was anciently the inner part of the tree (liber) on which men used to write, and which is now unfortunately again used in the making of paper, no longer obtained from rags but from wood pulp.

The libraries of Assyria and Egypt, those for instance of Assur-Bani-Pal and of Rameses I., consisted of clay tablets, of inscribed stones, or of papyrus rolls; the libraries of Greece, those of the Ptolemies and of the kings of Pergamus, the libraries of Rome, first opened to public use by the efforts of Asinius Pollio; the Byzantine libraries, which arose within Christian churches or in monasteries; and lastly, the rich and splendid collections made at great expense by the patrons, by the builders, of the culture of the Renaissance—all these, compared with the modern libraries, of which the most perfect specimens may be found in this land, are like an ancient trireme beside a twin-screw steamer. And the essential difference between the ancient and the modern library, between the conception of a library as it existed up to the times of Frederic, Duke of Urbino and of Lorenzo il Magnifico, and that existing in the minds of Thomas Bodley, or Antonio Magliabecchi, is to be found in the different objects represented by the same word, *liber*.

A study of the fate of this word would lead us step by step through the varying forms of the library, from those containing clay tablets, from those filled with rolls covered with cuneiform characters, to the codices brilliant with the art of Oderisi da Bobbio, splendid with gold and miniatures, to the first block books, to the printed books of Fust and Schoeffer, and of Aldo Manuzio, of William Caxton, and of Christopher Plantin.

The invention of printing caused a great revolution in the world of books. The new art was, as we well know, received at first with scorn and indifference. The incunabula were but rough, vulgar things as compared with the beautiful manuscripts clearly written on carefully prepared parchment, and glittering with brilliant colors. They were fit at most to be used by the masses—by women, by children, to be sold at fairs, to be put into the hands of cheap-jacks and charlatans; but they were quite unfitted for the valuable collections guarded with so much care in perfumed cases carved with damask or with the softest of leathers, made from the skins of sucking animals. We can easily understand that fastidious art patrons such as the Duke of Urbino should scorn this new form of book, and should proclaim it unworthy of a place in a respectable library. But this tempest of scorn gradually subsided before the advantages which the new invention offered and before the marvellous progress it made. It sought, moreover, the favor of the miniaturists by leaving, in the margins of the new codices, sufficient space for ornamentations and for initials of burnished gold; it sought the favor and the help of the learned Humanists by employing them to revise and correct the texts; it won the favor of the studious and of clerks, who have at all times been poor, by spreading abroad the texts of the classics, by offering for a few half-pence that which could at first be obtained only with gold or silver florins, by imparting to all that which had been the privilege of the few. And we must not forget the help given to typography by the invention of the minor arts, calcography and xylography, which added new value to the pages of the no longer despised book; so that printed codices (codices impressi) might stand side by side with the manuscript codices (codices manuscripti).

The word, the sign of the thought, first took on visible form with the invention of the alphabet. But other ways of revealing thought were to be discovered in the future. No one in the ancient world, no one before the very culminating point of the Renaissance, could have supposed it possible that a library might contain anything but manuscripts; just as we, to-day, are incapable of imagining a library containing anything but books. We have seen that the conception of the book underwent expansion, when printed books were added to those written by hand; and in the same way, the library underwent expansion, gradually rising, between the fifteenth and twentieth centuries, from a simple collection of codices, to the vast and wonderful proportions it has at present reached, assuming the duty of receiving within itself any kind of graphic representation of human thought, from clay tablets and inscribed stones and papyrus rolls, to phototypes and monotype or linotype products, from books for the blind written in Braille alphabet to the new manuscripts of the typewriters.

From this brief compendium of bibliographical history one essential feature emerges. As though directed by an unswerving law, by the law of reproduction, human thought feels the necessity of expanding, and of multiplying and perpetuating itself; and it is ever searching for new means of carrying out this intent. Thus the copyist or the scribe is replaced by the compositor, the miniaturist by the engraver, the draughtsman by the lithographer, the painter by the color-printer, the engraver by the photographer and zincographer; thus the machine replaces the hand of man—the machine which is only concerned with working quickly, with producing as many copies as possible with diminished effort, with snatching her secrets from Mother Nature herself. We have replaced the *note tironiane* of the Roman scribes by the typewriter, the wax tablets by the pages of the stenographer; for drawing and painting we have substituted photography and three-color printing; wireless telegraphy has taken the place of messages sent by the post-horses.

And not content with these singular and wondrous modes of reproducing graphically the thought and word, we have found another means of reproduction still more stupendous in the immediateness of its action. Sound, the human voice, whose accents have hitherto been lost, may now be preserved and repeated and produced like other graphic signs of thought. When the graphophone was first invented, we little thought that the cylinders upon which the vibrations of the voice had traced so slight and delicate an impression, would ever be reproduced as simply as, by electrotyping, we reproduce a page of movable characters. Neither have we yet, or I am much mistaken, grasped the whole of the practical utility which the graphophone may have it its further applications and improvements. Up to the present time the graphophone has been kept as a plaything in the drawing rooms or in the bars, to reproduce the last roulades of some well-known singer, the bangings of some military band, or the pretended uproar of some stormy meeting. At the present day, the librarian would probably refuse to receive within his library this faithful reproducer of the human voice, just as Frederic, Duke of Urbino, banished from his collection the first examples of printed books. But without posing as a prophet or the son or a prophet, we may surely assert that every library will before long contain a hall in which the discs of the graphophone may be heard (as already is the case at the Brera in Milan), and shelves for the preservation of the discs, just as the libraries of Assyria preserved clay tablets inscribed with cuneiform characters. This is a new form of book, strange at first sight, but in reality simply a return to ancient precedents, yet a return which marks the upward movement of progress.

An Italian Jesuit, Saverio Bettinelli, undertook toward the middle of the eighteenth century to give laws to Italian writers. He produced certain letters which he assumed Virgil to have written from the Elysian fields to the Arcadia at Rome. In two of these twelve tablets which he put forth under the names of Homer, Pindar, Anachreon, Virgil, Horace, Propertius, Dante, Petrarch and Ariosto, in the poetical meetings held in Elysium, he laid down as a rule: "Let there be written in large letters on the doors of all public libraries: 'You will be ignorant of almost everything which is within these doors, or you will live three centuries to read half of it;' and a little further on: 'Let a new city be made whose streets, squares and houses shall contain only books. Let the man who wishes to study go and live there for as long as may be needful; otherwise printed matter will soon leave no place for the goods, for the food, of the inhabitants of our towns.'"

This anticipation, which dates from 1758, still seems an exaggeration; but I know not whether a century and a half hence, posterity will think it so, so great is the development of the industries, the succession of ever new inventions for preserving any graphic representation of human thought. Not even the life of Methuselah would be long enough to read as much as the tenth part of all that a modern library contains; and I know no whether we could invent a more terrible punishment than to insist upon this for our criminal. How many repetitions of the same ideas, how much superfluity, how many scientific works cancelled and rendered useless and condemned to perpetual oblivion by those which succeeded them. By welcoming everything, without discrimination, the modern library has lost its ancient and true character. No longer can we inscribe over its entrance the ancient motto, "Medicine for souls:" few indeed of the books would have any salutary influence on body or on mind. Now that the conception of books and of library has been so enormously expanded, now that the library has become the city of paper, however printed, and of any other material fitted to receive the graphic representation of human thought, it will become more and more necessary to classify the enormous amount of material, to separate it into various categories. The laws of demography, whatever they may be, must be extended also to books: they may be, must be extended also to books: the dead must be divided from the living, the sick from the sound, the bad from the good, the rich from the poor; and cemeteries must be prepared for all those stereotyped editions of school books, of catechisms, or railway time-tables, for all that endless luggage of printed paper has only the form of a book and has nothing to do with thought. Sanatoria must be provided for books condemned to uselessness because already infected with error or already eaten away with old age, and the most conspicuous places much be set apart for books worthy to be preserved from oblivion and from the ravages of time, either on account of the importance of their contents or of the beauty of their appearance. In this great Republic of books, the princes will stand high above the countless mass, and an aristocracy of the best will be formed which will be the true library within the library.

But even this will not have the exclusive character of the ancient library. It will receive divers and strange forms of books: next to parpyrus of Oxyrinchos, with an unknown fragment of Sappho, may be placed a parchment illuminated by Nestore Lenoi or by Attilio Formilli, a graphophone disc containing Theodore Roosevelt's latest speech or a scene from "Othello" given by Tommaso Salvini, the heliotype reproductions of the Medicean Virgil, or some phrases written on palm leaves by the last survivor of a band of cannibals. The great abundance of modern production will render even more rare and more valuable ancient examples of the book; just as the progress of industrialism has enhanced the value of work produced by the hand of man.

Thought as it develops is undergoing the same transformation which has occurred in manual labor: mental work also has assumed a certain mechanical character visible in formalism, in imitation, in the influence of the school or of the surroundings. Industrialism has made its way into science, literature and art, giving rise to work which is hybrid, mediocre, without any originality, and destined therefore soon to perish. The parasites of thought flourish at the expense of the greater talents, and they will constitute, alas, the larger part of future bibliographical production. The greatest difficulty of future librarians will be to recognize and classify these hybrid productions, in choosing from among the great mass, the few books worthy of a place apart.

The appraisal of literature, which has already been discussed in books and congresses, will continue to increase in importance; and in this work of discrimination we shall need the aid of critics to read for other men and to light up the path for those who shall come after. "The records of the best that has been thought and done in the world," said George Iles, "growing volume and value every hour. Speed the day when they may be hospitably proffered to every human soul, the chaff winnowed from the wheat, the gold divided from the clay."

One of the special characteristics of the library of the future will be co-operation, and internationalism applied to the division of labor. We may already see premonitory symptoms of this in the "Catalogue of scientific literature" now being compiled by the Royal Society of London, in the Concilium Bibliographicum of Zurich, in the Institut de Bibliographie of Brussels, and in the card catalog printed and distributed by the Library of Congress at Washington. This co-operation, however, will have to be more widely extended and must assert itself not only by exchanges of cards and of indices but also by means of the lending of books and manuscripts, of the reproductions of codices or of rare and precious works. The government libraries of Italy are united under the same rules and correspond with all institutions of public instruction and with several town and provincial libraries, with free postage; so that books and manuscripts journey from one end to the other of the peninsular, from Palermo to Venice, without any expense to those who use them, and the different libraries of the state become, in this way, one single library. And so the day will come when the libraries of Europe and of America and all of the states in the Postal Union will form, as it were, one single collection, and the old books, printed when America was but a myth, will enter new worlds bearing with them to far off students the benefit of their ancient wisdom. The electric post of the airships will have then shortened distances, the telephone will make it possible to hear at Melbourne a graphophone disc asked for, a few minutes earlier, from the British Museum. There will be few readers, but an infinite number of hearers, who will listen from their own homes o the spoken paper, to the spoken book. University students will listen to their lectures while they lie in bed, and, as now with us, will not know their professors even by sight. Writing will be a lost art. Professors of paleography and keepers of manuscripts will perhaps have to learn to accustom their eye to the ancient alphabets. Autographs will be as rare as palimpsests are now. Books will no longer be read, they will be listened to; and then only will be fulfulled Mark Pattison's famous saying, "The librarian who reads is lost."

But even if the graphophone does not produce so profound a transformation as to cause the alphabet to become extinct and effect an injury to culture itself; even if, as we hope will be the case, the book retains its place of honor, and instruction through the eyes be not replaced by that through the ears (in which case printed books would be kept for the exclusive benefit of the deaf); still these discs, now so much derided, will form a very large part of the future library. The art of oratory, of drama, of music and of poetry, the study of languages, the present pronunciation of language and dialects, will find faithful means of reproduction in these humble discs. Imagine, if we could hear in this place to-day the voice of Lincoln or Garibaldi, of Victor Hugo or of Shelley, just as you might hear the clear winged words of Gabriele D'Annunzio, the moving voice of Eleonore Duse or the drawling words of Mark Twain. Imagine, the miracle of being able to call up again, the powerful eloquence of your political champions, or the heroes of our patriotic struggles; of being able to listen to the music of certain verses, the wailing of certain laments, the joy that breaks out in certain cries of the soul: the winged word would seem to raise itself once more into the air as at the instant when it came forth, living, from the breast, to play upon our sensibilities, to stir up our hearts. It is not to be believed that men will willingly lose this benefit, the benefit of uniting to the words the actual voices of those who are, and will no longer be, and that they should not desire that those whose presence has left us should at least speak among us. We may also believe that certain forms of art, such as the novel and the drama, will prefer the phonetic to the graphic reproduction, or at least a union of the two. And the same may be said of poetry, which will find in modern authors its surest reciters, its most eloquent interpreters. The oratory of the law-court and of the parliament, that of the pulpit and of the cathédra, will not be able to withstand the enticement of being preserved and handed on to posterity, to which their triumphs have hitherto sent down a but a weak uncertain echo. "Non omnis moriar;" so will think the orator and the dramatic or lyric artist; and the libraries will cherish these witnesses to art and to life, as they now collect play-bills and lawyers' briefs. But internationalism and co-operation will save the future library from the danger of losing altogether its true character by becoming, as it were, a deposit of memories or of embalmed residua of life, among which the librarian must walk like a bearer of the dead. The time will come when, if these mortuary cities of dead books are not to multiply indefinitely, we must invoke the authority of Fra Girolamo Savonarola, and proceed to the burning of vanities. A return to ancient methods will be a means of instruction, and those centenary libraries which have preserved their proper character, which have not undergone hurtful augmentations, which have reserved themselves for books and manuscripts alone, which have disdained all the ultra-modern rubbish which has neither the form nor the name of book, these libraries will be saluted as monuments worthy of veneration. And then some patron who from being a multi-millionaire, as was his far-off ancestor, will have become at least a multi-billionaire, will provide here in America for the founding of libraries, not of manuscripts, which will no longer be for sale, but of reproduction of codices in black or in colors; and we shall have libraries of facsimiles most useful for the study of the classics, just as we now have museums of casts for the study of the plastic arts. The application of photography and of photogravure to the reproduction of texts which are unique rather than rare, makes it possible for us not only to have several examples of a precious codex or manuscript, but to fix the invisible deterioration which began in it at a certain date so that, as regards its state of preservation, the facsimile represents an anterior stage to the future state of the original. By thus wonderfully forecasting the future these reproductions render less disastrous the effects of a fire such as that which lately destroyed the library of Turin. They have therefore found great favor among students and have excited the attention of the most enlightened governments. If the means for carrying on what have hitherto been but isolated efforts do not fail, if generous donors and institutions and governments do not deny their aid, we might already begin a methodical work of reproduction, and come to an agreement concerning the method of fulfilling a vast design which should comprehend all the most precious archetypes of the various libraries in the world, those which are the documents of the history of human thought and which are the letters-patent of the nobility of an ancient greatness. This, I think, would, nay, should, be the most serious and principal duty assumed by the library of the future: to preserve these treasures of the past while hoping that the present and the future may add to them new ones worthy of public veneration. Think how vast a field of work: to seek through all nations the autographs or archetypes to which have been entrusted the thought of great men of every age and of every race, and to explain them so as to render them accessible to modern readers. Thus should we form the true library of the nations, which, with the facsimiles, would bring together the critical editions of their authors and the translations and the texts made for the explanations of the works. But the first and most urgent duty would be that of making an inventory, an index, of what should constitute this collection; and, first of all, we should know and search out such authors as may have influenced the history of the human race by their works in all times and among all peoples; and we should have to find the venerable codices which have handed on to us the light of their intellect, the beating of their hearts. Every nation which is careful of its own glory should begin this list, just as we are now beginning that of the monuments of marble or of stone which have value as works of art. We should thus begin to prepare the precious material to be reproduced, while at the same time it would be possible to calculate the expense needed for carrying out the magnificent design. The Belgian government has appointed a congress to meet at Liège next year for this purpose, but its programs are too extended; for they take in also the documents in archives and in museums. More opportune and more practical would be an inquiry affecting libraries alone and beginning with oriental and classical authors, with those who represent the wisdom of the ancients. Thus the library of to-day would gradually prepare its work for the future library, which will surely want something more than the editions, however innumerable, supplied to it by the bibliographical production of the years to come.

Internationalism will also be able to render great service to science, in the field of photo-mechanic reproductions, if it find a way of directing them to some useful goal, and if it prevent them from taking a merely material advantage of the precious collections which every nation is justified in guarding with jealous care. Photography with the prism, which has no need of the plate or of the film, coasts so little and is so easy of execution, especially if the process of the late Mlle. Pellechet be adopted, that one can in a few hours carry away from a library the facsimile of an entire manuscript. No doubt many learned men of the new style find it more convenient to have these collections at their own house, instead of wandering from one library to another to collect them a the expense of their eyes, their patience and their money. To be able to compare the various texts and to have the various readings of them under one's eye is an inestimable benefit; but the true philologist will never be contented with simply studying these facsimiles, however perfect they may be; he will want to examine for himself the ancient parchments, the time-yellowed papers, to study the slight differences between the inks, the varieties in the handwritings, the evanescent glosses in the margins. In the same way an art critic is not content with confining his study simply to the photographs of pictures, but he observes the pictures themselves, their patina, their coloring, their shadows, their least gradations of tones and half-tones. In the same way, too, a musician would not presume to the knowledge of an opera which he had only studied in a pianoforte arrangement. If this manner of shunning fatigue took root, our splendid collections of manuscripts would no longer be the goal of learned pilgrims, but would become the easy prey of the photographer, who would certainly embark upon a new speculation: that of retailing these collections to the manifest injury of the libraries and of the states which would thus lose the exclusive literary and artistic possession of what is a national glory. Meanwhile a just jurisdiction will avoid these dangers without injuring or hindering studies and culture. We shall adopt for manuscripts, which excite other people's desires, the proposition made by Aristophanes in the *Ecclesiazuse* (that charming satire on Socialism) to bridle the excesses of free love. We shall permit a man to have a copy of a manuscript when he has first had one of another and older manuscript and when the latter, which is about equal in value to the first, has already been given up to the library, which will thus lose none of its property. "*Do ut des*," "I give to make you give," base and foundation of international treatises for customs duties, must be applied also in a reasonable manner to the intellectual traffic that will be the characteristic of future civilization, which will never permit one nation to grow poor while another grows rich, and will insist that wealth be the bearer of equality and fruitful in good. A well regulated metabolism, as it ensures the health of our organic bodies, will also serve to maintain the health of that great social body, which we all desire and foresee, notwithstanding political struggles and the wars which still stain the earth with blood. When the time comes in which we shall be able to use for ideal aims the millions which are now swallowed up by engines of war, of ruin and of assault, the library will be looked upon as the temple of wisdom, and to it will be turned far more than at present the unceasing care of governments and of peoples. When that time comes, the book will be able to say to the cannon, with more truth than Quasimodo to Notre Dame de Paris, "*ceci a tué cela*," and it will have killed Death with all her fatal instruments.

But another and more important aspect of scientific internationalism which will preserve the library of the future from becoming a bazaar of social life, will be the importation of the most wholesome fruits of ancient wisdom collected with wonderful learning by the great scholars of the 17th and 18th centuries, hitherto looked upon by experimental science with disdain, was collected with laborious detail all the learning of past centuries, that of the Holy Books, of the Oriental world, that which the Fathers of the Church and after them the Arabs, and later on the Encyclopaedists of the Middle Ages, and then the astrologists and the alchemists and the natural philosophers, condensed into encylopaedias, into chronicles, into treatises, into all that congeries of writings which formed the libraries of the Middle Ages and of the Renaissance, into that infinite number of printed books which still fill the ancient and classical libraries of Europe with voluminous folios and quartos. The desire of classifying and bringing into line all human knowledge, of reading this immense amount of material and gaining a thorough knowledge of it, armed those first solemn scholars with patience, formed those legendary librarians who, like Antonio Magliabecchi or Francesco Marucelli themselves, were living libraries. The Latin anagram of the celebrated founder of the Florentine Library, Antonius Magliabechi, is well known: "*Is unus bibliotheca magna;*" but it may be, and at that time also could be equally applied to others. These devourers of books were the first inventors and asserters of the scientific importance of a card catalog, because armed with cards they passed days and nights in pressing from the old books the juice of wisdom and of knowledge and in collecting and condensing it in their miscellanies, in those vast bibliographical collections compared with which the catalog of the British Museum is the work of a novice. They not only appraised the known literature of their time, but they classified it; not by such a classification as we make now, contenting ourselves with the title of the book, but by an internal and perfect classification, analyzing every page and keeping record of the volume, of the paragraph, of the line. The skeleton of the encyclopaedia, of the scientific dictionary, which at the end of the 18th century underwent in France a literary development, may be found within these bibliographical collections now forgotten and banished to the highest shelves of our libraries. Any one who has looked through and studied one of these collections as I have done, has wondered at the treasures of information, of learning, of bibliographical exactitude contained in those dusty volumes. Above all, the precision of the references and of the quotations, the comprehensiveness of the subjects and of the headings, render them, rather than a precious catalog, an enormous encyclopedia, to which we may have recourse not only for history, for geography, for literature, for moral sciences, but also, impossible as it may seem, for natural sciences, for medicine and for the exact sciences.

In the library of the future, classified on the Decimal system, or Cutter's expansive, every section should contain a sheaf of cards on which should be collected, arranged, verified and even translated this ancient material, which may thrown light on new studies and on new experiments; for the empirical methods of our forefathers, like tradition and legend, have a basis of truth which is not to be despised. Meanwhile the modern library, which in this land prospers and exults in a youth strong and full of promise, should collect this material and thus spare the students at your universities the long researches needed to assimilate the ancient literature of every subject. The modern library, the American library, would not need to acquire and accumulate with great expense all the ancient mass of human knowledge in order to make use of the work of past generations; it need only collect the extract of this work, opportunely chosen, sifted, classified and translated. This would be an immense advantage to its scholars, and the internationalism of science, of whose certain advent I have spoken to you, would find in this first exchange, in this fertile importation, its immediate application. Why should students and specialists be sent to begin new researches in learned and dusty volumes, when this work has been already done by the great champions of erudition in their miscellanies, in their bibliographical encyclopaedias? Let us rather try to spread abroad a knowledge of this treasure, this well of science; let us publish information about it; let us draw largely from its pure and health-giving waters. You will not be without guides who will lead you to it, who can and will give you to drink of its fresh waters. Thus shall these noble and solitary spirits who worked unknown in the dark of the 17th century and in the wan 18th century, be joined, by an invisible chain, to the vigorous intellects which, in the last century and in that upon which we have just entered, are working, are toiling, in the diffused light of civilization, and will continue to work and will continue to toil for Science, for Humanity.

And the card, the humble card, the winged arrow of the librarian and of the student, will fly from continent to continent, a messenger of knowledge and of concord.

The Library as Social Centre

The opening address at the Red Wing Meeting of the Minnesota Library Association, October 12, 1905, by Miss Gratia Alta Countryman. *Public Libraries,* 1906, p. 5.

During these latter days of enormous library activity, we have been conscientiously examining the functions of the library; we have been trying all sorts of methods to popularize it, to advertise it. We have asked for and listened to the criticism of outsiders, and by the light thrown upon it through this prism have separated our work into its elemental parts and seen its various hues.

We used to erect a library as an altar to the gods of learning; now, to use Mr. Dana's words, we erect it as an altar to the "gods of good fellowship, joy and learning." So you see, our ideals are constantly rising, our horizons ever broadening, and our work continually increasing, both in extent and in depth. We might well have considered our hands fairly full to have dealt alone with this god of learning, but we find ourselves embracing the opportunity for additional service to the gods of good fellowship and joy.

It might do us good to consider tonight what we are doing for the cause of learning, what the library has done to increase serious reading and study, and how it may further the educational work of the world. This question is ever present with us, and can stand any amount of discussion. But it is the gods of good fellowship and joy that we are discussing tonight, the library not as a center of learning but as a social center.

We are dealing with a small crowd of people whom we may call "our public." Who are the public? Why, you and I, and my family, and others just like us. They want just the same things that we do, and to be accommodated in just the same way that we do. The public is no indefinite, intangible somebody, it is just "we."

We talk about the people being hungry for books and information. Have you found it so? Then why do we have free libraries and free schools? People are willing to sacrifice for something that they are very hungry for. Do you hunger and thirst to read Homer and Shakespeare, and Emerson and Arnold, and good histories and literature? Do you, when you are tired after a day's work, take home a scientific work or a treatise of civics? No, you are just a little sample of the public, and you think you need to read a pleasant, entertaining, restful book. You aren't hungry for information, and, as a matter of fact, the person who delights in study and has a fine taste for the best in literature has one of the "gifts extremely rare." Most of us are practical, everyday, working people, with a very limited time for reading, and this public whom we serve is just like us. A few of them will love to read the best, many of them will want information at intervals, a large proportion want recreative reading, and the vast majority use the library not at all. Now the former, who want and love the library, you need not be troubled about. They will naturally come to the library, and you will find pleasure in serving them. But these latter classes who either come for pleasure or come not at all must be drawn and held through the social instincts, and through their desire for pleasure. We may find it in friendly gatherings, social clubs, or music or conversation or games, but social pleasure of some sort is sought by all of us, great and small, in town and country alike. In the city there is usually plenty of opportunity—I might almost say that there is a surfeit—and one must pick and choose. But in the towns and villages it is often different; good amusement and profitable pleasures are not always to be had, and being social beings, the social craving is satisfied with whatever means may be at hand. Young people especially can not isolate themselves, or live unto themselves. Just where is the library going to stand in this matter? Is there anything which we can do to satisfy these natural desires and to enter more vitally into the lives of the people? This is the question to take home and think about.

As individuals, we are coming to have an enormous interest in other human lives, there is a sense of social obligation upon us; we have come to know that personal righteousness is not all that is required of us, but that we must help to realize the social righteousness. The library has the duty of being all things to all men. It is no longer simply a repository of books, it is exactly what Mr. Carnegie calls it, the cradle of democracy, filled with the democratic spirit, and it endeavors, as far as circumstances permit, to minister to all the needs of the community in which it dwells. The library stands for progress, the progress of its town, and this does not mean increasing the material prosperity of the people, though that may follow, but it chiefly means the raising of the moral, social and intellectual standards of all its people, and helping men and women to be more effective in every way. The library does not exist for one side only of the life of the people, but for every side, and if it fails to provide for those who seek amusement, it shirks a good duty and renounces a privilege. The sooner we unveil the "gods of joy and good fellowship" in our library the better; and sooner we make the library a centre for all the activities among us that make for social efficiency the better.

Of course there are natural limitations to the kind of work which a library can do, and in helping to further the spirit of good fellowship and to furnish pleasure, we must keep within such limits as are consistent with the spirit of a library. The library can appeal to people in other ways than by books alone, as we shall consider later, yet as books are our chief tools, it is natural to think first of giving pleasure by that method. One of our chiefest ways of late years has been through the children's room. The children get books instruction and supplementary reading and enforced book interests, all of which are needed for their development, in the schoolroom. But in the children's room at the library furnished especially for them, with low tables, picture books and low shelves containing fairy stories and all their favorite authors, they settle down to satisfy their own especial individual tastes. Then there is the story hour, of which we shall hear to-morrow. Many of the children have never learned the pleasure of reading. They do not belong to cultured homes and the presence of books. Many of them never heard a Mother Goose jingle or a nonsense verse, and a book is an unlearned delight. But what child, even of this kind, does not love to hear stories, and listening breathlessly, would not come again and again. Somehow it seems as if we could not discharge our social obligation until we had gone into the byways and hedges and gathered in these scraps of society, and taught them the pleasures of a book. The children, once acquainted with the library, will always count it among their friends, and it will forever remain a social centre to them. We grown ups are not so different from the children; we, too, like a story, and we, too, want to read the things that cheer and entertain us. We agreed a moment ago that we, as well as our public, were liable to leave the serious books for the infrequent study hour and to spend our leisure evenings with the fascinating novel. Well, I do not know of any better way to give amusement and pleasure than to furnish the people with the books they want, in which they can be interested and absorbed. The "cares that infest the day" will fold their wings better under the spell of a good story than any other way. I think we need not be frightened when libraries are accused of being only fiction distributors, for it is a library's function to amuse as well as to instruct, and if people will seek amusement through the library, so much the better for the people. It is natural that the people should feel a curiosity about the newest book and want to read what other people are talking about. This adds also to pleasant social intercourse, and gives people a common subject of conversation. Fiction is bound to be more and more an interpretation of life by which we see the motives and currents in other souls. We need not be afraid to supply good, wholesome fiction and to use it in establishing social relations with our people, so that the adults as well as the children shall feel a real pleasure in coming to the library.

Many of our libraries are now housed in beautiful buildings, in which case, the building as well as the books becomes a means of social influence. If there is need of a home for social intercourse and amusement, the library may legitimately attempt to furnish such a home within its walls. If there are social or study clubs, organized labor guilds or missionary societies, or any other organizations, encourage them to meet at the library, find out what they need, let them find out that the library is their cooperative partner. And so with the schools and industries, of which I have not time to speak. The whole building at all times should be managed in the broadest spirit of hospitality; the atmosphere should be as gracious, kindly and sympathetic as one's own home. Then do away with all unnecessary restrictions, take down all the bars, and try to put face to face our friends the books and our friends the people. Introduce them cordially, then stand aside and let them make each other's blessed acquaintance.

Some have tried smoking rooms, had boy's club rooms and games, and many have tried simply to make the rooms homelike and cheery, and all of their experience is valuable to us.

It may be that no one of the plans used by other libraries may fit your case, for it is not necessarily good for you because some one else has used it successfully. But with any plan do not expect immediate results, for almost everything that succeeds permanently has a slow, gradual development; that which flashes up quickly usually dies down suddenly. Be willing to work out a good plan if you have one, and be willing to study your people and all of their interests before you shape your plans.

Phones Installed in Free Library

Patrons Now May Save Themselves Needless Trips for Books That Are "Out"

San Francisco Call (daily newspaper), April 7, 1912, p. 64.

Oakland, April 6.

A telephone service has been installed at the Oakland free library and all its branches, with the result that busy readers may now call by wire and receive desired information concerning books. A feature of the new system is that books may be renewed over the telephone. Information along general lines will also be given and questions answered as to whether certain books are on the shelves. At the branches requests may be made for books from the main library, and if this is done before 2 o'clock in the afternoon the volume will be sent by messenger on the same day.

Letter to the Editor of *The Nation* on "The librarian who reads is dead."

Published Nov. 7, 1912.

Sir: In a volume published last year, entitled "Facts for Freshmen Concerning the University of Illinois," there occurs, in the chapter on Library Science, the following sentence: "There is a saying that 'the librarian who reads is dead,' which means that the up-to-date librarian is too busy to find time to read books; he must know what is in them without reading them." Aside from the fact that the saying is wrongly quoted and wrongly applied, whoever penned the above sentence is preaching a false philosophy.

There is a tendency, I know, among librarians who regard themselves as "up to date" to deprecate, consciously or not, the fundamentals of librarianship, and to suppose that a librarian must be an administrator and *nothing else*. Let it be said once for all that no one is a true librarian who is not a lover and student of books. That he must be an administrator besides is another matter—he must be both. If he is *not* a student and lover of books he will never be able to find out "what is in books without reading them."

There is a legend about Justin Winsor that he could get the meat out of a book merely by glancing at the title page, preface, and index, and dipping into the text here and there. Therefore, so runs the popular application, this trick is the first that the tyro should learn. When, however, Justin Winsor learned the trick, he had behind him a lifetime as a student of books.

"The librarian who reads is *lost*," wrote Mark Pattison in his life of Isaac Casaubon, that is: the librarian who reads, and reads, and does *nothing more*, is lost as far as a real understanding of his function goes. The saying has been repeated again and again since that day, in decrying the old-fashioned librarian, who regards himself as a watchdog of the books in his charge. The saying speaks the truth—as far as it goes. But when it is used for the purpose of demonstrating that librarians do not need to know anything but methods and technique, then it is made to preach a false philosophy.

Aksel G. S. Josephson, Chicago, October 28, 1912

The Heyday of Librarians

The Nation, July 3, 1913.

Any one who has followed the meetings of the American Library Association, which ended last Saturday, after a week's session at Kaaterskill, N. Y., must have been set reflecting seriously in several directions. The public library, with a lifetime in this country of scarcely more than sixty years, has already reached that highly specialized development which characterizes the public school. The old-fashioned browsing which used to unearth many a delightful book that one wasn't looking for is largely a thing of the past. Books must be classified in reference rooms according to the divisions of knowledge which now form the plan of public instruction. This serves a purpose which should not be hastily minimized. The library is attempting to-day as never before to meet the needs of a most heterogeneous public. Particular attention is given to those who cannot readily help themselves. Experts are employed to pick out books best suited to immigrants, to ambitious farm-hands and factory workers, to children, legislators, and business men. Volumes are also lent by one community to another. No better illustration of the contrast of former conditions with modern could be found than that furnished by one who took part in the Conference. She visited a library in England where the tradition was still maintained of chaining the books to the shelves; yet the same day she saw books in trucks on the way to the provinces. So greatly has the spirit changed that the up-to-date librarian, she said, had to restrain himself from running out into the highway and chaining books to the passer-by.

With the minute organization which is now the rule in public libraries goes a sense of power and responsibility which has given even those possessed of it some pause. Mingled with much talk about highly specialized efficiency was frequently heard a note of warning lest the library should have a disintegrating effect. As President Legler put it, the public is tending towards a "rag-time" habit of mind which the library can help correct only by installing a director and assistants with proper personalities. However detailed its system, an institution should strive to allure its readers to its best possessions in general fields of knowledge. Mr. Legler would probably not go so far as one of several outsiders whose criticism was invited by the Conference. According to this very zealous gentleman, the head of a public library should be the mayor of thoughts in his community, and above all should be personally acquainted with the interests of the young people. Find the boy and connect him with the right book, that is the first duty. But in the case at least of children the library has virtually been doing this. The space and thought given to juveniles in institutions of New York, Boston, and Chicago makes the task of parents easy and delightful. And librarians are now hoping to render other departments equally inviting. The necessity is clear, the problem is how to meet it. Much could be accomplished, it is felt, if heads and attendants had leisure for daily reading. Then we might hope for more of such outstanding figures as Winsor, and especially certain Englishmen who, while carrying on their duties in the British Museum or the Bodleian, have shown by their publications how wide-ranging were their minds.

Closely connected with this, though it received but brief discussion by the Association, is the amount of attention which any large public library should devote to scholars. What with all the thought bestowed upon those who have to be driven to the shelves, it is a question whether the natural bookman is not somewhat neglected. To compare the New York Public Library with the British Museum is not altogether fair, yet the mere physical conveniences in London might be reproduced. The scholar is not so easily distracted as the poet, but to sit at a great flat table with no division into desks, and to be obliged to walk into a distant room to consult the card catalogue, is distracting to even prosaic moods. If more warmth of personality is really desired for the public library, and if it is to be an intellectual centre, there is no better way to begin than to heed the comfort of those who by their equipment are intellectual leaders.

One other important problem which confronted the Association was that of selecting new books. The general public hardly appreciates how much is involved. Here the power exercised affects not only readers, but the very life of a large class of publications. For to the discerning it is well known that unless publishers could count on the public library patronage, they would not dare to issue certain volumes at all. Works selling at three or five dollars may be highly important, even though they cannot expect large private sales. But other works got out at these prices in attractive bindings are utterly worthless, and here librarians might do much more than they have done to keep them off the market. The case of fiction is very different. The demand for stories being what it is, librarians have no such power of veto, but they have begun to see that every best seller need not be acquired. Yet if fiction is in their province, where shall they draw the line? Mr. Robert Herrick, to whom the question was put, complicated the matter still farther by insisting that "The Kreutzer Sonata" was much less harmful to young readers than, say, "The Rosary." And other writers urged great caution in instituting censorship; they would set up truth to life as the proper standard of selection. Unanimity is not to be expected from the Council, with whom the subject was left. But it would appear that some thoroughgoing policy ought to be adopted. The function of a good library should be not only to acquire but quite as much to reject; and just now fiction is sorely in need of weeding.

Note on 1913 ALA Annual Conference in *The Dial*

The Dial: Semi-monthly Journal of Literary Criticism, Discussion, and Information.
July 16, 1913. Vol. 55, No. 650.

The annual discussion of library problems which has recently occupied the attention of our librarians in conference assembled impresses the observer with the library's increasing closeness of relationship to the varied interests and activities of modern life. So eager, in fact, has the librarian become to enlarge and strengthen this relationship to every conceivable legitimate device, that Mr. Legler, in his presidential address, felt called upon to admonish his hearers against letting the methods of the moment encroach upon the library's larger general usefulness. The importance now attached to efficiency and specialization does indeed threaten to overshadow the vital human element, and to make us forget that even the most wonderfully efficient machine is an absolutely soulless, heartless, lifeless piece of mechanism. Hence it is well that the broadly human factor in library work received timely emphasis in the speeches and debates at Kaaterskill. Among minor matters pressing for attention were the probable future effect of the commission form of municipal government upon public-library administration; the ever-present problem of book-selection; more particularly of novel-selection; the helpfulness or harmfulness of novels in the solution of social and economic problems; the amount of attention that the public library, especially the large library, should give to the special needs of scholars; the question of granting librarians sufficient leisure for both the reading and the recuperation that are necessary if the daily grind is not speedily to result in lessened efficiency; and (this from the delegate of the British Library Association) the detrimental effect of an excessive employment of women in library work, not by reason of any inferiority in such service, but because the salaries offered to young girls and women are so low as to tend to diminish the remuneration of men also, and to cause hardship in an already underpaid profession. On the whole, the attendance at this thirty-fifth annual conference, the addresses and discussions, the interest shown, and the whole atmosphere of the convention, give encouraging evidence of the growing importance and usefulness of the public library, which, as an appreciable factor in promoting the public good, is not yet much more than half a century old, and which in its modern development we are justified in proudly regarding as preeminently an *American institution*.

The Region of the Unromantic

The Dial: a Semi-monthly Journal of Literary Criticism, Discussion and Information. December 1, 1913, p. 465.

The region of the unromantic, where statistics displace sentiment, and hard-and-fast certainty crowds out all the delightful possibilities that love to lurk in the penumbra of the uncertain and the problematical, is deemed by some to be the chosen abiding-place of librarians. Especially does the presiding genius of the information desk have the reputation of one who scorns the delights of vagueness and lives laborious days in clearing the cobwebs of dubiety from his mind and in flooding its every nook and corner with the pitiless glare of the light of positive knowledge. The English delegate who attended our late A.L.A. annual conference reports to his fellow-librarians at home on this zeal of our librarians for reducing the unknown if not the unknowable to its lowest terms. "It is difficult, perhaps," he says in the course of his report, "just at this time to estimate the intellectual and spiritual loss entailed on the race of men by the reaching of the two poles, reducing almost to the vanishing point those places of the earth where imagination may still lose itself untrammeled by the deadening reality of the topographer and the map-maker, and foreshadowing the time when it will be as easy to get to the poles as it is to Bournemouth. Let us express the hope that librarians may leave the poles and a few other areas of what Bacon calls the Globe Intellectual in their virgin remoteness, untouched as long as may be by the 'civilizing' influences of the cataloguer, the bibliographer, and all those agencies for hustled information which centre themselves in that generally speaking excellent, but unromantic, department of the American public library known as the Information Desk." But after all, there is no real cause for alarm. As Herbert Spencer long ago reminded his readers, the enlarging of the sphere of the known, so far from diminishing the volume of the unknown, only increases the amount of surface exposed to that circumjacent element, or, in other words, multiplies our points of contact with it and makes its magnitude more appreciable to the senses.

First Aid to the Enquiring Reader

The Dial; a Semi-monthly Journal of Literary Criticism, Discussion and Information. June 1, 1914; Vol. 56, No. 671.

First Aid to the Enquiring Reader is freely and expertly rendered by most librarians, though some insist that the visitor should reach the end of his own resources in catalogue and reference-book consultation before soliciting professional assistance. Probably a judicious mixture of self-help and expert aid is wisest as a general rule. In sharp contrast to the Lethbridge plan (described in our last issue) of mechanizing the public library by bringing it into gear with the post-office machinery, thus eliminating much waste, including that of time taken up in personal intercourse between librarian and patron, an "ex-librarian" has something to say, in the May "Public Libraries," in favor of extending that personal side of library work which the Lethbridge scheme would abolish. We quote a few sentences: "With no reflection upon any library in particular, it is the experience of many readers that the atmosphere among the assistants of the average free library is of a forbidding type. Many library helpers seem to be so afraid that they will give an inquirer one word too many in extending information. Perhaps the writer erred in the other direction; but in her experience in library work she was never so happy as at a time when an earnest reader made inquiries, and an opportunity presented itself to gather together all the literature upon a specified subject which might be found in indirect ways—hidden chapters of books with irrelevant titles, etc. Certain experiences in library work in one of the largest libraries in the country, together with two seasons of lecture-recital programmes, have brought to vision the possibility of broadening the influence of the free library as an educational centre—in all branches." Of course there is liability of imposition upon a too complaisant librarian: he may find that he is expected to write club papers, prepare outlines for debates, decipher difficult manuscripts, translate whole books from the lesser-known foreign tongues, and in other similar ways occupy his supposedly abundant leisure; but the competent and tactful librarian will know how to decline an unreasonable request and at the same time maintain his reputation for urbanity and omniscience.

Some Old-Time Old-World Librarians

By Theodore W. Koch
The North American Review, Aug 1914. vol. 200, no. 705, p. 244.

Mr. Herbert Putnam, in an address before the Ottawa meeting of the American Library Association, expressed a hope for a recognition, a recognition, in our library organization of that type which gave personality to the old-time libraries. However indifferent the old-time librarians may have been, or might be to-day, to the mere mechanism in our modern library organization, Mr. Putnam said, "they succeeded in producing an atmosphere which had a potency of its own. It was that which at once took the visitor out of himself, away from affairs, and gave him touch with a different world, a sense of different values. Does he not miss it now? I think he does; and that, however he may respect the efficiency of the modern librarian as administrator, his really affectionate admiration turns back to the librarian of the old school, whose soul was lifted above mere administration or the method of the moment, or the manner of insistent service, and whose passionate regard was rather for the inside of a book than the outside of a reader—even the librarian to whom a reader seemed indeed but an interruption to an abstraction that was privileged."

The prevailing ideas concerning librarianship have changed so radically within the last generation or two that it may be worth while to study a few types of the old-fashioned librarian. The modern librarian has been so concerned with schemes of classification, card catalogues, and new methods of housing the present-day avalanche of books that he has not had time to familiarize himself with his forebears.

I must resist the temptation to go back to antiquity as a starting-point for our study, and simply allow myself one illustration to show that the ancients knew a good librarian when they saw him. For the library of Pergamos, Eumenes the Second tried to secure the services of Aristophanes of Byzantium, librarian to Ptolemy the Fifth. To assure his remaining in Alexandria the librarian was cast in prison, a simple device for keeping an efficient worker when he had a call elsewhere. But in this paper we can concern ourselves only with librarians who have come on to the scene since the invention of printing. In 1475 Pope Sixtus the Fourth made Platina librarian of the newly organized Vatican Library. Platina's account-book has been preserved and published, and from this can be seen the varied nature of his duties. The librarian had to attend to the purchase of books, send out copyists, procure skins for binding, and supervise in the making of books as well as their use. He had charge of the reading-room in which the books were chained to the desks, and was allowed discretionary power in the lending of books to high officials of the Church, to scholars, and even to strangers sojourning in Rome. His account-book shows that he looked very carefully after the comfort of the readers, and that he knew the men whom he could trust. Platina and his three pages slept in a room adjoining the library, and they were diligent in the use of juniper in fumigating the rooms, in sweeping the library with brooms, and dusting the books with foxtails. Montaigne, in the Journal of his travels in Italy in 1581, says that he inspected the Vatican Library without any difficulty. "Indeed," he adds, "any one may visit it and make what extracts he likes; it is open almost every morning. I was taken to every part thereof by a gentleman who invited me to make use of it as often as I might desire." Des Brosses, in his letters on Italy, published at the end of the eighteenth century, in writing of the Vatican Library says that "as Cardinal Quirini, the librarian, is also Bishop of Brescia, he is always away in his diocese. His portrait in the antechamber has to do duty instead." The copyists, he added, are ignorant and dear. The most picturesque figure in the annals of Italian librarianship is undoubtedly Antonio Magliabecchi. While his official position as librarian to Cosmo III., Grand Duke of Tuscany, gave him considerable prominence, he is remembered more especially for his personal characteristics and his vast store of self-acquired learning. He has been described as a literary glutton, and the most rational of bibliomaniacs, inasmuch as he read everything he bought. His own library consisted of 40,000 books and 10,000 MSS. His house literally overflowed with books; the stairways were lined with them, and they even filled the front porch. Many stories are told of his marvelous memory that was "like wax to receive and marble to retain." One of the best known of these stories is that when Cosmo asked him for an extremely rare book he replied, "Signore, there is but one copy of that book in the world; it is in the Grand Signore's library at Constantinople, and is the eleventh book in the second shelf on the right hand as you go in."

In worldly matters Magliabecchi was extremely negligent. He even forgot to draw his salary for over a year. He wore his clothes until they fell from him, and thought it a great waste of time to undress at night, "life being so short and books so plentiful." He welcomed all inquiring scholars, provided they did not disturb him while at work. He had a hearty dislike for Jesuits. One day in pointing out the Palazzo Riccardi to a stranger he said, " Here the new birth of learning took place," and then turning to the college of the Jesuits, "There they have come back to bury it." The Jesuits, on hearing of this, characterized him rather cruelly as "Est doctor inter bibliothecarios, sed bibliothecarius inter doctores." Magliabecchi rejoined with this sally:

> "Some say that, after all, his learning is not so great; The learned allow him but librarian's state; And yet in sober truth it must be said All go to him for flour to make their bread."

Unlike some scholarly librarians of the past, ever watchful and jealous of manuscript material, which they themselves planned to edit, Isaac Casaubon, the humanist, was only anxious to read the manuscripts under his charge. For the most part, he was ready to leave the printing to others. Casaubon, too poor to buy books of his own, said of his father-in-law, Henri Estienne, who jealously kept him from gaining access to his books and manuscripts, that he guarded them "as griffins in India do their gold."

When Casaubon visited the library of the learned historian De Thon, of which he had heard so much, he found it far surpassed his expectations, and his heart sank at the thought of the little that he knew. In 1604 Casaubon was appointed sub-librarian in the Royal Library under De Thou, with the title garde de la librarie du Roi. His years there were the happiest of his life; his ideal was to read from early morning till late at night. In his *Ephemerides*, a diary in which he recited the progress of his studies day by day, there are such entries as: " To-day I got six hours for study. When shall I get my whole day?" And again, "This morning not to my books till seven o'clock or after; alas me! and after that the whole morning lost—nay, the whole day." When he was able to have a whole day for his studies he gratefully recorded the fact in his diary in the words *Hodie Vixi*. Frequently the only entry is: "My daily tasks, thanks be to God!" Not knowing how long he should remain in Paris, he early resolved to read all the books in the Royal Library which he might not be able to find elsewhere. Consequently he did nothing in the way of classifying or cataloguing the material under his charge. When any one asked for a particular book he tried to find it. In 1608, four years after Casaubon entered the library, Hoeschel wrote him, asking whether the library contained any manuscripts of Arrianus. Casaubon replied that he did now know, but would look, and upon searching found two. In reply to Scaliger's request for manuscript fragments of a chronological nature, he says that he will have a thorough search made through all the cases. No wonder that Mark Pattison in his life of Casaubon said that "the librarian who reads is lost." Casaubon was forcibly reminded that he was the King's librarian, and as such shared the obligations which the court imposed on all its entourage. He was not permitted while librarian to write a critical review of the *Annals of Baronius*, for fear of offending the Church, and Roman influence was paramount at the French court. When Casaubon visited Oxford he was hospitably entertained, but he succeeded in reserving many hours of each day for his studies in the Bodleian, and over-indulgence for which he paid the penalty during the second week in a sudden sense of dizziness which seized him one day while on his way to the library. "None of the colleges have attracted me so much as the Bodleian, the work rather for a king than for a private man," said Casaubon. He describes his own feelings when he writes Saumaise, who was reveling in the treasures of the Palatine, that he "must be suffering the torment of Tantalus, not being able to read all the books at once." A younger contemporary of Casaubon, Gabriel Naudé by name, was destined to build up for Cardinal Mazarin a library which outstripped the one belonging to the King. In 1642 Naudé was invited to return to his native city of Paris and begin the task of laying the foundations of a new public library. Naudé had previously catalogued the library of Descordes, a Canon of Limoges, who had died, leaving his collection of 6,000 volumes to be sold, and Naudé prevailed upon Mazarin to purchase the entire lot. Then all the bookshops of Paris and all the wastepaper dealers were canvassed for possible treasures. Naudé had been at his task but little more than a year when there was opened in the Mazarin Palace a public library larger than anything that had been seen before in the French capital. The reading-room was open once a week on Thursdays, from eight until eleven and from two until five. Naudé himself counted as many as from eighty to a hundred readers, among whom were such scholars as Hugo Grotius, Aubrey, the historian, and René Moreau, Professor of Medicine at the University of Paris. Before long the number of volumes reached the respectable total of twelve thousand, thus exceeding the royal collection at that time by approximately two thousand volumes. Naudé was still far from satisfied, and undertook a book-hunting journey in Flanders, which brought such good results that in April, 1645, he went to Italy in search of additional volumes. This last trip brought into the library fourteen thousand books. An Italian friend, Vittorio di Rossi, who met him in Rome on this trip, has left an account of Naudé's method of book-buying. According to this writer, Naudé would enter a bookshop with a foot-rule in hand, and without going too much into details about the titles, would ask the bookseller to name a price at random, which Naudé would beat down by degrees, and eventually buy in the books at such a low figure that the bookseller, seeing too late how he had been duped, would regret that he had not sold the lot to a grocer or a butter-man, who would surely have given him a larger sum for so much paper. After a visit from Naudé, the bookshops, says di Rossi, appeared to have been swept by a hurricane rather than visited by a bibliophile, and when one met him with a smile of satisfaction beaming through the dust and cobwebs that covered him, his lean figure swelled by the volumes which filled his pockets, one might readily conjecture that he had just come from a particularly satisfactory victory. Naudé claims that in book-collecting, as in love and war, all means are fair. He was famous for his ability in driving a hard bargain. There is on record, however, one instance of his being outwitted in the buying of a book, but it will not be laid to his discredit when it is known that the other party to the transaction was a Scotchman. Perhaps the most extraordinary librarianship was that enjoyed by Diderot, who about 1765 decided to sell his library in order to provide a dowry for his daughter. The Empress Catherine of Russia heard through Grimm of the straits to which Diderot had been reduced, and instructed her agent to buy in the library at the owner's valuation. In this way Diderot received not only sixteen thousand livres, but he was graciously requested to consider himself the librarian of the new purchase at the salary of one thousand livres a year. Moreover—and this begins to sound like a fairy tale—Diderot was paid the salary for fifty years in advance! Needless to say, this was only a pension in disguise. Catherine wrote to Madame du Deffand:

> "I should never have expected that the purchase of a library would bring me so many fine compliments; all the world is bepraising me about M. Diderot's library. But now confess, you to whom humanity is indebted for the strong support that you have given to innocence and virtue in the person of Cales, that it would have been cruel and unjust to separate a student from his books!"

Lessing may be taken to typify one class of old-fashioned librarians, the men of letters who regarded an appointment to a library position as a sinecure. Installed as librarian of the ducal library at Wolfenbüttel, Lessing took advantage of the privilege of the librarian of his day by substituting the writing of books for the less attractive duty of classifying and cataloguing them. His successor in office, Langer, was very bitter in his criticism of Lessing's administration, claiming that he had left much of his work undone. He even offered a reward to any one who could show him a trace of Lessing's handwriting in the library. To this day the only scrap of it is a note attached to a collection of engravings. Geissler wrote Langer in 1781, saying "that Lessing left you far too much to do was natural, because he was a genius, and this class seldom do their duty, but always follow their inclinations. "While Lessing was confessedly weak in matters of routine, he was strong where the general welfare of the library was concerned. He proposed a good plan for disposing of duplicates and filling the gaps in the library. It was also specified that "to the mere mechanical duties, the librarian was to attend to just as much or just as little as he pleased. For these he was to have two assistants and a man-servant. His main function would be to investigate thoroughly the library and to bring to light its chief treasures. "This last was Lessing's principal concern. "A catalogue of treasures," said he, "is good enough, but it is no new treasure," which is a point hardly conceded by the librarian of to-day who is in the midst of making over an old card catalogue.

So much for the old-fashioned librarian on the Continent. Let us now look at a few of this class in Great Britain and gather some illustrations of early ideas of library management in that country. The Bishop of Worcester in 1464 stipulated that his librarian be a graduate in theology and a good preacher, and in addition he was expected to explain hard passages in the Bible, to make lists of books in his keeping, and take an inventory of the library each year on the Friday after the Feast of Relics. Sir Thomas Bodley, in the first draft of the Statutes which he drew up for the administration of the library founded by him, explicitly states that the keeper shall open and close the library doors at certain hours, varying with the season, and that "at these prescribed hours he shall cause to be rung the warning bell of his ingress and egress, that men may shun the discommodities of repairing thither oversoon, or abiding there too long, which the difference of clocks may occasion very often, to the prejudice and hindrance of himself as well as others."

The keeper is to see that a register of gifts shall be kept, "written with a special, fair, and pleasing hand; and withal to be exposed where it may be still in sight, for evry man to view, as an eminent and endless token of our thankful acceptation of whatsoever hath been given, and as an excellent inducement for posterity to imitate these former good examples." The founder ruled that before any graduate or any person of note would be given the privilege of the Bodleian Library he should appear before the Vice-Chancellor or his substitute, and there in the presence of the Library Keeper he should take the oath of fidelity to the library, which was to be administered with these words:

"You shall Promise and Swear in the Presence of Almighty God, That whensoever you shall repair to the Publik Library of this University, you will conform yourself to study with Modesty and Silence; and use, both the Books, and everything appertaining to their Furniture, with careful Respect to their longest Conservation; And that neither your self in Person, nor any other whatsoever, by your Procurement or Privity, shall either openly or underhand, by way of embezzling, changing, razing, defacing, tearing, cutting, noting, underlining, or by voluntary corrupting, blotting, blurring, or any other manner of mangling or misusing, any one or more of the said Books, either wholly or in part, make any Alteration; But shall hinder and impeach, as much as lieth in you, all and every such Offender or Offenders, by detecting their Demeanour unto the Vice-Chancellor, or to his Deputy then in place, within the next Three Days after it shall come to your Knowledge; so help you God by Christ's Merits, according to the Doctrine of His Holy Evangelists." King James I was so appreciative of the work of Bodley that he granted letters patent the year after the library was opened, naming the library after the founder, whom he later knighted, and whose name, said he, should have been not Bodley, but Godley.

Richard Bentley was an intellectual prodigy who in early life fell heir to the cloak of librarianship. He coupled with his genius for scholarship a large enthusiasm for the advancement of learning, and with a daring almost insolent he shook off the "clamors of the half-learned who are always noisy against their betters." This ever-pugnacious determination to carry all projects through a maze of falsities is seen even in his career as royal librarian. At thirty-one, already well on the highway to scholarly recognition, he was induced to take the vacant office of the King's Librarian. His first step was characteristic. To such good use did he put the few months left before the evaded Licensing Act expired, that the significant record remains that he "exacted near a thousand volumes." Bentley's next step was to endeavor to secure some vacant rooms to relieve the cramped condition of his library at St. James's Palace. The duke of Marlborough, his neighbor across the hall, with obliging diplomacy, undertook to plead his cause, with the result that the future hero of Blenheim "got the closets for himself." Not disheartened by this perfidy, the young librarian, after declaring that the royal library was "not fit to be seen," started on what Lord Evelyn warmly called his "glorious enterprise" of building a new library. The Treasury consented to the proposal, but the bill to Parliament was shelved, owing to the press of public business. In the mean time Bentley took the library's chief treasure, the Alexandrine MS. of the Greek Bible, to his own rooms in St. James's Palace in order that "persons might see it without seeing the library," thereby establishing a new and original precedent in library economy. Out of one incident in his early tenure of office grew a quarrel resulting in several curiosities of literature and one masterpiece of scientific criticism. Dr. Aldrich, the dean of Christ Church, had induced a young Oxford man, the Honorable Charles Boyle, to edit the *Epistles of Phalaris*, and, in preparing his work for the printer, Boyle desired to consult a manuscript in the King's Library. Accordingly he wrote to a bookseller in London, asking him to have some one collate it for him. When Bentley took charge of the library, in May, 1694, he granted the loan of the manuscript for the purpose, and allowed ample time for the work to be done, but the collator failed to complete his task before the expiration of the time of the loan. The bookseller then very unfairly represented to Boyle that Bentley had acted churlishly in the matter, and Boyle, without verifying the story, said in his preface: " I have also procured a collation as far as epistle No. 40 of a manuscript in the Royal Library; the librarian, with that courtesy which distinguishes him, refused me the further use of it." Bentley happened to see an early presentation copy before the bulk of the edition was issued, and he at once wrote to Boyle, saying that the statement was incorrect, and gave him the true facts. Boyle sent an evasive reply, but let the statement stand as written. While Bentley was urged to refute the slander, he remained silent. "Out of a natural aversion to all quarrels and broils," he wrote, with what later seemed refined irony, "and out of regard to the editor himself, I resolved to take no notice of it, but to let the matter drop." A few years later Bentley reviewed Boyle's work in a way that incited Boyle, with the aid of half a dozen Oxford wits, to publish the book popularly known as *Boyle against Bentley*, in which insults were heaped upon the royal librarian. In 1699 Bentley was appointed Head Master of Trinity College, Cambridge, and, though still continuing to hold the office of King's Librarian, he removed to Cambridge. Here he continued the policy displayed in connection with the Alexandrine manuscript. When Dr. Conyers Middleton became librarian of Trinity College he published a plan for the classification of the books, and took occasion to attack Bentley for retaining some manuscripts, including the precious Codex Bezae, in his own house. But Bentley was always able to fight his own battles, and he inaugurated, by what his enemies were pleased to call his "insolent erudition," that famous series of bitter college feuds which ended only with the death of their vigorous and valiant instigator. Even the admiring, kindly Pepys was brought to admit that "our friend's learning wants a little filing," while Bishop Stillingfleet was heard to agree that did his friend Richard but possess the "gift of humility he would indeed be the most extraordinary man in Europe."

The name of Bentley brings to mind that of a later classical scholar who was an interesting misfit in the library world of a century ago, Richard Porson. his professorship of Greek at Cambridge paid only forty pounds a year, and so he welcomed the additional appointment of librarian to the newly founded London Institution in 1806, at a salary of two hundred pounds per year, with a suite of apartments thrown in. "I am sincerely rejoiced," wrote Richard Sharp, one of the electors, in notifying Porson of the appointment, "in the prospect of those benefits which the institution is likely to derive from your reputation and talents, and of the comforts which I hope that you will find in your connection with us." To-day the only existing indications of his tenure of office are the acquisition during his time of some Greek and Latin classics, and some manuscript notes in a few volumes in the library. He made no attempt to catalogue the books. The managers of the Institution wrote him to the effect that "they only knew him to be their librarian by seeing his name attached to the receipts for his salary." He reciprocated by characterizing the managers as "mercantile and mean beyond merchandize and meanness." While Porson had three essentials of librarianship—a good memory, a knowledge of books, and imagination, and was always willing to dispense information to such as called upon him for it—yet he was lacking in methodical attention to work. Dr. Parr once remarked that "if the Duke of Brunswick at the head of his Huns and Vandals were to burn every book of every library in Cambridge, Porson, being as Longinus was said to be, a living library, would make the University hear without books more than they are likely to read with books."

In 1752 David Hume was appointed librarian of the Faculty of Advocates in Edinburgh. Hume described it as "a petty office of forty or fifty guineas a year," and again as a "genteel office." He accepted it because it gave him "the command of a large library." A member of the Faculty was a candidate at the same time, but Hume got the majority of votes. "Then," says Hume, "came the violent cry of Deism, atheism, and skepticism. 'Twas represented that my election would be giving the sanction of the greatest and most learned body in this country to my profane and irreligious principles." The ladies sided with Hume, and one of them broke with her lover because he voted against he philosopher-historian. After he had been in office two years, Hume was censured by three of the curators of the library for buying the *Contes* of La Fontaine, Bussy-Rabutin's *Histoire amoureuse des Gaules*, and Crébillon's *L'écumoire*, deemed indecent and "unworthy of a place in a learned library." The absurdity of the resolution of censure is shown by the fact that these works are now in almost every library which makes any pretension of being classed among the learned.

Hume wrote to Lord Advocate Dundas, claiming that in his opinion the impropriety did not matter if it were executed with decency and ingenuity! "Being equally unwilling to lose the use of the books, and to bear an indignity, I retain the office, but have given Blacklock, our blind poet, a bond of annuity for the salary. I have now put it out of these malicious fellows' power to offer me any indignity, while my motive for remaining in this office is so apparent." The assistant librarian, Goodall, who was seldom sober, was busied with his *Vindication* of Mary, Queen of Scots, while Hume was writing his history of England, and the library was left to run itself.

The director of the British Museum formerly had only the title of Principal Librarian, which was, to a certain extent, a misnomer, as he had always had as much to do with the antiquities as with the books. To him is entrusted the custody of the entire museum, his duty being to look after the welfare of the whole institution and to see that the respective duties of the various officers and subordinates are properly performed. The Principal Librarian, as housekeeper, had also the nomination of the housemaids, until the doubtful privilege passed, in Sir Henry Ellis's day, to the principal trustees. The head of each department is called its "Keeper," and in most departments there is also an Assistant Keeper. These titles are reminiscent of the prime duty of the old-time librarian. One of them once consulted the trustees on the question of the acceptance by the Museum of a certain anti-Christian manuscript by a learned Jew—which he argued would not be pernicious, as the ignorant would not read it, and the souls of the learned were of little importance.

Dr. Templeman, the first superintendent of the Reading Room, seems to have found his duties rather onerous. After occupying the position eight months he asks to be relieved from what he considers the excessive attendance of six hours each day, as this "is more than he is able to bear." Under date of March 18, 1760, it is recorded that "last Tuesday, no company coming to the reading-room, Dr. Templeman ventured to go away about two o'clock." Twenty readers per month during the first few months was a high average, and after the novelty had worn off the average dropped to ten or twelve. The early librarians at the British Museum were little more than guides appointed to show visitors around the institution. In 1802, three attendants were appointed to relieve the "Under and Assistant Librarians from the daily duty of showing the Museum," and they were given an increase in pay. As late as 1837 no less a person than the Rev. Henry Francis Cary, Keeper of Printed Books, gave poor health as an argument for his promotion to Principal Librarianship, which, as he said, would give him less to do. Sir Henry Ellis, when he was Principal Librarian, defended his closing of the Museum for three weeks each autumn, and argued that if that were not done the place would become "unwholesome," and that to open it during Easter holidays would be dangerous, as " the most mischievous portion of the population is abroad and about at such a time." He further argued for the closing of the institution for public holidays, on the ground that "people of a higher grade would hardly wish to come to the Museum at the same time with sailors from the dockyards and the girls whom they might bring with them." From this it can be clearly seen that he was not in touch with the growing liberality in the administration of public institutions and the influx of democratic ideas.

In the opinion of many, modern librarianship begins with Sir Anthony Panizzi's administration of the British Museum. An Italian carbonaro, under indictment for the publication of a pamphlet attacking the judicial system of Modena, he escaped to London, where, in 1831, he had an opportunity to enter the service of the Museum. The administration was then at its lowest ebb. The Elgin marbles and the King's Library had just been acquired, but the regime was antiquated and the policy very narrow. Panizzi was put to work at cataloguing the pamphlets in the King's Library. Owing to dissatisfaction with the progress of the subject catalogue, the trustees, in 1834, outlined a plan for an alphabetical catalogue. The plan was an unsatisfactory one, but Panizzi was put in charge of the work. As he did more work than any two of his colleagues, the trustees raised his salary, and when there was an investigation of the administration of the British Museum it was Panizzi who contributed the most important evidence. Valuable reforms were introduced, and Panizzi became Keeper of Printed Books in 1837. This appointment brought out a certain British anti-foreign prejudice against Panizzi which pursued him throughout his official career. There were meetings held to arouse sentiment against the promotion of this "foreigner," and a speaker on one of these occasions made an open statement that Panizzi had been seen on the streets of London selling white mice! At the time of his appointment, the collections were just being removed from Montague House to new quarters, serious attempts were being made to fill the gaps in the collections, and the catalogue was being attacked in real earnest. The transfer of the collection was accomplished with remarkable expedition, but the progress of the catalogue was less satisfactory. The responsibility for accepting or rejecting the supervision of this work was left by the trustees to Panizzi, and with his usual courage he decided to undertake the task. With the assistance of Jones, Watts, and others, he framed a set of catalogue rules which in many respects have never been superseded. An insufficient staff and an unfortunate decision of the trustees (overruling Panizzi's advice) to proceed in strict alphabetical order, occasioned a good deal of trouble and criticism. The attempt to print out one portion of the catalogue while another part was in preparation, before it had been definitely decided as to what the main entry for many items would be, was responsible for the breakdown of the scheme. After the publication of one volume in 1841, the decision to print the catalogue was abandoned, and Panizzi persuaded the trustees to engage an efficient staff of transcribers to copy the titles on slips, and he was thus enabled to put before the public a plan for a comprehensive catalogue. He failed to see the advantage of a printed catalogue over a slip catalogue, and was more concerned with supplying the deficiencies of the library, a task in which he had no rivals. By submitting a list of the needs in nearly every branch of literature, he procured, in 1845, an annual grant of ten thousand pounds, and through the judicious administration of this fund the Museum rose in rank from the sixth or seventh to the second, if not the first, place among the libraries of the world. In 1848 dissatisfaction with conditions in the Museum, due to lack of space, was so great that a royal commission of inquiry was instituted, and as a result of Panizzi's success, the administration of the Museum was put into his hands.

In temperament Panizzi was strong and masterful, but his nature was warm and generous. "He governed his library as his friend Cavour governed his country," said Dr. Garnett, "perfecting its internal organization with one hand while he extended the frontiers with the other." When traveling abroad he always rushed to visit the chief libraries first. At Bologna he found a manuscript catalogue so carefully made that he at once asked whose work it was, and when told that it had all been done by one man who had written every title with his own hand, Panizzi insisted upon seeing him. A tall, thin-faced, threadbare individual appeared whom Panizzi plied with questions, and then, to the astonishment of the attendants, Panizzi in an outburst of Italian enthusiasm hugged and kissed the timid cataloguer on both cheeks.

Panizzi was one of the most conscientious of officials and was rarely absent from his post. Sydney Smith wrote him several times inviting him to dinner on a certain date. "Receiving no answer," the wit wrote later, "I concluded you were dead, and I invited your executors. News, however, came that you were out of town. I should have thought of St. Paul's or the Monument being out of town, but as it was positively asserted, I have filled up your place." Next to Panizzi, the most attractive personality in the annals of the British Museum, to us at least, is Richard Garnett. Like another native of Lichfield, Dr. Samuel Johnson, Garnett will be remembered more for what he was than for what he wrote. To carry the comparison still further, both were interpreters and left volumes of critical biography, both were poets of no mean order, both were story-tellers and entertainers of repute, famed alike for their friendships, their love of learning, and their erudition. While Dr. Johnson's most enduring monument is his famous dictionary, Dr. Garnett left behind a printed catalogue of the British Museum containing four and a half million entries, thereby earning the gratitude of scholars throughout the world. The British public never quite forgave Panizzi for claiming that a printed catalogue of their national library was too big a task to undertake. Richard Garnett may be said to have spent his whole life in the British Museum. His father was an assistant keeper, and at the age of sixteen the young man was made an assistant in the Printed Books Department. Promotions came rapidly until in 1875 he was made Assistant Keeper and superintendent of the reading-room. Garnett's work as "placer" or classifier, combined with his rare memory, gave him a remarkable command of the resources of the library. There seemed to be nothing that he had not read and few subjects that he had not studied intimately. Few men of his time knew both the inside and outside of books as he did. Whatever the subject, he gave the impression that his knowledge of it was fresh and waiting for use. Only one fall from grace is recorded. Mrs. Garnett had brought home, after a country holiday, what she believed to be a squirrel's nest which she placed on the drawing-room table to show her friends. A dispute arose as to whether squirrels made nests. Mrs. Garnett appealed to her husband. "Richard, do squirrels guild nests?" He hesitated, then replied: "I really do not know; I do not think so. I must look it up."

Dr. Garnett was so endowed with a sense of good humor that he was never perturbed by the chronic fussers who frequented the place. A blank-book in which the public can jot down suggestions for the improvement of the service or of titles recommended for purchase has for years been found to ease the public mind. The authorities make a practice of entering in the margin a reply to each suggestion made. When a reader entered a request that somebody's life of Satan be obtained, the official comment read: "Purchase not thought necessary." Another suggestion was: "Best sixpenny cookery by Josiah Oldfield does not appear in the catalogue, but should, I think, be procured, as it is a useful vegetarian work." This was applied for on December 26th—note the date—and was promptly ordered. There is a class of beings to whom it is a great joy to discover a book that is not in the British Museum, or, if there, cannot be found for the time being, or is wrongly described, as they think, in the catalogue. "So you see, sir," said Dr.

Johnson on an occasion of this kind, "when it was lost it was of immense consequence, and when found it was no matter at all."

Garnett's administration of the reading-room was characterized by a large increase in the number of readers, the placing of special bibliographies in the room to supply as far as possible the want of a subject catalogue, the formation of a second library of reference in the gallery in the reading-room, and the introduction of electric light. The mere mention of electric light shows that we have come down to our own day, and we must take leave of the old-time librarian. Naturally the atmosphere of the modern public library, with its rush and hustle, proved uncongenial to the old-fashioned librarian. The less rapidly changing college and university libraries harbored him much longer, but with modern efficiency tests I suppose that he, too, is to be driven even from that last resort. The following has been suggested as an appropriate epitaph for him:

"He loved his library and his books more than the service of his fellow-men."

Upon the librarian of to-day devolves many problems not dreamed of by his forerunners. But the success of the library and its utility always have been and always must be measured, to quite Lord Goschen, largely by the "affability and competence of the librarian." What is wanted, according to this wise statesman, is a librarian who will suffer fools gladly and who, when asked foolish questions, will guide the questioners aright.

The People's Share in the Public Library

By Arthur E. Bostwick, Librarian, St. Louis Public Library.
Read before the Chicago Woman's Club, Jan. 6, 1915.
Published in *Library Journal*, April, 1915.

The change that has come over the library in the last half century may be described, briefly but comprehensively, by saying that it has become predominantly a social institution; that is, that its primary concern is now with the service that it may render to society—to the people. Books, of course, were always intended to be read, and a library would have no meaning were it never to be used; yet in the old libraries the collection and preservation of the books was primary and their use secondary, whereas the modern institution exists primarily for public service, the collection of the books, their preservation and whatever is done to them being directed to this end. To a social institution—a family, a school, a club, a church, a municipality—the persons constituting it, or served by it are all-important. A family without parents and children, a school without pupils, a club without members, a church with no congregation, a city without citizens—all are unthinkable. We may better realize the change in our conception of the public library by noting that it has taken its place among bodies of this type. A modern library with no readers is unthinkable; it is no library, as we now understand the word; though it is teeming with books, housed in a palace, well cataloged and properly manned.

It is no longer possible to question this view of the library as a social institution—a means of rendering general service to the widest public. We have to deal not with theories of what the library ought to be, but with facts indicating what it actually is; and we have only to look about us to realize that the facts give the fullest measure of support to what I have just said. The library is a great distributing agency, the commodities in which it deals being ideas and its customers the citizens at large, who pay, through the agency of taxation, for what they receive. This democratic and civic view of the public library's functions, however does not commend itself to those who are not in sympathy with democratic ideals. In a recent address, representative librarian refers to it as "the commercial-traveler theory" of the library. The implication, of course, is that it is an ignoble or unworthy theory. I have no objection to accepting the phrase, for in my mind it has no such connotation. The commercial traveler has done the world service which the library should emulate rather than despise. He is the advance guard of civilization. To speak but of our own country and of its recent years, he is responsible for much of our improvement in transit facilities and hotel accommodations. Personally, he is becoming more and more acceptable. The best of our educated young men are going into commerce and in commerce to-day no one can reach the top of the ladder who has not proved his efficiency "on the road." Would that we could place men of his type at the head of all our libraries!

We need not think, however, that there is anything new in the method of distribution by personal travel. Homer employed it when he wished his heroic verse to reach the great body of his countrymen. By personal travel he took it to the cross-roads—just as the distributor of food and clothing and labor-saving appliances does today; just as we librarians must do if we are to democratize all literature as Homer democratized a small part of it. Homer, if you choose to say so, adopted the "commercial-traveler theory" of literary distribution; but I prefer to say that the modern public library in laying stress on the necessity of distributing its treasures and in adopting the measures that have proved effective in other fields, is working on the Homeric method.

Now, without the people to whom he distributed his wares, Homer would have been dead long ago. He lives because he took his wares to his audience. And without its public, as we have already said, the public library, too, would soon pass into oblivion. It must look to the public for the breath of life, for the very blood in its veins, for its bone and sinew. What, then, is the part that the community may play in increasing the efficiency of a public institution like the public library? Such an institution is, first of all, a medium through which the community does something for itself. The community employs and supports it, and at the same time is served by it. To use another homely illustration, which I am sure will not please those who object to comparing great things with small, this type of relationship is precisely what we find in domestic service. A cook or a housemaid has a dual relation to the mistress of the house, who is at the same time her employer and the person that she directly serves. This sort of relation does not obtain, for instance, in the case of a railroad employee, who is responsible to one set of persons and serves another. The public library is established and maintained by a given community in order that it may perform certain service for that same community directly. It seems to me that this dual relationship ought to make for efficiency. If it does not, it is because its existence and significance are not always realized. The cook knows that if she does not cook to suit her mistress she will lose her job—the thing works almost automatically. If the railroad employee does not serve the public satisfactorily there is no such immediate reaction, although I do not deny that the public displeasure may ultimately reach the railroad authorities and through them the employee. In most public institutions the reaction is necessarily somewhat indirect. The post office is a public institution, but public opinion must act on it generally through the channels of Congressional legislation, which takes time. Owing to this fact, very few postmen, for instance, realize that the persons to whom they deliver letters are also their employers. In all libraries the machinery of reaction is not the same. In St. Louis, for instance, the library receives the proceeds of a tax voted directly by the people; in New York City it receives an appropriation voted by the Board of Apportionment, whose members are elected by the people. The St. Louis Public Library is therefore one step nearer the control of the people than the New York Public Library. If we could imagine the management of either library to become so objectionable as to make its abolition desirable, a petition for a special election could remove public support in St. Louis very soon. In New York the matter might have to become an issue in a general election, at which members of a Board of Apportionment should be elected under pledge to vote against the library's appropriation. Nevertheless, in both cases there is ultimate popular control. Owing to this dual relation, the public can promote the efficiency of the library in two ways—by controlling it properly and by its attitude toward the service that is rendered. Every member of the public, in fact is related to the library somewhat as a railway stockholder, riding on a train, is related to the company. He is at once boss and beneficiary.

Let us see first what the public can do for its library through its relation of control. Besides the purse-strings, which we have seen are sometimes held directly by the public and sometimes by its elected representatives, we must consider the governing board of the institution—its trustees or directors. These may be elected by the people or appointed by an elected officer, such as the mayor, or chosen by an elected body, such as the city council or the board of education. Let us take the purse-strings first. Does your public library get enough public money to enable it to do the work that it ought to do? What is the general impression about this in the community? What does the library board think? What does the librarian think? What do the members of his staff say? What has the library's annual report to say about it? It is not at all a difficult matter for the citizen to get information on this subject and to form his own opinion regarding it. Yet it is an unusual thing to find a citizen who has either the information or a well-considered opinion. The general impression always seems to be that the library has plenty of money—rather more, in fact, than it can legitimately use. It is probably well for the library, under these circumstances, that the public control of its purse-strings is indirect. If the citizens of an average American city had to go to the polls annually and vote their public library an appropriation, I am sure that most libraries would have to face a very material reduction of their income. The trouble about this impression is that it is gained without knowledge of the facts. If a majority of the citizens, understanding how much work a modern public library is expected to do and how their own library does it, should deliberately conclude that its management was extravagant, and that its expenditure should be cut down, the minority would have nothing to do, as good citizens, but the idea, so generally held, that libraries are well off, does operate in the long run to limit library appropriations and to prevent the library from doing much useful work that it might do and ought to do.

It is, then, every citizen's business, as I conceive it, to inform him or herself of the work that the public library is doing, of that which it is leaving undone, and of the possibilities of increased appropriations. If the result is a realization that the library appropriation is inadequate, that realization should take the form of a statement that will sooner or later reach the ears and tend to stimulate the action, of those directly responsible. And it should, above all, aid in the formation of a sound public opinion. Ours is, we are told, a government of public opinion. Such government will necessarily be good or bad as public opinion is based on matured judgment or only on fleeting impressions. Inadequacy of support is responsible for more library delinquency than the average citizen imagines. Many a librarian is deservedly condemned for the unsatisfactory condition of his institution when his fault is not, as his detractors think, failure to see what should be done, or lack of ability to do it, so much as inability to raise funds to do it with. This is doubtless a fault, and its possessor should suffer, but how about the equally guilty accessories? How about the city authorities who have failed to vote the library adequate support? How about the board of trustees who have accepted such a situation without protest? And what is more to our purpose here, how about the citizens who have limited their efforts to pointing out the cracks in the edifice with not a bit of constructive work in propping it up and making possible its restoration to strength and soundness? In conversation with a friend, not long ago, I referred to the financial limitations of our library's work, and said that we could add to it greatly and render more acceptable service if our income were larger. He expressed great surprise, and said: "Why, I thought you had all the money you want; your income must be all of $100,000 a year." Now our income actually is about $250,000, but how could I tell him that? I judiciously changed the subject.

Let us look next, if you please, at the library board and examine some of its functions. There appears to be much public misapprehension of the duties of this body, and such misapprehension assumes various and opposing forms. Some appear to think that the librarian is responsible for all that is done in the library and that his board is a perfunctory body. Others seem to believe that the board is the direct administrative head of the library, in all of its working details, and the librarian is its executive in the limited sense of doing only those things that he is told to do. Unfortunately there are libraries that are operated in each of these ways, but neither one relationship nor the other, nor any modification of either, is the ideal one between a librarian and his board. The board is supreme, of course, but it is a body of non-experts who have employed an expert to bring about certain results. They ought to know what they want, and what they have a right to expect, and if their expert does not give them this, the relation between him and them should terminate; but if they are men of sense they will not attempt to dictate methods or supervise details. They are the delegated representatives of the great public, which owns the library and operates it for a definite purpose. It is this function of the board as the representative of the public that should be emphasized here. Has the public a definite idea of what it wants from the public library, and of what is reasonable for it to ask? If so, is it satisfied that it is represented by a board that is of the same mind? The citizens may be assured that the composition of the library board rests ultimately upon its will. If the board is elective, this is obvious; if appointive, the appointing officer or body would hardly dare to go counter to the expressed desire of the citizens.

What has been said above may be put into very few words. The public library is public property, owned and controlled by the citizens. Every citizen, therefore, should be interested in setting standards for it and playing his part toward making it conform to them—in seeing that its governing body represents him in also recognizing those standards and trying to maintain them—in laboring for such a due apportionment of the public funds as shall not make an attempt to live up to such standards a mere farce. So much for the things that the citizen can and should do in his capacity of library boss. His possibilities as a beneficiary are still more interesting and valuable.

Perhaps you remember the story of the man who attempted to board the warship and, on being asked his business, replied, "I'm one of the owners." One version of the tale then goes on to relate how the sailor thus addressed picked up a splinter from the deck, and handing it to the visitor, remarked: "Well, I guess that's about your share. Take it and get out!"

I have always sympathized with the sailor rather than his visitor. Most of us librarians have had experiences with these bumptious "owners" of public property. The fact has already been noted that in a case like this the citizen is both and owner and a beneficiary. He has duties and privileges in both capacities, but he sometimes acts the owner in the wrong place. The man on the warship was doubtless an owner, but that that particular moment he was only a visitor, subject to whatever rules might govern visitors; and he should have acted as such. Every citizen is a part owner of the public library; he should never forget that fact. We have seen how he may effectively assert his ownership and control. But when he enters the library to use it his roles is that such of beneficiary, and he should act as such. He may so act and at the same time be of the greatest service to the institution which he, is a member of the public, has created and is maintaining.

I know of no way in which a man may show his good citizenship or the reverse—may either demonstrate his ability and willingness to live and work in community harness, or show that he is fit for nothing but individual wild life in the woods—better than in his use of such a public institution as a library. The man who cannot see that what he gets from such an institution must necessarily be obtained at the price of sacrifice—that others in the community are also entitled to their share, and that sharing always means yielding—that man has not yet learned the first lesson in the elements of civic virtue. And when one sees a thousand citizens, each of whom would surely raise his voice in protest if the library were to waste public money by buying a thousand copies of the latest novel, yet find fault with the library because each cannot borrow it before all the others, one is tempted to wonder whether we really have here a thousand bad citizens or whether their early education in elementary arithmetic has been neglected.

Before the present era there were regulations in all institutions that seemed to be framed merely to exasperate to put the public in its place and chasten its spirit. There are now no such rules in good libraries. He who thinks there are may find that there is a difference of opinion between him and those whom he has set in charge of the library regarding what is arbitrary and what is necessary; but at any rate he will discover that the animating spirit of modern library authority is to give all an equal share in what it has to offer, and to restrain one man no more than is necessary to insure to his brother the measure of privilege to which all are equally entitled.

Another way in which the citizen, in his capacity of the library's beneficiary, can aid it and improve its service is his treatment of its administrators. Librarians are very human: they react quickly and surely to praise or blame, deserved or undeserved. Blame is what they chiefly get. Sometimes they deserve it and sometimes not. But the occasions on which some citizen steps in and says "Well done, good and faithful servant," are rare indeed. The public servant has to interpret silence as praise; so sure is he that the least slip will be caught and condemned by a vigilant public. No one can object to discriminating criticism; it is a potent aid to good administration. Mere petulant fault-finding, however, especially if based on ignorance or misapprehension, does positive harm. And a little discriminating praise, now and then, is a wonderful stimulant. No service is possible without the men and women who render it; and the quality of service depends, more than we often realize, on the spirit and temper of a staff—something that is powerfully affected, either for good or for evil, by public action and public response.

Years ago, at a branch library in a distant city, a reader stood at the counter and complained loudly because the library would not send her a postal reserve notice unless she defrayed the cost, which was one cent. The assistant to whom she was talking had no option in the matter and was merely enforcing a rule common, so far as I know, to all American public libraries; but she had to bear the brunt of the reader's displeasure, which she did meekly, as it was all in the day's work. The time occupied in this useless business spelled delay to half a dozen other readers, who were waiting their turn. Finally, one of them, a quiet little old lady in black, spoke up as follows: "Some of us hereabouts think that we owe a great debt of gratitude to this library. Its assistants have rendered service to us that we can never repay. I am glad to have an opportunity to do something in return, and it therefore gives me pleasure to pay the cent about which you are taking up this young lady's time, and ours." So saying, she laid the coin on the desk and the line moved on. I have always remembered these two points of view as typical of two kinds of library users. Their respective prefects on the temper and work of a library staff need, I am sure, no explanation. In what I have said, which is such a small fraction of what might be said, that I am almost ashamed to offer it to you, I have in truth only been playing the variations on one tune, which is—Draw closer to the library, as it is trying to draw closer to you. There is no such thing, physicists tell us, as a one-sided force. Every force is but one aspect of a stress, which includes also an equal and opposing force. Any two interacting things in this world are either approaching each other or receding from each other. So it should be with library and public. A forward movement on the one hand should necessarily involve on to meet it.

The peculiarity of our modern temper is our hunger for facts – our confidence that when the facts are known we shall find a way to deal with them, and that until the facts are known we shall not be able to act—not even to think. Our ancestors thought and acted sometimes on premises that seem to us frightfully flimsy—they tried, as Dean Swift painted them in his immortal satire, to get sunbeams from cucumbers. There are some sunbeam-chasers among us to-day, but even they recognize the need of real cucumbers to start with; the imaginary kind will not do. I recently heard a great teacher of medicine say that the task of the modern physician is merely to ascertain the facts on which the intelligent public is to act. How different that sounds from the dicta of the medicine of a past generation! It is the same everywhere" : we are demanding an accurate survey—an ascertainment of the facts in any field in which action, based on inference and judgment, is seen to be necessary. Now the library is nothing more nor less than a storehouse of recorded facts. It is becoming so more truly and more fully every day, thereby adjusting itself to the modern temper of which I have already spoken. The library and its users are coming more closely together, in sympathy, in aims and in action, than ever before – partly a result and partly a justification for that Homeric method of popularizing it which has been characterized and condemned as commercial. The day when the librarian, or the professor, or the clergyman could retire into his tower and hold aloof the herd is past. The logical result of such an attitude is now being worked out on the continent of Europe. Not civilizations as some pessimists are lamenting, but the forces antagonistic to civilization are there destroying one another, and there is hope that a purified democracy will arise from the wreckage. May our American civilization never have to run the gantlet of such a terrible trial! Meanwhile, there can be no doubt that the hope for the future efficiency of all our public institutions, including the library, lies in the success of democracy, and that deepens on the existence and improvement of the conditions in whose absence democracy necessarily fails. Foremost among these is the homogeneity of the population. The people among whom democracy succeeds must have similar standards, ideas, aims, and abilities. Democracy may exist in a pack of wolves, but not in a group that is half wolves and half men. Either the wolves will kill the men or the men the wolves. This is an extreme case, but it is true in general that in a community made up of irreconcilable elements there can be no true democracy. And the same oneness of vision and propose that conduces to the success of democracy will also bring to perfection such great democratic institutions as the library, which have already borne such noteworthy fruit among us just because we are homogeneous beyond all other nations on the earth. And here progress is by action and reaction, as we see it so often in the world. The unity of aims and abilities that makes democracy and democratic institutions possible is itself facilitated and increased by the work of those institutions. The more work the library does, the more its ramification multiply, and the further they extend, the more those conditions are favored that make the continuance of the library possible. In working for others, it is working for itself, and every additional bit of strength and sanity that it takes on does but enable it to work for others the more. And if the democracy whose servant it is will but realize that it has grown up as a part of that American system to which we are all committed—to which we owe all that we are and in which we must place all our hopes for the future—then neither democracy nor library will have aught to fear. Democracy will have its "true and laudable" service from the library and the library in its turn will have adequate sympathy, aid and support from the people.

It is no accident that I make this appeal for sympathy and aid to a club composed of women. The bonds between the modern public library and the modern woman's club have been particularly strong in this country. The two institutions have grown up together, making their way against suspicion, contempt and hostility, aided by the same public demand, and now, when both are recognized as elements in the intellectual strength of our nation, they are rendering mutual service. The club turns to the library daily. Hitherto the library has turned to the club only in some emergency—a bill to be passed, an appropriation to be made, an administration to be purified. I have tried to show you how, apart from these great services, which no one would think of minimizing, the women of this country, as citizens, can uphold the hands of the library daily. Ours is a government of public opinion, and in the formation of that opinion there is no more powerful element than the sentiment of our women, especially when organized in such bodies as yours.

"To be aristocratic in taste and democratic in service," says Bliss Perry, "is the privilege and glory of a public library." In appealing thus to both your aristocracy and your democracy, I feel, then, that I have not gone astray.

Women Assistants and the War

Published in *Library World* 17 (January 1915).
By M.F.

One result of the present disastrous war is the fact that certain doors in various professions and trades are being opened to women – doors which would otherwise have long remained closed to our sex.

Although we must all regret the cause of the opening of these doors, women cannot regret the effect—the fact that certain advantages must accrue, and in our direction.

In France we hear of women successfully filling positions which have been rendered vacant by the men who have left their work and answered the call of their country—positions which have hitherto been held only by men. As yet, in England, the services of women have not to any great extent been called for but we cannot say what may happen in the near future if some form of compulsory military training calls out still more of our men.

There is unlimited scope today for the capable woman with originality, grit and initiative, for already one sees advertisements for women workers in all branches of work to fill the place of the men who have gone; vacancies for lectureships in colleges where a year or so ago the merits of a woman professor would not have been discussed; vacancies in offices where men only have been employed; vacancies in public libraries, the staffs of which have previously been composed entirely of men.

The women who mean to win through must make up their minds they will be a success by putting their very best into their work; the exercise of tact and understanding, and the necessity for keeping cheerful are some of the means we can employ towards this end, and we must remember that it is the woman with initiative, the woman who does something no one has done before, who gets promotion and who earns the pleasing verdict—"most efficient."

The problem that we are now called upon to face is, that we as women workers are to be put on our trial, and the result of that trial depends on the individual and her work.

For years past women library assistants have been steadily qualifying themselves, only to find in many instances after they have reached a certain point, that the path is blocked to them, and there is no chance of further advance.

One of the chief causes of complaint in our profession has been that the senior positions have invariably fallen to men; the justice or injustice, the truth or untruth of this statement does not, at the present time, concern us.

The most unimaginative of us now admit that when the war is over a great many changes will have taken place, not only nationally and politically, but socially and individually.

It is too early as yet to determine where in the general reorganization of national life our profession will be; the optimist may foresee brighter days ahead – the pessimist, the end of libraries and librarians for all time.

Who shall say which will prove to be the correct prophet?

But with regard to woman's work there is one thing we can prophesy, and that is, that when the war is over and things are once again straightened out, the library committees who have experienced the services of capable women assistants who have been engaged "for the period of the war" will, as a result of the quality of the work rendered, be unanimous in their desire to retain such services permanently.

There are many ways in which girls can help. A circular has been sent by the Secretaries of the Women's Committee to the women members of the Library Assistants' Association asking them by their presence at the meetings of the Association, both in town and the provinces, to fill up the absent places caused by the large number of men of the profession who have answered the call of the flag. If the girls will respond to this appeal and fill up the ranks at the meetings during the coming sessions, when our men return they will find at least one profession in as flourishing a condition as it has ever been, possibly more so. Who can tell?

Another of the many ways in which they can help is by making the library in which they work as cheerful and bright a place as possible to the many harassed and anxious people who may turn to it for relaxation during this time of stress and worry. They may be assured that they will be doing as patriotic a duty as the war poet who is so rampant, or as the women who carry irritating odds and ends of knitting about them where they go. Those who know the reception these poems and discomforts receive will have the added satisfaction of knowing that their work is of use!

There are chances today for the "one talent" assistant.

A small library which the writer know has furnished a good instance of this; a practically unknown member of the staff who has failed to obtain any certificates of the Library Association, has, during the last few months proved to be of great value, entirely owing to the fact that she speaks French fluently.

It will be argued that French is a most ordinary accomplishment, all educated assistants speak French, and so on; but how many of our assistants have been able to converse with ease with the many Belgians who have used our libraries recently?

We are constantly coming across the "Business as usual" phrase—it is a good motto for a public library, and if women will only remember that if they do their best it will be largely through their efforts that the flag of our profession can be kept flying as proudly as ever.

It must be remembered that this is not a time when we must look for material advantages merely, the girl who is out wholly with that idea today will probably find herself as badly off when the war is over, as the man who, for the sake of what he terms his "professional prospects" is hesitating to fulfill his share of the duty he owes to his country.

But remembering the salaries paid to the Mid-Victorian working women and those paid today, we may well be cautious in guessing what are the limits which the future will establish and it is well therefore to stimulate the ambition and hopefulness in the junior assistants. They should be reminded that their goal is not such "a long, long way" off as it was even a year ago, that "these are the days of the side car and the one will drive who can best do it" —so learn to drive and teach your juniors.

We have claimed that we are as competent as men and that our work in the library world is as good as that of our male confreres, our claims are now to be tested, it is up to every girl and woman in our profession to show "of what stuff she is made!"

Napoleon's exclamation, "How rare are men!" is still unfortunately true, but the dreary significance of this statement need not hinder library work.

M.F.

Letters to the Editor of *The Library World*

Sir—As a woman librarian I should like to express my sympathy, up to a certain point with M.F.'s article. There is much in it to stimulate us to do our best work and there is good advice in it for those who are in senior positions. Nor can it be anything but right and sensible for us to make the most of our opportunities and to strain every effort to fit ourselves for such duties as we may be called upon to perform. But, whatever happens, we must not lose sight of the services rendered by the men at the front, in almost every case at great personal sacrifice.

When they return to fill the places kept open for them, as we truly hope they may, we want them to fell that women are better able to work side by side with them, each doing whatever is best suited to his or her respective qualifications. Conditions which can bring about a kindly understanding between the men and women who by force of circumstances have to earn a living, must be welcome and to their mutual advantage, and to such conditions we all look forward in the future; if possible at the close of this terrible war.

I am Sir, &c., *A Woman Librarian*

February, 1915

Dear Sir—In the tumult of feeling which the outbreak of war caused throughout the Empire, hundreds of thousands of men, without thought of the check it might mean to their worldly advancement and prosperity, left their work and their offices, and took the oath which would in all probability lead them into terrible danger—perchance to some ghastly death on the filed of battle. Let it be granted that the change from the routine and monotony of everyday life and work was pleasant; that the call to arms thrilled the adventure spirit; that some of the men are having the time of their lives; and that, after all, they are only ding their duty. Those who know of something other than the surface gaiety and glory as portrayed in the newspapers, or by the men who are ever- anxious to save their woman fold from a true appreciation of the hardships they undergo, know that doing what is "only their duty" is making men face a strain and horrors which have turned tried and seasoned soldiers into gibbering idiots! Having regard to these things, it is inconceivable that anyone should be found capable of suggesting that the present is a time in which women should strain every nerve to oust and supplant their men competitors in any department of life. It is, I suppose, inevitable that those who are left at home—men as well as women—should meet with professional opportunities which would not have come their way had not the war claimed the other works; but coldly and deliberately to attempt to occupy permanently places left open by them is to break every rule of fair play. To say that women workers have had to suffer from men's unfairness does not mitigate the offence in the very least. I have sufficient faith in the eternal rightness of things to believe that, should the women of our libraries adopt this attitude of fighting a man when he is down—and that is what it amounts to—their cause would suffer irretrievably, and the day would never dawn when their work would be judged as work and not as the product of a very much cheaper machine than man!

Let them give of their best to their work; let them cheerfully accept more work and longer hours, so that the work of their men colleagues may not be allowed to come to a standstill; let them offer themselves as *voluntary* workers in districts which are too heavily handicapped by the absence of men; let them attend meetings of professional associations, read papers, and take part in debates, so that there shall still be living organizations for the men to come back to. That is the right thing for women as workers to do during the course of the war; that is the thing which the women of France have been doing; that is the thing which the leaders and members of the various woman suffrage and feminist societies have shown that they consider the right thing—the only thing. They have stopped all acts of militancy, all propaganda work, all diatribes against men and their doings.

Let us not be led astray by a chimera!

Olive E. Clarke

Sir—Napoleon' exclamation, "How rare are men!" is evidently much more true than I thought when I first quoted it. It was the men who first asked me to write the notes for *The Library World;* it is now the men who write or inspire the criticism of my efforts to please them. I commenced by that that "we must all regret the cause of the opening of these doors." I then wrote the truth. Yet some of your correspondents apparently deny that I was then sincere. Heaven forbid that I should lead any member of the Library Association or of any other Association, astray—but I am gratified to be referred to as "a fabled fire-breathing monster of Greek mythology, with a lion's head, a goat's body, and a serpent's tail. A horrible and fear-inspiring phantasm, a bogey." This I find is a chimera! Miss Clarke has evidently unintentionally flattered me. A real "Woman Librarian," seems to have correctly interpreted the spirit of my notes. My point is that in most libraries the men have seen to it that the women have not had an opportunity of showing their ability, and I may add in some cases the women have not grasped the opportunity. The opportunity has now arisen, and I was urging women to be sufficiently manlike in their methods to take it. As to dear old Eratosthenes—his ancestor was a grammarian and a philosopher. "How are the might fallen!" His descendants have deteriorated—this one cannot make even an inapt quotation from Shakespeare correctly. However, it is apparent that my notes have been of sufficient interest to be read and criticized, and I therefore presume I shall be receiving some acknowledgment for my efforts if only in order to enable me to cover up my "lion's head," or to assist in clothing my "goat's body."

Yours, &c. M.F.

How Far Should the Library Aid the Peace Movement and Similar Propaganda?

By George F. Bowerman, Librarian, The Public Library of the District of Columbia. An address at the American Library Association National Conference in Berkeley, California, 1915. *Papers and Proceedings of the Thirty-Seventh Annual Meeting of the American Library Association*, pp. 129-134.

I suppose it may be taken for granted that the members of no other profession could have been more surprised and shocked at the outbreak of the great European war than were American librarians. Living in an atmosphere of peace and good will and enlisted in the work of spreading enlightenment, joined by many strong ties with our professional colleagues in other lands, we had assessed the spirit of the world to be in harmony with the spirit of our profession and with the American spirit, strong for universal peace, and had thought that the world had become sufficiently civilized so that war, or at least a great continental war, involving the most advanced European peoples, was no longer possible. Even now it hardly seems comprehensible that many of the European libraries are either closed or are running shorthanded because librarians are serving with armies in the field where they are fighting their professional colleagues of other nations, being killed or maimed or contracting diseases that will cut short their careers. Almost incredible also is it that the great library of the University of Louvain should have been destroyed in war in this the twentieth century. It is all so bewildering as almost to defy belief.

Although our country has happily kept out of the war through the wise leadership of the President and the fundamental devotion to peace of our people, yet the country in general has suffered heavily and many American libraries in particular have had appropriations much curtailed as a result of the business depression brought on by the war. With our sympathies aroused and our professional interest enlisted, ought we to allow an annual meeting of our national association falling while the war is still in progress to pass without asking whether there is anything that we librarians and the libraries we represent can do to further the cause of international peace, whether we can assist in bringing about the peace that shall last, that will make all wars impossible, unthinkable? I am sure that we librarians "look forward," in the words of William James, "to a future when acts of war shall be formally outlawed among civilized peoples." How far is the library justified in going and what specific methods are we as librarians justified in taking to help in causing this view to be generally accepted?

In attempting to answer these questions it is desirable first to lay down certain principles that should guide the library in its attitude toward propaganda in general and then to inquire whether there are special considerations that may properly affect our attitude toward the peace movement.

The librarian is constantly confronted with demands for the purchase of books and magazines, the offer of free copies of books, magazines and pamphlets issued on one side or the other of controverted questions, cults and isms. The main guiding principle should be that of interested neutrality. The library seeks complete enlightenment on the part of the constituency and to that end affords the fullest possible representation to both sides, to all sides of every controverted question. The library should encourage a broad and liberal spirit of free inquiry; its purpose is not to restrain but foster comprehensive curiosity. The offers of literature or the requests for its purchase may have propaganda in mind; the proponents very probably intend to use the machinery of the library, expensive to the public but cheap for their use for the dissemination of their own views. The library in lending itself to such use is not playing into the hands of the propagandist, but is rather availing itself of offers and requests to afford the inquiring and curious public, interested in subjects of current discussion, with material for the study of the questions at issue. Care should of course be taken when material representing one side only is offered, to procure the best material on the other side, together with the writings of capable neutral critics, if such exist. Even though the subjects of discussion may sometimes seem relatively unimportant or even at times rather foolish to the matter-of-fact librarian, the library cannot best meet the needs of the public unless it furnishes such material. The library wishes to be fair and escape the criticism of being narrow-minded or biased. Some subjects which provoke only a smile or faint interest among sophisticated persons like librarians, may be of surpassing interest to certain readers of character and standing in the community. This position of hospitality is, I believe, the proper attitude of the librarian toward the many controverted questions with which he is constantly dealing such as vivisection, vaccination, Roman Catholicism, Christian Science, socialism, the single tax, the recall, capital punishment, immigration restriction, prohibition and women's suffrage. The individual librarian or member of a book committee may have strong opinions on some or all of these subjects; he may be superior in his personal attitude toward some of them and hostile toward others; officially, however, he must be sympathetic toward various points of view, for they are vital questions to large sections of the community and to ignore them is to render a public library unresponsive to the needs of its public.

The word that libraries may appropriately do with respect to a sharply controverted question may be well illustrated by what has been done by them in the case of the present war, involving as it has disputes over causes, atrocity charges, infractions of international law, etc., on the one hand, and an American public divided in its sympathies on the other. Ever since its outbreak the public has been closely following the war not only by means of the newspapers, but numerous readers have flocked to libraries to study with eagerness books, reviews and controversial pamphlets. The war has created an entire new and voluminous literature that libraries have properly collected and made available, in many cases by means of maintaining a series of special shelves devoted to the material about the war. Several libraries have printed for distribution reading lists, compiled in their own libraries or have distributed the list issued by the Publishers' Weekly. In gathering this material, libraries have collected widely and impartially, in order to afford the amplest opportunity for the forming of independent judgments. The wise librarian has utilized this occasion to bring to the attention of his readers not only material about the immediate and controverted questions at issue, but also books about the historical aspects of the controversy, about the conditions in times of peace in the nations involved and also especially the literature of peace and international arbitration.

How far should the library definitely promote the peace movement itself, if at all? Should its attitude be strictly that which it occupies toward any other controverted question? If so, the peace advocate may hope much from what the library can do for it is believed that the literature favorable to peace and international arbitration is far stronger than that opposed to peace. Simply for the library to possess full resources on both sides of the question and to exploit it by displays, annotated lists and the other usual methods will of itself powerfully aid the peace movement. This war has forcibly dragged the question out of the academic shades where it has for the most part previously rested and made it the most vital question before the bar of the world's opinion. It can no more be neglected than can the question of the cost of living. Every library at all responsive to public questions must provide full resources and make them available to the public. That of itself inevitably promotes the peace movement. But I believe that the library is justified in occupying a more advanced position on this particular controverted question. It is likely that few librarians or library trustees, whatever their individual opinions may be, would *officially* advocate omission to provide for suitable national defense, or for proper development of army and navy and other elements of preparedness, at least until such time as armies and navies, if retained at all, are made into international military and police forces. These are immediate questions of public policy with which he has nothing *officially* to do. I believe, however, that it is entirely in consonance with the purpose of the library, as an integral part of the public educational system, as an institution devoted to the spread of democracy and the promotion of enlightenment, as an institution with books in many languages, containing information about all the peoples of the world, and as an institution with many international friendships with librarians and other scholars throughout the world, to promote in every suitable way the strongest ties of international friendship.

Librarians are also interested in peace and should, I believe, promote it as a matter of self-preservation. Many observers have predicted that the present war will cease only with the complete economic exhaustion of one or more of the combatant nations. In any event the rehabilitation of all of the countries involved will be a long and painful process. Money spent on armies and navies and for interest on piled up debts cannot be spent for social objects or for education; and since the library is perhaps the youngest and least considered of all educational agents, it will doubtless suffer most from the enforced economies resulting from war preparations. We are told that more than 70 per cent of income of our own national government is spent on wars past and future. Can anyone doubt that library appropriations would be larger if military and naval expenditures were smaller?

Most librarians would agree not only that war and preparations for war are entirely at variance with the purposes for which the library exists, but that war versus peace is no longer a controverted question of public policy at all. It is rather a question of fundamental ethics: Is the world willing to go on sanctioning a system that puts all of the resources of modern technical science into commission for wholesale murder and theft? The failure to adopt at the close of the present war some plan that will eliminate war from the earth except as a measure of punishment by an international police force would be to postpone the time when the library may hope to do its full work.

We the librarians of today want to see the scope of the library enlarged instead of having it kept to its present narrow limits. We want to see libraries have larger and better paid staffs in order adequately to meet present demands. We need money to foster larger demands on the part of the public. Both as citizens and as librarians we want to see promoted all of the other movements that make for social well-being and enlightenment, knowing that thereby the opportunities and demands for our work will most surely be enlarged. The reduction of the burden of armaments offers, I believe, the best hope for the expansion of the library and of library work. Although I have been arguing that the library by reason of its essential character as well as because of self-interest ought definitely to promote the peace movement yet I do not think that the specific measures I shall advocate will prove unacceptable even to those librarians and library trustees who conceive the peace movement as strictly falling within the field of controverted questions. In proposing that the library stress the peace movement there is no suggestion of neglect to provide the fullest possible resources for the study of literature favoring war and controverting pacifist arguments.

In an enumeration of the ways in which the library can appropriately aid the peace movement I should put foremost the efficient and liberal development of the library itself and the compelling extension of its resources to the entire reading population. If only the library is generously stocked with travel literature, books in foreign languages and literatures, technology, fine arts, economics, sociology and history; if it has branches and other agencies and expert administration so that it is really used by approximately the entire population, it becomes a great leavening influence, improving the economic efficiency of the population, increasing their general enlightenment, counteracting the jingoism of the yellow journal, making good Americans of recent immigrants and increasing the sympathetic interest of persons of American birth in foreign lands and peoples. The great agent for the amalgamation of those of foreign birth is the public school and the library is or should be its strong right arm. In other words, if the library is able by proper support to cease being a static institution simply responding to calls made upon it and can become more a more dynamic institution that shall reach out and influence the entire population and join in a big way in the forward social movements, it can powerfully influence public opinion. Who can doubt that this influence would be for general progress, including international peace?

It must be confessed that some of the influence of the library has been in the direction of fostering warlike sentiments. Many of the books, most popular in libraries, fiction, juvenile books and histories, glorify war and inflame international hatreds. I make no suggestion of a censorship that would eliminate such books. It is desireable, however, that libraries should furnish an ample stock of the books that depict the horrors of war an that they should encourage the writing of books of history that record the work of heroes of peace and that recognize the fact that real history is a record of the development of pacific civilization and international harmony. The Carnegie Endowment for International Peace might well enlist some geniuses in the work of writing masterpieces of fiction for adult and juvenile readers—books that will do for the cause of peace what "Uncle Tom's Cabin" did for the slavery question. It is a perfectly fair proposition, I believe, for the library as an educational institution to stress such a part of its collection. Of course it goes without saying that the library should have the best possible stock of books on international law and on the economic and social phases of war and peace.

The literature of peace, internationalism and war may well be exploited by the methods already mentioned and by the publication of lists such as those issued by the Brooklyn Public Library in 1908 (57 pages), by the public libraries of Boston, Denver, Salem and Buffalo, by the Library of Congress and the Wisconsin Free Library Commission. The American Association for International Conciliation has issued two lists on "Internationalism," compiled by Mr. Frederick C. Hicks, and has distributed them to libraries generally. Mr. Hicks also prepared and the American Association issued, two or three years ago, about a dozen "best book catalog cards," each card listing, with annotation, several titles of books and periodicals on various phases of the peace question. These cards have been inserted in the card catalogs of a large number of American libraries. This work should be continued. The American Association has issued for free distribution a reference list and a syllabus for the study of international polity, by Dr. John Mez. It is also believed that the American Peace Society or one of the other American peace agencies, would, if the American Library Association or any considerable number of American libraries should make the suggestion, issue a brief and a comprehensive annotated list of books on peace in very large editions for distribution by libraries to their readers. The call for literature on the peace question in libraries is already large. The distribution of such lists would stimulate such calls.

Librarians might well let it be known to the Carnegie Endowment and the local peace societies that they would welcome lectures and debates on the peace questions in their lecture halls in their main libraries and branches. In common with most lectures given in library auditoriums, they need not be directly under library auspices, but might be under the patronage of the peace societies. The public library is now generally becoming a feature in the social and civic center movement by which public school buildings are coming to be used for public lectures, meetings and debates. Here are opportunities for the popularization of knowledge of the peace movement and for library co-operation in furnishing the literature for the study of the question. the story-telling now done in library children's rooms or in schools by children's librarians, or with library co-operation, offers another opportunity for implanting peace ideas in the minds of coming citizens. If heroes of war form the subject of the stories, care should be taken not to leave the idea that war of today is the romantic thing it may possibly have been once—or more probably never was, except in the minds of the romancers. Perhaps the horrors of war should not be detailed to younger children, but the deeds of heroes of peace might well be utilized in story-telling. More material in the interest of peace suitable for story-telling should be published. It ought also to be listed in bibliographies for children's librarians and teachers, and for the children themselves. Something has been done in this direction in the publication by the New York Public Library of its pamphlet list entitled "Heroism."

The scope of the American School Peace League might well be enlarged to include the library. One of its objects is to secure the writing of histories for children which will be truthful but will not unduly emphasize international and racial antipathies. The library surely needs such help, should use it and might well join in the movement.

So far as I am aware, this is the first time that the relation of the library to the peace question has ever been specifically discussed at the meeting of the American Library Association. The New York Library Club devoted a meeting in November, 1912, to the subject. The speakers were President Nicholas Murray Butler, Professor Samuel T. Dutton and others, who discussed the movement generally, the literature of peace, the library and peace, international bureaus of information and the international exchange and loan of books. I believe that the topic ought frequently to appear on the programs of the national and local library associations.

If the practical suggestions here offered seem few, it should be stated that the purpose of my address is more to enlist librarians and the library in the cause of peace than to point out specific measures, to appeal to the spirit rather than definitely to outline the practical. If I have offered sufficiently convincing arguments that the library might properly assist in this movement, appropriate measures will suggest themselves to alert librarians.

Even if the advocates of internationalism should at the close of this war see their dreams realized by the establishment of a supreme international tribunal and the stable development of a body of international law enacted by regularly recurring sessions of the Hague Peace Conference, by the organization of a League of Peace, a Federation of the World or a World

State, the task of making any such plan work, of holding any such organization together when some crisis arises, or of securing the acceptance of the decrees of any such international tribunal would be a difficult one. In order to be successful, behind the world organization and the international court there must be the sympathetic world spirit. This can only be secured by education, in which the library should have an increasingly large part.

The Libary's Primary Duty

President's Address, ALA Annual Conference, Berkeley, CA, June 3-9, 1915
By Hiller C. Wellman, Librarian, City Library, Springfield, Massachussetts.
Papers and Proceedings of the Thirty-Seventh Annual Meeting of the American Library Association, pp. 89-93.

Fellow Members: This gathering of the American Library Association is but the thirty-seventh annual conference. The fact is significant, because it reminds us how brief is the history of the public library. Our other teachers are even more venerable. Books we have had since the world was young; the church, through the ages; schools and universities and great reference libraries for scholars, hundreds of years; the newspaper, some three centuries; but the public library—free to all the people—only a few decades. That is an amazingly brief period to witness the rise and development of a great educational agency—so widespread and so far-reaching.

Yet, rapid as it has been, the spread of the public library is in a sense not surprising. It is a truism to say that the safety of a republic rests on the enlightenment of its people; and wise men were quick to see in the library a sound instrument of popular instruction. More slowly, they are recognizing that is also contributes, in a measure equaled by few other institutions save the public school, toward realization of the great ideal—still dear to America—equality of opportunity. It is not strange, therefore, that American communities everywhere are coming to deem it proper that all men have access to books; and for the spread of public libraries, we as librarians need feel no great concern. It will go on whether we urge or no; for the public library has become an essential of democracy. But the shaping of the libraries is a different matter; it lies often in the hands of the men and women who administer them. And if it is peculiarly the librarian's responsibility, so, too, it is a responsibility demanding foresight and judgment. For the library—to use a mathematical term—is not a constant but a variable. It has assumed new functions and today is still changing to a degree hardly realized save when we regard it in perspective.

That the public library should have started with traditions inherited from scholars' or research libraries is but natural. For a whole generation librarians laid more stress on garnering books and on perfecting the admirable machinery of their organization, than on finding readers for them; and it did not seem anomalous in the late 'sixties—though it does now to us—to find the trustees of a great public library virtually congratulating themselves that the poorest books were the most read, for they reported "It is in many respects fortunate that the wear and tear of the Library falls mainly upon the class of works of the smallest relative importance," while the librarian lamented that "It had become very common for visitors to demand the use in the Hall of costly books of engravings, for mere purposes of curiosity." As late as 1868, when the foremost public library in the country—that of Boston—stood second in size only to the Library of Congress, the classes in the community chiefly served may be guessed from the fact that its reference collections and reading rooms were closed, not only Sundays and holidays, but every evening as well; while a population numbering a quarter of a million souls, less than twelve thousand held cards. The proportion would be the same if at present all the public libraries in the United States should reach a clientage no larger than the number of people living in New York City.

But about that date, under the leadership of a scholar, Justin Winsor, began the great work of popularization, a process which was without doubt hastened by the influence of the American Library Association, with its opportunities for conference and comparison. In former times there had even been question as to the status of women in libraries, or at least protest against admitting them to "the corrupter portions of the polite literature"; but in an early report the trustees of the Boston library gave assurance that they regarded it as "one of the most pleasing and hopeful features...that its advantages are equally open to both sexes." Nowadays libraries besides making extensive provision for the general reader are striving more and more to meet the special needs of every class in the community. Municipal reference collections are being established for our legislators and officials, technical books are supplied in profusion for the artisans in every branch of industry, commercial books for the business men, books for the blind, books for the aliens, even for the sick, the insane, and the criminal, and above all, for the children who have in recent years come to absorb such a large share of attention. Furthermore, this great public has been admitted freely to the books on the library shelves; while outside, through branch libraries and stations, by collections in schools and other institutions, by traveling libraries and deposits in factory and office building, in shop and grange and club—in short, by placing books wherever they will be accessible—the library alike in the small town and the great city is being carried to the people.

More significant still, is the changed conception of library work. To supply demand is now regarded as by no means enough; the library must create demand. It must be aggressive, not passive. By booklists and bulletins, by addresses to societies and personal visits to the working men in shop or club, by exhibitions, by circulars, by a constant fire of articles and notes in newspapers and magazines, in short by all the arts and wiles of modern publicity, librarians are expected to make known their resources, to spread a realization of the opportunities both cultural and practical afforded by the library; and the ideal is not fulfilled until in every man, woman and child capable of comprehending, there has been awakened an appreciation of the benefits and the delights to be derived from books.

Thus has evolved the modern public library. No similar institution in a community touches the lives of so many of its people. Consider how rapid has been this development. Much of it has taken place within a generation, much within the years still be regarded as tentative. With so large a sum of achievement, librarians do not fear frank criticism of details; and a prime purpose of these annual gatherings is to scrutinize the wisdom of our various activities. For example, in these days when the utilitarian is coming to be a fetish even in education, is there danger of the cultural ideal of the library becoming overshadowed? Is there a temptation to overemphasize the bread-and-butter side of the library—the excellent practical work of helping men and women in all callings to advance materially, of furnishing aid to men in business and commerce—all of which appeals so readily to the taxpayer? Are our methods of publicity in keeping with the dignity of an educational institution? With limited funds, is the share of the library's money and energy allotted to the extensive work with children justified by the returns? It is well to consider questions like these, to endeavor to make sure that in all directions results are commensurate with the cost, and to weigh the relative emphasis to be given different phases of the work.

Whether there be or be not room for some advancement of relative effort as regards the activities already described, it will be agreed without question that they are in the main wise and successful, that they are approved by the taxpayer, and that they constitute but a logical development for accomplishing the ends for which the public library is maintained. But in recent years there has become evident a somewhat different nature. They are often grouped under the term library extension, which might be taken to imply that they extend beyond the field of library work in its strictest sense. It is becoming increasingly common for lectures— not simply on library or literary topics, but popular courses on all manner of subjects—to be provided by libraries and occasionally delivered by librarians themselves. Here and there has been further adventuring in the field of direct instruction, with classes for children in science, for foreigners learning English, and even tentative correspondence courses. Exhibitions of all kinds are held by libraries, including not simply books, bindings, and prints, but paintings, rugs, porcelains and other objects of art, frequently natural history specimens, flower shows, occasionally industrial displays or commercial exhibits; and some libraries have installed permanent museums. Story-telling for children on an elaborate scale has become not unusual, with the avowed purpose of interesting them in good literature, but sometimes conducted at playgrounds and other places where there is no distribution of books; and in general the work with children has been extended in manifold directions. We read here and there of games, dances, parties—particularly for the holidays, plays, aeroplane contests, athletic meets, and other entertainments, and children's clubs of many kinds. In one city the branch libraries were centers for collection in the "fly-swatting" contests. Such work is sometimes carried on by outside agencies in rooms furnished by the library; more often it is conducted by the library itself. One large library offered prizes to boys and girls making articles during the summer for exhibition last fall; and exhibitions of model aeroplanes, bird houses and other results of manual training seem not infrequent. The adults, too, are not neglected. We are lending library halls freely for literary, educational, civic and charitable purposes, and to a growing extent for social gatherings and entertainments as well. Here a library has established a social center for young women where "all the various useful arts and handicrafts [can] be taught, free of charge," and there another has opened public debates each week on topics of timely interest, with speakers chosen by the trustees. Photographs and prints of all kinds, music rolls, scores, lantern slides, phonographic records, which are often supplied for circulation, perhaps fall within the legal definition of book or writing, and the lending of historical and scientific specimens, and of stereoscopes, radiopticons, and lanterns, is a function that is closely allied.

In one or two cities branch librarians are employed in friendly visiting among the families of the neighborhood or for social service work with factory girls. One library is reported to maintain close relations with the probation officer and juvenile court; another publishes an excellent magazine giving large space to matters of civic and commercial interest; elsewhere libraries are said to be aiding in social surveys. Not only is the reading of foreigners fostered, but their welfare in other ways is looked out for. Semi-social gatherings are held, talks on citizenship sometimes planned, and in at least a few places, exhibitions of their handiwork have been arranged. Concert-giving by libraries with victrolas is becoming not unusual; and now we are introducing moving pictures.

Most of the practices enumerated are as yet by no means common enough to be characteristic of the American public library; but whether general or sporadic, they are of sufficiently frequent occurrence to show a strong trend. It has been said by one friendly critic that librarians are peculiarly alert to social needs, and so eager to render possible service, that once convinced of a real want in the community, they are prone to undertake to meet it without always considering whether the work falls properly within the sphere of the library or could be better conducted by some other agency. No doubt it is true that an institution like the public library, which has developed so rapidly, with few hampering traditions, is especially pliable, and possibly extends its scope more readily than it might otherwise. But the truth is, as a matter of fact, somewhat larger, for the tendency seems but in keeping with the spirit of the times observable elsewhere in the church, in playgrounds and public centers of recreation and education of diverse sorts, and, some critics hint, even in school curricula. Yet, if these signs really mark the beginning of library evolution toward institutions of wider social activity, the path should be chosen consciously and with deliberation, for it is obvious that the change is likely to affect the library itself profoundly—either for good or ill.

Some of the papers and discussions at the present conference will bear directly or indirectly on various phases of the questions I have raised; and it is not my purpose to anticipate by offering here my own conclusions. But I should like to plead that however occupied with executive cares, and whether engaged in supplying with books the *practical* needs of the community, or turning to work of wider social application, the librarian should never forget or slight what seems to me to be a primary duty of the public library—a service so fundamental that, as I shall try to show, it may be said without exaggeration to touch the springs of our civilization itself.

For this twentieth century civilization of ours, which the world so easily takes for granted, is nevertheless regarded with misgiving by many who examine its evolution and condition. Within the past two or three years alone, not a few thoughtful writers have questioned its solidity and permanence. The Italian historian, Ferrero; the brilliant English churchman, J. N. Figgis; A. J. Hubbard in his "Fate of Empires," S. O. G. Douglas, Guy Theodore Wrench, Mrs. John Martin—all are impressed with the transitoriness of the phenomenon known as civilization. Macaulay's famous New Zealander taking his stand on a broken arch of London bridge to sketh the ruins of St. Paul's, in his "vast solitude" may count at least on the ghostly fellowship of a goodly number of our contemporary writers who have been solicitous as to the laws of modern civilization and its decay.

Perhaps the most interesting of these treatises is the immensely suggestive little volume in which the archaeologist, W. M. Flinders Petrie, has traced the rise, the flourishing, and the decay of eight successive civilizations in Egypt during the period of ten thousand years, and five distinct eras of civilization in Europe from the early Cretan down through the classical and that of our own day. It is only in recent years that, owing to the discovery and study of archaeological remains, it has become possible to take the long view. Hitherto, students have been confined largely to comparisons between our own civilization and the classical which immediately preceded it. Professor Petrie uses as criteria the development of the different arts, especially the period when each passes from a stage of archaism to a condition of full artistic freedom; and he finds that in all the civilizations he has presented, so far as discernible, the arts have reached their highest development in the same sequence. First comes sculpture, followed by painting, and then literature; these in turn are succeeded after a somewhat longer interval by the development of mechanics, of science, and the results of applied science, or wealth. There appears to be a striking conformity, not only in the sequence, but roughly, in the relative time, suggesting that the same laws are operative throughout the entire period. The intervals between the successive waves of civilization as shown by the point when sculpture, the first of the arts, reaches the stage when it is fully freed from archaism averages between thirteen and fourteen hundred years, with an apparent tendency towards lengthening in the case of the later civilizations. Our modern European civilization, according to Professor Petrie, reached the turning point of freedom in sculpture about 1240 A. D.; in painting, about 1400; in literature during the Elizabethan age, or about 1600; in mechanics possibly in 1890; while the full development in science and in the production of wealth is still to come.

Of course, I have not cited the interesting and ingenious conclusions of Professor Petrie, which are bristling with debatable points, nor referred to the works of the other authors, who differ much among themselves, as proving any definite theory of civilization. I merely wish to impress on you the well-recognized fact that civilization is an intermittent phenomenon. Nor can I personally see that our own civilization, though covering so much wider area than any which have preceded it, differs essentially from them, except in two respects. One of them is the possession of a religion so ennobling that if its principles were valid in the hearts of men, it would seem in itself to afford a strong preservative, at least against the corruption and ill living that accompany a decaying civilization. But one of the phenomena that all students point out is the weakening in our times of the hold of religion on the minds and actions of men. The other essential difference, as I see it, between our civilization and previous ones lies in the remarkable development of the arts of communication. The facilities for travel by steamship and railroad, and for the transmission of information by mail and telegraph, have so united the world and brought into contact differing civilizations as to produce a condition without parallel in earlier ages.

But incomparably greater in its effect is the ease of communication from mind to mind resulting from the invention of printing. One would be rash, indeed, to assume that this new force in the world, powerful though it be, and aptly termed the art preservative of arts, has yet within itself sufficient virtue to overbalance the laws which, working through human nature for ages past, have caused one great civilization after another to rise, reach its zenith, and decay. Yet, when we consider that not simply in preserving knowledge, but in diffusing it among the whole people, it has produced a condition of general enlightenment that has never before been known; and when we remember also the immense acceleration given to the renascence of the very civilization we now enjoy through the recovery by scholars of the Greek manuscripts and classical texts, it may not be immoderate to hope that this great art of printing will have an incalculable influence in deepening, strengthening, carrying higher, and prolonging this present wave of our civilization; and should this likewise be destined to recede, in alleviating man's intervening low estate and hastening the world's next great advance. And in carrying to the whole people the solider and more vital product of the printing press, no such agency has ever before existed as the modern free public library.

This, then, I conceive to be the great fundamental obligation of the public library—to make accessible to all men the best thought of mankind, whether it be found in the classic works of the older civilizations that preceded our own, or in the master intellects of a later day, or in the innumerable derivative writings of lesser minds. And this function is one that I trust may never be forgotten, however far it may seem well to extend the province of the library in other directions. While striving in every wise way to further the material or ephemeral interests of our communities, above all, we as librarians should prize and cherish the things of the mind and of the spirit. Only those gifted by God can hope for the supreme joy of feeding the pure, white flame that lights man's pathway through the ages. Few they be and blessed. It is privilege enough for us to strive to hold aloft the light, and carry ourselves staunchly and worthily as torchbearers.

Some Tendencies of American Thought

By Dr. Arthur E. Bostwick, Librarian, St. Louis Public Library. Read before the New York Library Association at Squirrel Inn, Haines Falls, Sept. 28, 1915. *Library Journal*, vol. 40, no. 10 (October 1915) pp. 771-777.

The modern American mind, like modern America, itself, is a melting pot. We are taking men and women of all races and fusing them into Americans. In the same way we are taking points of view, ideas, standards, and modes of action from whatever source we find them, combining them and fusing them into what will one day become American thoughts and standards. We are thus combining the most varied and opposing things—things that it would seem impossible to put together. Take our modern American tendency in government, for instance. Could there be two things more radically different that despotism and democracy?—the rule of one and the rule of the many? And yet I believe that we are taking steps toward a very successful combination of the two. Such a combination is essentially ancient. No despotism can hold its own without the consent of the governed. That consent may be unwilling and sooner or later it is then withheld, with the result that a revolution takes place and the despot loses his throne—the oldest form of the recall. Every despotism is thus tempered by revolution, and Anglo-Saxon communities have been ready to exercise such a privilege on the slightest sign that a despotic tendency was creeping into their government.

It is not remarkable, then, that our own Federal government, which is essentially a copy of the British government of its day, should have incorporated this feature of the recall, which in England had just passed from its revolutionary to its legal stage. It was beginning to be recognized then that a vote of the people's representatives could recall a monarch, and the English monarchy is now essentially elective. But to make assurance doubly sure, the British government, in its later evolution, has been practically separated from the monarch's person, and any government may be simply overthrown or "recalled" by a vote of lack of confidence in the House of Commons, followed, if need be, by a defeat in a general election. We have not yet adopted this feature. Our President is still the head of our government, and he and all other elected Federal officers serve their terms out, no matter whether the people have confidence in them or not. But the makers of our Constitution improved on the British government as they found it. They made the term of the executive four years instead of life and systematized the "recall" by providing for impeachment proceedings—a plan already recognized in Britain in the case of certain administrative and judicial officers.

As it stands at present we have a temporary elective monarch with more power, even nominally, than most European constitutional monarchs and more actually than many so-called absolute monarchs such as the Czar or the Sultan. In case he should abuse that power that we have given him, he may be removed from office after due trial, by our elected representatives.

In following out these ideas in later years, we are gradually evolving a form of government that is both more despotic and more democratic. We are combining the legislative and executive power in the hands of a few persons, hampering them very little in their exercise of it, and making it possible to recall them by direct vote of the body of citizens that elected them. I think we may describe the tendency of the public thought in governmental matters as a tendency toward a despotism under legalized democratic control. It may be claimed, I think, that the best features of despotism and democracy may thus be utilized, with a minimum of the evils of each.

It was believed by the ancients, and we frequently see it stated today, that the ideal government would be government by a perfectly good despot. This takes the citizens into account only as persons who are governed, and not as persons who govern or help to govern. It is pleasant, perhaps, to have plenty of servants to wait upon one, but surely health, physical, mental, and moral, waits on him who does most things for himself. I once heard Lincoln Steffens say: "What we want is not 'Good Government;' it is Self-Government." But is it not possible to get the advantage of government by a few, with its possibilities of continuous policy and its freedom from "crowd-psychology," with its skillful utilization of expert knowledge, while admitting the public to full knowledge of that is going on, and full ultimate control of it? We evidently think so, and our present tendencies are evidence that we are attempting something of the kind. Our belief seems to be that if we elect our despot and are able to recall him we shall have to keep tab on him pretty closely, and that the knowledge of statecraft that will thus be necessary to us will be no less than if we personally took part in legislation and administration—probably far more than if we simply went through the form of delegating our responsibilities and then took no further thought, as most of us have been accustomed to do.

Whether this is the right view or not—whether it is workable—the future will show; I am here discussing the tendencies, not their ultimate outcome. But it would be too much to expect that this or any other eclectic policy should be pleasing to all.

"The real problem of collectivism," says Walter Lippmann, "is the difficulty of combining popular control with administrative power.... The conflict between democracy and centralized authority...is the line upon which the problems of collectivism will be fought out." In selecting elements from both despotism and democracy we are displeasing the adherents of both. There is too much despotism in the plan for one side and too much democracy for the other. We constantly hear the complaint that concentrated responsibility with popular control is too despotic, and at the same time the criticism that it is too democratic. To put your city in the hands of a small commission, perhaps of a city manager, seems to some to be a return to monarchy; and so perhaps it is. To give Tom, Dick and Harry the power to unseat these monarchs at will is said to be dangerously socialistic; and possibly it is. Only it is possible that by combining this two poisons—this acid and this alkali—in the same pill, we are neutralizing their harmful qualities. At any rate this would seem to be the idea on which we are now proceeding.

We may now examine the effects of this tendency toward eclecticism in quite a different filed—that of morals. Among the settlers of our country were both Puritans and Cavaliers—representatives in England of two moral standards that have contended there for centuries and still exist there side by side. We in America are attempting to mix them with some measure of success. This was detected by the German lady of whom Mr. Bryce tells in his "American Commonwealth," who said that American women were "furchtbar frei und furchbar fromm" —frightfully free and frightfully pious! In other words they are trying to mix the Cavalier and Puritan standards. Of course those who do not understand what is going on think that we are either too free or too pious. We are neither; we are trying to give and accept freedom in cases where freedom works for moral efficiency and restraint where restraint is indicated. We have not arrived at a final standard. We may not do so. This effort at mixture, like all our others, may fail; but there appears to be no doubt that we are making it. To take an obvious instance, I believe that we are trying with some success, to combine ease of divorce with a greater real regard for the sanctity of marriage. We have found that if marriage is made absolutely indissoluble, there will be greater excuse for disregarding the marriage vow than if there are legal ways of dissolving it. Americans are shocked at Europeans when they allude in ordinary conversation to infractions of the moral code that they treat as trivial. They on the other hand are shocked when we talk of divorce for what they consider insufficient causes. In the former case we seem to them "frightfully pious"; in the latter, "frightfully free." They are right; we are both; it is only another instance of our tendency towards eclecticism, this time in moral standards. In some directions we find that this tendency to eclecticism is working toward a combination not of two opposite things, but of a hundred different ones. Take our art for instance, especially as manifested in our architecture. A purely native town in Italy, Arabia, or Africa, or Mexico, has its own atmosphere; no one could mistake one for the other any more than he could mistake a beaver dam for an ant hill or a bird's nest for a woodchuck hole.

But in an American city, especially where we have enough money to let our architects do their utmost, we find streets where France, England, Italy, Spain, Holland, Arabia and India all stand elbow to elbow, and the European visitor knows not whether to laugh or to make a hasty visit to his nerve-specialist. It seems all right to us, and it is all right from the standpoint of a nation that is yet in the throes of eclecticism. And our other art—painting, sculpture, music—it is all similarly mixed. Good of its kind, often; but we have not yet settled down to the kind that we like best—the kind in which we are best fitted to do something that will live through the ages.

We used to think for instance that in music the ordinary diatonic major scale, with its variant minor, was a fact of nature. We knew vaguely that the ancient Greeks had other scales, and we knew also that the Chinese and the Arabs had scales so different that their music was generally displeasing to us. But we explained this by saying that our scale was natural and right and that the others were antiquated, barbaric and wrong. Now we are opening our arms to the exotic scales and devising a few of our own. We have the tonal and the semi-tonal scales and we are trying to make use of the Chinese, Arabic and Hindu modes. We are producing results that sound very odd to ears that are attuned to the old-fashioned music, but our eclecticism here as elsewhere is cracking the shell of prejudice and will doubtless lead to some good end, though perhaps we can not see it yet.

How about education? In the first place there are, as I read the history of education, two main methods of training youth—the individual method and the class method. No two boys or girls are alike; no two have like reactions to the same stimulus. Each ought to have a separate teacher, for the methods to be employed must be adapted especially to the material on which we have to work. This means a separate tutor for every child.

On the other hand, the training that we give must be social—must prepare for life with and among one's fellow beings, otherwise it is worthless. This means training in class, with and among other students, where each mind responds not to the teacher's alone but to those of its fellow-pupils.

Here are tow irreconcilable requirements. In our modern systems of education we are trying to respond to them as best we may, teaching in class and at the same time giving each pupil as much personal attention as we can. The tutorial system, now employed in Princeton University, is an interesting example of our efforts as applied to the higher education.

At the same time, eclecticism in our choice of subjects is very manifest, and at times our success here seems as doubtful as our mixture of architectural styles. In the old college days, not so very long ago, Latin, Greek, and mathematics made up the curriculum. Now our boys choose from a thousand subjects grouped in a hundred courses. In our common schools we have introduced so many new subjects as to crowd the curriculum. Signs of a reaction are evident. I am alluding to the matter here only as another example of our modern passion for wide selection and for the combination of things that apparently defy amalgamation. What of religion? Prof. George E. Woodberry, in his interesting book on North Africa, says in substance that there are only two kinds of religion, the simple and the complex. Mohammedanism he considers a simple religion, like New England Puritans, with which he thinks it has points in common. Both are very different from Buddhism, for instance. Accepting for the moment his classification I believe that the facts show an effort to combine the two types in the United States. Many of the Christian denominations that Woodberry would class as "simple"—those that began with a total absence of ritual, are becoming ritualized. Creeds once simple are becoming complicated with interpretation and comment. On the other hand we may see in the Roman Catholic Church and among the so-called "High Church" Episcopalians a disposition to adopt some of the methods that have hitherto distinguished other religious bodies. Consider, for example, some of the religious meetings held by the Paulist Fathers in New York, characterized by popular addresses and the singing of simply hymns. As another example of the eclectic spirit of churches in America we may point to the various efforts at combination or unity, with such results as the Federation of the Churches of Christ in America—an ambitious name, not yet justified by the facts—the proposed amalgamation of several of the most powerful Protestant bodies in Canada, and the accomplished fact of the University of Toronto—an institution whose constituent colleges are controlled by different religious denominations, including the Roman Catholic Church. I may also mention the present organization of the New York Public Library, many of whose branch libraries were contributions from religious denominations, including the Jews, the Catholics and the

Episcopalians. All these now work together harmoniously. I know of nothing of this kind on any other continent, and I think we shall be justified in crediting it to the present American tendency to eclecticism.

Turn for a moment to philosophy. What is the philosophical system most widely known at present as American? Doubtless the pragmatism of William James. No one ever agreed with anyone else in a statement regarding philosophy, and I do not expect you to agree with me in this; but pragmatism seems to me essentially an eclectic system. It is based on the character of results. Is something true or false? I will tell you when I find out whether it works practically or not. Is something right or wrong? I rely on the same test. Now it seems to me that this is the scheme of the peasant in later Rome, who was perfectly willing to appeal to Roman Juno or Egyptian Isis or Phoenician Moloch so long as he got what he wanted. If a little bit of Schopenhauer works, and some of Fichte; a piece of Christianity and a part of Vedantism, it is all grist to the mill of pragmatism. Any of it that works must of necessity be right and true. I am not criticizing this, or trying to convert it; I am merely asserting that it leads to eclecticism; and this, I believe, explains its vogue in the United States.

It would be impossible to give, in the compass of a brief address, a list of all the domains in which this eclecticism—this tendency to select, combine and blend—has cropped out among us Americans of to-day. I have reserved for the last that in which we are particularly interested—the Public Library, in which we may see it exemplified in an eminent degree. The public library in America has blossomed out into a different thing, a wider thing, a combination of more different kinds of things, than in any other part of the world. Foreign librarians and foreign library users look at us askance. They wonder at the things we are trying to combine under the activities of one public institution; they shudder at our extravagance. They wonder that our tax-payers do not rebel when they are compelled to foot the bills for what we do. But the taxpayers do not seem to mind. They frequently complain, but not about what we are doing. What bothers them is that we do not try to do more. When we began timidly to add branch libraries to our systems they asked us why we didn't not build and equip them faster; when we placed a few books on open shelves they demanded that we treat our whole stock in the same way; when we set aside a corner for the children they forced us to fit up a whole room and to place such a room in every building, large or small. We have responded to every such demand. Each response has cost money and the public has paid the bill. Apparently librarians and public are equally satisfied. We should not be astonished, for this merely shows that the library is subject to the same laws and tendencies as all other things American.

Hence it comes about that whereas in a large library a century ago there were simply stored books with no appliances to do anything but keep them safe, we now find in library buildings all sorts of devices to facilitate the quick and efficient use of the books both in the building and in the readers' homes, together with other devices to stimulate a desire to use books among those who have not yet felt it; to train children to use and love books; to interest the public in things that will lead to the use of books. This means that many of the things in a modern library seem to an old-fashioned librarian and an old-fashioned reader like unwarranted extensions or even usurpations. In our own Central building you will find collections of postal cards and specimens of textile fabrics, an index to current lectures, exhibitions and concerts, a public writing-room, with free note-paper and envelopes, a class of young women studying to be librarians, meeting places for all sorts of clubs and groups, civic, educational, social, political and religious; a bindery in full operation, a photographic copying-machine; lunch-rooms and rest-rooms for the staff; a garage, with an automobile in it, a telephone switchboard, a paint-shop, a carpenter-shop, and a power-plant of considerable capacity. Not one of these things I believe, would you have found in a large library 50 years ago. And yet the citizens of St. Louis seem to be cheerful and are not worrying over the future. We are eclectic, but we are choosing the elements of our blend with some discretion and we have been able, so far, to relate them all to books, to the mental activities that are stimulated by books and that produce more books, to the training that instills into the rising generation a love for books. The book is still at the foundation of the library, even if its walls have received some architectural embellishment of a different type.

When anyone objects to the introduction into the library of what the colleges call "extra-curriculum activities," I prefer to explain and justify it in this larger way, rather than to take up each activity by itself and discuss its reasonableness—though this also may be undertaken with the hope of success. In developing as it has done, the Library in the United States of America has not been simply obeying some law of its own being; it has been following the whole stream of American development. You can call it a drift if you like; but the Library has not been simply drifting. The swimmer in a rapid stream may give up all effort and submit to be borne along by the current, or he may try to get somewhere. In so doing, he may battle with the current and achieve nothing but fatigue, or he may use the force of the stream as far as he may, to reach his own goal. I like to think that this is what many American institutions are doing, our libraries among them.

They are using the present tendency to eclecticism in an effort toward wider public service. When in a community, there seems to be a need for doing some particular thing, the library, if it has the equipment and the means, is doing that thing without inquiring too closely whether there is logical justification for linking it with the library's activities rather than with some others. Note, now, how this desirable result is aided by our prevailing American tendency toward eclecticism. Suppose precisely the same conditions to obtain in England, or France, or Italy, the admitted need for some activity, the ability of the library and the inability of any other institution, to undertake it. I submit that the library would be extremely unlikely to move in the matter, simply from the lack of the tendency that we are discussing. That tendency gives a flexibility, almost a fluidity, which under a pressure of this kind, yields and ensures an outlet for desirable energy along a line of least resistance.

The Englishman and the American, when they are arguing a case of this kind, assume each the condition of affairs that obtains in his own land—the rigidity on the one hand, the fluidity on the other. They assume it without stating it, or even thoroughly understanding it, and the result is that neither can understand the conclusion of the other. The fact is that they are both right. I seriously question whether it would be right or proper for a library in a British community to do many of the things that libraries are doing in American communities. I may go further and say that the rigidity of British social life would make it impossible for the library to achieve these things. But it is also true that the fluidity of American social life makes it equally impossible for the library to withstand the pressure that is brought to bear on it here. To yield is in its case right and proper and a failure of response would be wrong and improper.

It is usually assumed by the British critic of American libraries that their peculiarities are due to the temperament of the American librarian. We make a similar assumption when we discuss British libraries. I do not deny that the librarians on both sides have had something to do with it, but the determining factor has been the social and temperamental differences between the two peoples. Americans are fluid, experimental, eclectic, and this finds expression in the character of their institutions and in the way these are administered and used. Take if you please the reaction of the library on the two sides of the water to the inevitable result of opening it to home-circulation—the necessity of knowing whether a given book is or is not on the shelves. The American response was to open the shelves, the British, to create an additional piece of machinery—the indicator. These two results might have been predicted in advance by one familiar with the temper of the two peoples. It has shown itself in scores of instances, in the front yards of residences, for instance—walled off in England and open to the street in the United States. I shall be reminded, I suppose, that there are plenty of open shelves in English libraries and that the open shelf is gaining in favor. True; England is booming "Americanized" in more respects than this one. But I am speaking of the immediate reaction to the stimulus of popular demand, and this was as I have stated it. In each case, the reaction, temporarily at least, satisfied the demand; showing that the difference was not of administrative habit alone, but of community feeling. This rapid review of modern American tendencies, however confusing the impression that it may be give, will at any rate convince us, I think, of one thing—the absurdity of objecting to anything whatever on the ground that it is un-American. We are the most receptive people in the world. We "take our good things where we find them," and what we take becomes "American" as soon as it gets into our hands. And yet, if anything does not happen to suit any of us, the favorite method of attack is to denounce it as "un-American." Pretty nearly every element of our present social fabric has been thus denounced, at one time or another, and as it goes on changing, every change is similarly attacked.

The makers of our Constitution were good conservative Americans—much too conservative, some of our modern radicals say—yet they provided for altering that Constitution, and set absolutely no limits on the alterations that might be made, provided that they were made in the manner specified in the instrument. We can make over our government into a monarchy tomorrow, if we want, or decree that no one in Chicago shall wear a silk hat on New Year's Day. It was recently the fashion to complain that the amendment of the Constitution has become so difficult as to be now practically a dead letter. And yet we have done so radical a thing as to change absolutely the method of electing senators of the United States; and we did it as easily and quietly as buying a hat—vastly more easily than changing a cook. The only obstacle to changing our constitution, no matter how radically and fundamentally, is the opposition of the people themselves. As soon as they want the change, it comes quickly and simply. Changes like these are not un-American if the American people like them well enough to make them. They, and they alone, are the judges of what peculiarities they shall adopt as their own customs and characteristics. So that when we hear that this or that is un-American, we may agree only in so far as it is not yet an American characteristic. That we do not care for it today is no sign that we may not take up with it tomorrow, and it is no legitimate argument against our doing so, if we think proper.

And now, what does this all mean? The pessimist will tell us, doubtless, that it is a sign of decadence. It does remind us a little of the later days of the Roman empire when the peoples of the remotest parts of the known world, with their arts, customs and manners, were all to be found in the imperial city—when the gods of Greece, Syria and Egypt were worshipped side by side with those of old Rome, where all sorts of exotic art, philosophy, literature and politics took root and flourished. That is usually regarded as a period of decadence, and it was certainly a precursor of the empire's fall. When we consider that it was contemporaneous with great material prosperity and with the spread of luxury and a certain loosening of the moral fiber, such as we are experiencing in America today, we can not help feeling a little perturbed. Yet there is another way of looking at it. A period of this sort is often only a period of readjustment. The Roman empire as political entity went out of existence long ago, but Rome's influence on our art, law, literature and government is still powerful. Her so-called "fall" was really not a fall but a changing into something else. In fact, if we take Bergson's viewpoint—which it seems to me is undoubtedly the true one, the thing we call Rome was never anything else but a process of change. At the time of which we speak the visible part of the change was accelerated—that is all. In like manner each one of you as an individual is not a fixed entity. You are changing every instant and the reality about you is the change, not what you see with the eye or photograph with the camera—that is merely a stage through which you pass and in which you do not stay—not for the thousand millionth part of the smallest recognizable instant. So our current American life and thought is not something that stands still long enough for us to describe it. Even as we write the description it has changed to another phase. And the phenomena of transition just now are particularly noticeable—that is all. We may call them decadent or we may look upon them as the beginnings of a new and more glorious national life.

"The size and intricacy which we have to deal with," says Walter Lippmann, "have done more than anything else, I imagine, to wreck the simple generalizations of our ancestors." This is quite true, and so, in place of simplicity we are introducing complexity, very largely by selection and combination of simple elements evolved in former times to fit earlier conditions. Whether organic relations can be established among these elements, so that there shall one day issue from the welter something well-rounded, something American, fitting American conditions and leading American aspirations forward and upward, is yet on the knees of the gods.

We, the men and women of America, and may I not say, we, the Librarians of America, can do much to direct the issue.

Librarianship: A Profession

W. E. Henry, Librarian, University of Washington, Seattle.
Librarianship: A Profession (University of Washington Press, 1922)

Foreword

On this day twenty-five years ago I entered upon whatever career I have had in librarianship. I entered not through that straight and narrow way known as a library school, but "climbed up another way," resigning a college professorship in English Language and Literature to enter this new, but not wholly different, field of education. Having been professionally prepared for teaching, I carried with me into the new activity professional ideals, and the transfer from one educational institution to another in many ways similar was rather natural and easy.

In this quarter of a century I have held firmly to the professional aspect of librarianship, believing that to be the most fundamental and essential view. On all occasions I have held that view before my staff and my classes, and I count this the most significant service I have rendered to my profession.

On this occasion I am I am reprinting for the service of my classes a paper which I prepared in December 1916. My hope is that they may get a professional viewpoint, and, if may be, adopt a professional attitude. I neither hope nor wish that all who take the professional attitude shall agree with all of my statements but rather that they may have a point of departure for their own thinking.

W. E. Henry, Librarian and Director of the Library School, University of Washington, Seattle, Wash.
April 1, 1922

First printed in the *Library Journal*, May 1917

Librarianship: A Profession

Our profession, if we may assume librarianship to be a profession, has at once the distinction and the handicap of being very young. Those of us who can remember 1876 have seen the beginnings and development of a profession. However many libraries there may have been before the Philadelphia meeting, or however many excellent and scholarly and devoted librarians there may have been, and there were many, the profession, to whatever degree we have one, began with the centennial year. Not until then did we begin to demand special training to see librarianship as a social service, to fix any standard, or to plan institutions thru which professional training may be secured. What are some of the more distinctive marks of a profession and a professional education that may set the profession off from the trade or occupation?

Every profession has set apart for its field of activity and devotion some phase or problem of human life that is fundamental to the social welfare. One group of men has thru the ages claimed for its province the essential principle prevalent among men that justice and equity must prevail because society as a living organizing and a working organization cannot exist unless there shall be some rule among men by which the weak can be protected from the vicious strong. In this effort they have developed a body of doctrine founded on human experience and thought known as the law. The mission of the law and its machinery, the court, is that justice may prevail. The lawyer then becomes the agent of this mission and every lawyer of honest purpose and high ideals lives and works that justice and right and fair dealing shall exist for society. Whether all nominal lawyers have held and practiced this conception need not be discussed; the principle obtains, the man may go wrong.

Another group has selected for its thesis that people cannot solve their problems, serve themselves, reach the end set up for them unless they are physically well and fit and efficient. To this end, this group has set for itself the problem and the task that our people shall be well, that health shall prevail not merely for the good of one who has it, but for the good of all. A well organized, well educated profession has grown up on the thesis that people shall be well.

On the thesis that life is permanent and logical another profession has grown up. Its instrument is the church and its mission the preparation of society for the fullest realization of the possibilities of life in harmony with its permanency. The agent is the clergy.

That society shall possess they key to intelligence as an aid to justice, health, efficiency and completeness is a doctrine that another group has evolved and the school has become its instrument and the teacher its agent. Its elementary mission is to teach us how to read.

Each of these professions, it will be noted, finds its mission in organized society and its distinctive feature is that it is a social service. Each of them finding itself in need of specialized education has organized schools for that purpose. Each of these schools has driven its roots deep into the fundamental principles of whatever phase of life it has selected for itself as the province of its activity.

May librarianship be considered a profession under such standards as are here suggested? Has librarianship found for itself or can it find a realm of opportunity, a phase, an area of human life that presents a social need which the professions named and others that might be named do not cover?

Many of us have come to believe and the world is rapidly coming to believe that there is a larger, more extended and more varied educational need than any or all other professions can reach. We believe that in this new field the education may be largely self-directed, indefinitely prolonged and largely the choice of the individual concerned; a large opportunity, equally free and open to all, yet under intelligent and expert direction—a social service but with the highest degree of individuality. We believe this service cannot be rendered without a recognized instrument—the library and the agent, the librarian—corresponding in all these characteristics to the recognized professions already named.

In this new institution the service is social, the problems vary as the individual tastes and experiences vary and the service must be sufficiently intelligent to diagnose the symptoms and prescribe a treatment. The problems of the present need the aid of all the past for light and guidance. No man and no social organization can solve its problems wisely without the aid of the concentrated intelligence and experience of the past and unto this end were books sent. The life of the individual is too short to reflect the perspective of any fair portion of the past so we must have the vicarious experience of others and the book is the agent of the past bringing to us this vicarious experience. All the past has lived for us and we must live for all the future's good.

Is there, then, a realm, an area, a mission in life that humanity can not realize without an unrestrained and self-directed access to the past which the individual alone cannot secure for himself? Can this mission be performed by any other institution? The library is the instrument and the librarian is the social agent which bring the past to the present in preparation for the future, and thru these the individual is self-educated for social ends.

The trade, the vocation, the occupation knows the practical service side of a limited field of activity. It has made no fundamental study of the principles that arise out of the very nature of life itself. I can think of a man being an excellent carpenter without being an expert in knowledge of woods or having the slightest conception of the philosophy of shelter or the dimmest shadow of a notion upon the housing problem as a social necessity. The street car motorman is a public servant and a very valuable one. He must know how to handle his car, but he may be totally indifferent to and even ignorant of any social principle or social need of a transportation system. The farmer may be able to produce good crops under the usual and ordinary circumstances, but let a crisis arise and he is helpless for he does not know chemistry or geology or entomology, so he sits helplessly by and sees his work fail.

He does not see the social significance of, nor even the fact that he who produces two stalks of corn where one grew before is a benefactor of the human race. The carpenter of rare ability and depth of insight may become an architect, but this is only as the individual rises above the mass. Farming might become a profession. It has not, perhaps, will not.

The professional men and women must everywhere and always be the guardians, guides, advisers, and directors of the people. Perhaps no other mark so distinguishes the professions.

Have we now some fairly definite demarcations setting off the nature of the profession from the trade or occupation? Assuming that we have, I want now to turn to questions within the professions. I have said that each profession has created and is sustaining training institutions for the preparation of its members and it may be worth noting that these professions are so clearly recognized as social needs that these institutions are created and sustained at the social or public expense.

And further, the social significance of the professions is so strongly felt that society has said thru its formulated laws that no one may practice the profession who has not taken the training offered by these training institutions and this demand is rapidly regulating the practice of many professions. If a social service comes at social expense, then society must control it guided by the professionally prepared.

The standard in all of these professional requirements is being placed higher and higher until now only the well selected may enter. The medical profession has advanced from no requirement above the ability to read and assume a title to the requirement that the applicant shall have at least two years of college academic work built upon a high school curriculum before he enters the professional school. Then his professional preparation shall consume from four to seven years including his hospital experience. The law school demands two years of college academic work at least, and then either three or four years of professional preparation. The best professional schools in these lines go further and demand college graduation before entering the specializing school. So it goes and so it will continue to go.

There was a time within the memory of men now living when a boy with the most meager scholastic preparation—little above the ability to read—could enter the office of a physician and by industriously sweeping out the office and caring for the physician's horse for a period of years and reading a few books on anatomy and materia medica in his leisure moments become a doctor. This was the apprentice system. Young men entered the law by the same easy road. But old things have passed away. Now we demand that any one assuming to direct the interest of others in the great crises of life must be one of experience and training, for training is only specialized experience.

Now what about the preparation for our profession if we are willing to admit that we are in a profession?

Is there a body of knowledge and information covering the field and is that body of information well formulated and organized? If we answer in the affirmative to these questions, as I presume we should without argument, then there is a place for a profession and a place for a professional school which shall transmit and enlarge upon this body of knowledge and put into practice the doctrine which the school stands for.

Whom can society (not librarians) economically admit to this great social service? I say *great* social service not because the library is a greater service in the sense of greater value than any of the others, but because it is more comprehensive, more inclusive than any of the other professions. Society then can economically admit that person to serve in the library who has this more comprehensive and inclusive view, not only of the library profession, but of all other professions and the whole realm of thought and its embodiment roughly called literature. If my characterization is not also an exaggeration then our professional standards must be high indeed. The profession of librarianship, coming to consciousness as a social need so recently as it did—forty-six years ago—and starting without estate or tradition, has secured for itself an enviable growth and a standing in the respect of many, but not of most. The marvel of it is that it has done so well. No profession perhaps has reached so high a level of intelligence and so strong a sentiment for professional preparation so early in its career as has librarianship, but we must recall that we are the youngest of the group and that we progress more now in forty years than older professions did in many centuries. Our profession must continue to elevate its standards, for, like the Golden Rule, it has infinite possibilities in its reinterpretations. The profession will grow in its own self-respect and in the respect of others just as it keeps its standards almost out of reach. All professional standards must of necessity be dual standards; one of general intelligence, comprehensive experience, general scholarship; the other of specific scholarship or professional education. If we have been remiss in our demands in either of the two standards I should say it is in the former rather than in the latter. Perhaps we have more adequately valued our professional education than we have appreciated the foundations upon which it should be built.

Specific training may be of value to the tradesman, to the artisan, to the mechanic without much concern about foundations beyond fair intelligence, but I hold it almost worthless and totally out of harmony with any reasonable conception of a profession to give specific training in librarianship to one who has had a very small round of experience and general education. I wish I might cite examples, but I dare not. I do think that in medicine, law, teaching, or librarianship, there are persons to whom it is a trade, an occupation, but in no sense a profession. There may be phases of library work where only a trade is required, but if so we should draw a fairly definite distinction and act in the light of that distinction. Whom shall we professionally educate? I should answer most emphatically that I would not sanction giving professional education to any one who, including the professional work, shall have had less than four years above the high school graduation or its equivalent in travel or reading, or home environment or in library service. This is not too high for any library service, and if it should be changed, I should consent only to an increase, and say all special preparation must be built upon college graduation, or its equivalent. As to equivalents I may frankly say that I have seen many who had never taken a college assignment who were better scholars and more capable of excellent library service than many who were loaded with degree symbols. I had rather have grown up in a great library or at home with a great scholar of good taste and social instincts than to carry the A.B. from any university without them, yet the A.B. degree is the best formal and recognized standard that can be named for it connotes four years of intelligent presence and cooperation and comprehensive scholarship. There is much in every college curriculum that one does not study, but he finds out that there is such a field and he cannot if he would wholly escape it. So, for the future let no one contemplate the profession of librarianship who has not lived long in the presence of culture or scholarship or both. Let it be understood both in and out of the profession that " not everyone who saith Lord, Lord, shall enter into the Kingdom."

There is a large field of personality here to be considered. It is so indefinable that we cannot discuss it, yet everyone knows what it means and what it implies, and that is a most essential attribute. I shall not attempt its discussion. Now what can we say as the necessity for education in the specific experience of the profession?

As has been said, not many years ago a man might become a lawyer of certain type with no special preparation from a professional school, indeed without even knowing that such institutions existed. Physicians came to their practice in the same way. Anyone who could not do anything else was popularly supposed to be able to teach in the public schools. By the popular conception we are now in that stage of librarianship. In the other professions above mentioned the state has interfered, and is making at least elementary requirements before one can enter upon practice in these lines. Except in a few instances no state or other governmental unit has even proposed to prevent unqualified librarians from drawing public money. Up to date, then, with few exceptions the only force behind librarianship has been the relatively few well prepared librarians and a few others who comprehend the situation.

This is not unique in the history of the profession; on the contrary it is quite the common experience. The problem, then, of better librarianship is with those librarians who comprehend the service as a large directing social service, whose possibilities are infinite, not those who think it a trade, a job an occupation, a mere makeshift, a waiting station. A profession comprehends a body of fundamental principles the practice of which shall render to the world an engrossing social service. A trade or an occupation sees an opportunity for a job, a wage, a day's work, and a day's pay with little comprehension of a primary service or of a world to be serviced. A profession knows no limit of working hours, the trade or occupation watches the clock. In library work we have both types as in other professions. I am trying to deal with the profession, not the trade, and into the profession the legitimate entrance is thru the Library School. By whatever name, it must be a professional school, not a trade school, not an apprentice relationship, but a school funded on a professional conception dealing with fundamental principles.

This professional school should be built upon general educational qualifications not less than the equivalent of the A.B. degree. The profession has made itself what it is and we in this generation must guard its interests and elevate its standards. Librarians must have all that I have described on both phases of the work. If we must have cheaper helpers they must know and the public must know that they are not librarians. Charging out a book is no more a part of librarianship than the bookkeeping by the physician's office girl is of the profession of medicine. Knowing what book to charge out and why, knowing the life and taste and needs of the patron and the community, and what book will serve is as much the profession as the most intelligent prescription of the finest surgery. It has been pointed out that the mass of people, even the very intelligent, does not yet know but what just anybody can do library work. That is the greatest obstruction in the way of our progress, and the sad feature of it is that librarians are much at fault. The belief has grown largely because we have not insisted as strongly as we might that no one shall do library work who is not prepared.

If our people think that the high school girl can come in and watch me " be a librarian" for a few days, and thereby become a librarian, they cannot respect, nor will they compensate the library profession. Apprentice lawyers and doctors and teachers have been out of date for a half century. England ruined her board schools (corresponding to our public schools) by her apprentice teacher system. No one had confidence in nor respect for teachers with such imitative preparation. The apprentice system will not work anywhere in a profession. It will serve in a trade or occupation and it is my candid and long considered judgment that no librarian can do a more detrimental act for a community or a greater indignity and injustice to the library profession than is done by admitting apprentices. If the apprentice system is to be condemned and not tolerated as a cheap and detrimental makeshift which at least retards the profession, what can we do? That is a practical question, and one that must ultimately be answered. If the system is pernicious and short sighted the answer to my question is worth not only minutes and hours in time spent in effort to find a solution, but it is worth years. If I cannot answer, as I probably cannot, then you others yet to come must answer.

The school answers this question by offering competitive examinations and issuing temporary license permits to teach. Whenever a supply of better prepared people are found these licenses are not renewed. Some such system may serve the library. It is understood that unless this preparation is improved and greatly strengthened up to a high standard and in a reasonable time the license permit shall be permanently withdrawn.

Or we may create a type of clerkship in which some apprentice work may be given, but wiht the definite understanding that it is only a clerkship and that without final and high grade preparation the grade of clerkship can never be passed and that no person can remain in it permanently. In this discussion I shall threat with brevity that institution that is doing excellent service half way between the apprentice course and the formal library school, i.e., the Public Library training class. It is rendering a great service and at present it is perhaps the best device for supplying a working staff for many of our large library systems. I am inclined to believe from a superficial and inadequate knowledge that general scholarship is frequently much below what any profession should demand and its nearness to the apprentice principle must handicap it in any professional consideration.

If we argue there are not enough library schools or that they are not the right type, let me say that every profession has been answered with adequate schools whenever the demand came for training. The normal school came when the schools were no longer willing to accept imitation for legitimate education in principles.

The university began to train teachers in historical and scientific principles based upon large general scholarship when the high schools could no longer succeed with the normal school product. Technical schools will always supply the demand if it is persistent.

The Larger Publicity of the Library

By Joseph L. Wheeler, Librarian, Youngstown Public Library
Presented at the ALA Annual Conference in Asbury Park, New Jersey, 1916. *Papers and Proceedings of the Thirty-Eight Annual Meeting of the American Library Association,* pp. 175-180.

At this late date, when librarianship has been an organized profession for forty years, we are making a small beginning in what always has been and always will be an important part of our work. If the goal of the library is to get as many good books read as possible; if the function of the librarian is to get two books read where only one was read before; then the library publicity is an ordinary, legitimate activity, calling for our best interest and effort. For, no matter how good his service, the librarian can never hope to reach the mass of people without advertising his wares.

The this is true, proof may be found in some of our well thumbed pages of library statistics, which show that even in those cities where the libraries are working for larger use of books, less than a fifth of the people are enrolled as library users. We have only begun to do library work, after these forty years. If we omit all of the population which is unable to read in any language, which is too young, too ill, to handicapped by distance and circumstance, to use the libraries in our cities and towns, can we prove to anyone that we have made much progress in our dealings with the remaining large part of the population?

The time may come when the technique of getting books read will be taught in library schools, along with instruction in marking numbers on their backs. One may arise among us and teach us the psychology of our profession, the appeal of colored book-covers, the lure of the book-line that reaches out to the sidewalk, the cause and cure of the craving for "something new," the origin of dull seasons and rush hours, the mind of him who comes for a light novel and takes away a biography of power and inspiration. Publicity is nothing more than the study of human nature, followed by a carefully planned appeal to it. A man in any other work or business would tell us that if we librarians hope to achieve a greater use of books, we should make more study of human nature, and more appeal to it.

A feeling still lingers in some corners that library publicity is a fad, a side-issue, a running after newspaper glory and large figures of circulation. It is true that we still are so elated over the publication of a booklist, circular, or news story, that our delight must often appear elementary even to our fellow workers. But it is not true that library publicity aims at size rather than quality of circulation, or that circulation of books is a less worthy object than their use in the library building. Why not assume that publicity can increase both quality and quantity of reading, that it can make steady book users out of persons who have previously used books but little, that it can be directed to building up reference work itself?

One thinks first of the publicity which works directly for a larger use of books. Even more important, in some respects, and in the long run, is the publicity which works for a larger public understanding of the library itself, and what it is trying to do. In all too many instances librarians are reminded of this public understanding and support only when the city council is voting on the annual appropriate. Why is it that in a great many cities and towns, the playgrounds, the public schools, the social centers, the Christian associations, and all the rest of the agencies for social advance, receive so much more attention than the library? Why is it that the state experiment stations can send out a column of news that describes the county adviser as a distributor of agricultural literature, and have the column appear in every newspaper in the state, when a news story on the same topic, if sent out by librarians, is almost sure to be ignored by the editors? The answer is that though we ourselves take our work with tremendous seriousness, we have not yet made much of a dent in public opinion.

It is only natural that a community where the library has followed a quiet course of handing out volumes to those who ask for them, distributing well-made booklists from the desk, trying to operate the library economically and according to the rules of Hoyle, we should become most oblivious to the great question: What is our real standing in the community, as a vital factor in the life of every citizen? It is easy to delude oneself into thinking that the small number who use the library are typical of the whole population. It is hard to realize that even among the crowds who are already borrowing library books, few know anything of the purpose, the plans and the methods of the work for which they themselves are paying. The library plays such a small part in the public mind, as compared with schools, for instance, that to the nine out of ten, education and school are completely synonymous terms. Chambers of commerce, women's clubs, and improvement societies gather to discuss and argue about the Gary system, vocational schools, the platoon plan. Librarians probably hope that the time will never come when the public will assemble to discuss the proper aims, methods and finances of library work. Perhaps it would be better for us if they did. Perhaps, our well-meaning efforts to do just the right thing for our "dear public," we have built a fence around our profession and have left our public too much on the outside.

To come down to facts instead of speculations, the public must know more about the library and the librarians, as well as about the books, if we are to gain a place in the sun. Conversely, unless the librarian himself has the outward vision, unless he studies and loves the crowd, and has his finger on the pulse of the community, he will find it slow work to build up enthusiasm, interest and support for his institution. The personal element plays a large part in library work, all the way up and down the staff. But nowhere is it so important as in the attitude which the librarian has toward one hundred per cent of his fellow citizens. People do not have to come to the library; they do not have to read books. There is no legal, social or moral obligation to use the library. We must use suggestion, attraction, enthusiasm and satisfaction, if we are to lead an ever growing stream of people to the open book, and secure for our libraries the increasing support to which they are entitled.

What then, more definitely, are some of the things which the librarian may do in this direction? Beginning close at home he can undertake to make each of his trustees into an active and zealous missionary. It is no easy matter. It is the librarian's self-punishment, that his willing, interested and conscientious trustee too often reflects the lukewarm attitude of the public. Rather should trustees act as bearers of the great truth that the library is vital to the community. Nothing can reveal to the librarian with such dismaying clearness his own neglect of this opportunity, as to have his trustees, perhaps at the threshold of some new development, assume that the library is doing well enough, that the public will not pass a bond issue, will not increase the millage, or that the city officials will not grant a larger appropriation, when current library practice points forward. With their standing in the community, the confident and outspoken leadership that trustees could take before the public, would be a new and priceless asset to most librarians. It is well to have the librarian given the responsibility for running the library. But we have made another great step toward an ideal situation when we know that each trustee is an active co-worker in some of these larger problems.

For the good of the library we have duties to our trustees other than making a weekly or monthly report. We must inform and inspire them, that they in turn may help us teach the public what the library means. We can keep them abreast with current library practice. We may inflict an occasional library magazine article on them. Bring them to the library between meetings, and visit them in their offices, not to bother them with troubles, but to tell them of constructive hopes, plans and problems, and to have them share the pleasure of directing the work, and realizing what it means in the community. One would hardly need to add, if it were not so often overlooked, that the staff members are likewise indispensable helpers in winning public opinion. A recent article in a library magazine gives the warning that staff members should not have their first knowledge of the librarian's policies from news articles or from readers. Beside the embarrassment of the assistants in having what they regard as their business told them from outside, the public cannot escape the thought that the librarian is not closely enough in touch with his own family of workers. There are conditions and developments of a general enough nature to allow the librarian to take his staff into his confidence, to some extent, especially in the smaller libraries. While it is difficult to know just how far to go, and one must be sure of himself, it is probably true that nearly every librarian could benefit by a larger discussion of general library problems with his staff.

Such an attitude would surely be reflected in the attitude of the staff toward the public, and in turn in the attitude of the public toward the library. The business man, especially, knows the value of team work in store or factory, and respects it in the library. Business men would take more interest in the library if they were shown how library operation follows many of the methods of business itself. To mention a few, there are: buying, turnover of stock, advertising, organization, operating costs, scientific layout of the working space, and good-will. This is a good outline of topics on which to base a talk before business organizations. A librarian ought to take advantage of every possible opportunity to appear before groups of business men, not only to encourage them to a larger personal use of the library, but even more to let this large class of citizens know something about the library's purpose.

In attempting to reach the business men, and indeed, in trying to uproot the whole of the old-fashioned idea that a library is merely a storehouse for novels and cultural books, we often have the appearance of going to the other extreme and emphasizing far too strongly the mere dollar value of library books. But is it not true, after all, that this emphasis is more apparent than real? It would be hard to find a library, which in developing its work with artisans, engineers, business men, has really neglected or even slackened its efforts to make the library what it always must be, a center and source of culture.

The emphasis on the dollar is natural and necessary. Though it may have been especially noticeable of late, it is doubtful if it will be abated. We cannot change human nature to meet our little ideas of what books people should read. Nor is there anything about our work which we can tell with such force, as the stories of men and women who find library books of some use in earning their daily bread, and in solving the merely physical, commercial problems that are to be found in every city and town. It does no good to stand proudly aloof from the crowd, whispering about culture and the classics. It does do good to meet the crowd on the basis of its work-a-day interests, and to have enough understanding and sympathy with its point of view, to be able to say in an effective way, "Here, too, are books for you. Books that will refresh and inspire, though they may not make your pay check larger." We take pride in knowing the single reader and his tastes. But we are on the right road when we try to know the taste and feeling of the great hundred per cent.

Therefore we must forever emphasize the mere commercial value of our work, in keeping the library in the public mind. It is because the public mind cares most for this presentation. There are three publicity methods which seem especially successful, and which have as one of their central motives this work-a-day value of books. The first of these has just had its best example in the Library Week that was carried out this spring by the joint efforts of the Toledo Public Library and Chamber of Commerce. We all know that in any town or city, the mass of people has practically no understanding of the library. It is reasonable to say that now, in Toledo, there is practically no one who has not at least heard of the library. The whole town was aroused an interested in the library. The business men were not only interested, but they did much of the actual planning and work. The Chamber of Commerce stood shoulder to shoulder with the library. Not that the library needed moral support, but that Business felt its personal connection with the realm of books. This campaign consisted of a whole week of widespread and active publicity of all kinds. There were circulars, posters, book-lists, window displays, a proclamation by the mayor, public meetings and speeches about the library. There were signs on the street cars, even. What librarian with the outward vision, can help wishing to follow so notable an example?

Yet it is possible that there are still a few who murmur to themselves, "This is not the library work of my grandfather's day." Even these would be inclined to approve of the second method that seems worth mention. This is the public exhibition of diagrams, charts and other material which shows what the library does with books and money. The purpose of such exhibits is not the larger use of books, except as an indirect result, but to tell the story that will bring greater interest and support for the library itself. Something is needed for the guidance of librarians in the preparation of such exhibits, and it is probable that the Publicity Committee of the Association will undertake something of this sort. At least the smaller cities, and many of the larger ones, could well use a traveling exhibit, as the nucleus for their local effort. The things which work most for success will be: choosing the few forcible facts and presenting them forcibly; the use of few and brief legends; the use of bold and clear-cut lettering, which should be done by an expert; the placing of the exhibit where it will be seen by the greatest number. Even the most conservative librarian could feel that exhibits of this sort were appropriate and useful, and they could be carried out in every community.

The third method is one which has been used in many cities, with marked success. This is the display of library books in store windows, to increase the use of books. By making a change in the display, the emphasis can be thrown onto the library and its work, as well as on the appeal of the books themselves. This means the use of placards and small diagrams which tell the important things about the library: How it is supported, how it spends its money, how it is used, increases in use, decreases in operating costs. In preparing window exhibits take advantage of the help that the advertising men and window-trimmers can give. In one city, at least, this cooperation went to the length of preparing a scene form a reader's home, with father and mother reading in their arm-chairs, while in the foreground a little girl lay at full length, reading "Alice in Wonderland." In this instance the library's exhibit occupied an entire window in a large department store, and during the same week ten other windows, equally valuable, were given to the library by other merchants. The money value of such cooperation meant the loss of hundreds of dollars to the stores, and simply shows that though they would never grant such a privilege to anyone else, they regard the library as on a different basis from other organizations, and are glad to help it.

This is not the best time to discuss the details of actual publicity. The point is, that we have lying at our hands many means for showing the public something of our plans, methods and purposes, and this education of the public is worth the time and trouble which it takes.

All of our plans, hopes, labor, for adequate appropriates come to their climax when the town or city council takes its vote on the annual budget. The fortunes of the average town or city library are practically dependent on a very few men, and most of all on the finance committee of the council. Librarians can well depart from the usual American custom of electing men to the City Hall, and then charging them, in a vague and careless way, with being dishonest, small minded and incompetent. The men who make the city appropriations are perhaps as honest and conscientious as we could desire, if we only took the trouble to find out. The librarian is only one of the swarm of busy bees who sing loudly at the councilman's ears at budget time, and if he pays more attention to the ones who sing loudest, who shall blame him?

The librarian's hum is not very loud, sad to say, and his singing seldom arouses any loud echoes from the public, we must admit, still more sadly. When we make library service mean as much to the public as schools do now, we may expect the same outspoken demands for more support, and complaints at any cuts in the budget.

Be actually acquainted with councilmen, or supervisors, or selectmen, or whatever their titles are. Know the city hall and its workers and their work. They will doubtless be as much interested in you and your work as you are in them, and not any more so. The librarian's temptation is to look on all the office holders as politicians, in the unhappy sense of the word, and to forget that he too must be a politician, but in the good sense of the word.

We need to go to council meeting, once or twice a year, to find out how little a part of the library plays in the grist of motions for street openings, paving, more police protection, tax payer's complaints, and all the rest. Interest the President of the council, and ask him for ten or fifteen minutes out of some session, so that you can give the members a bird's-eye view of the library system, what it means, how you buy books, how a budget is divided, how the accounts and bills are handled, how your library ranks with others in various respects. If you have any forcible figures or comparisons, perhaps they can be made into a large diagram that can be shown. One showing the population growth, and the increase in library support as compared with the growth of circulation, could be used to advantage in a great many cities. These men are busy, they are not predisposed to give their time, but on the other hand they will give close attention and be much interested and impressed by short, plain talk, that touches the main points.

Over and over, councilmen have been invited to visit libraries. It would be interesting to count noses and find out how many councilmen have ever been inside the libraries to which they apportion money. In one city, several invitations having had no effect, the library board descended upon the council chamber and brought the members to the building in their automobiles. Surprise at the amount of patronage was followed by deep interest in the methods of handling the work and helping readers in different departments. Still the wonder grew, as these men watched the steady stream of borrowers, that the library was doing so great and useful a work, and that library books are not all novels, by any means.

The librarian can maintain a mutually helpful acquaintance with many city officials and show them forcibly the value of the library if he makes a point of seeing that the library service connects directly with the problems, at least the occasional and important problems, which come before the council and its committees. The larger library is able to do this much more successfully than the small. But the small library can often select a topic which is sure to interest the public very widely and deeply, and endeavor to make the books, pamphlets, and reports of some actual assistance.

The campaign with mayor and council and city officers is not a temporary or sporadic thing, therefore. It ought to be based on a continuous acquaintance with the men in authority, and find its expression in ever-renewed efforts to show them the relative importance of the library in a well organized community.

Last of all, and very briefly, what about the librarian himself?

We have heard that the librarian should spend fifty per cent of his time inside of his building and fifty per cent of his time outside. Certainly every library worker feels the ever-lasting necessity of more books, the acquaintance with the inside of books, better service, attention to a host of details, and all the rest. It is in the worthy desire to perfect service that he forgets the people outside. Out of each day, or from his week, he should hold inviolate a few minutes, in an hour or two, in which he can forget details and project his mind into the community mind, get his ear to the heart of the crowd.

After all, the librarian is the library's greatest advertiser. To join the local historical, literary and scientific societies, has always been held in good repute. Join also the Chamber of Commerce, or the leading civic and business organizations of the city, not with the notion that mere membership produces support for the library, but to take active part in work that helps the people, and thereby show that the librarian is human as well as being a librarian. (Both in and out of libraries this interesting doubt still seems to exist in some localities.) We ought to seek and accept every opportunity to appear personally before clubs, social, business, religious organizations, labor unions, foreign societies and all other groups. We cannot stifle the personal element out of library work. We cannot even use the newspapers successfully without injecting the personal name, the human interest into them. The value of interviews, the personal touch, is understood well enough by newspaper men and by everyone but librarians, many of whom possess a false modesty that is based on self-consciousness rather than on the good of the library.

There should be no specialists on library publicity. Every librarian must be a publicity man, with his heart in the work of reaching his people. The motive of publicity is the great democratic ideal of librarianship. It is a sound, healthy, helpful motive. It is only a reflection of our chosen motto, under whose inspiration we have all been striving these many years.

"Human Interest" in the Public Library

By Marilla Waite Freeman, Librarian, Goodwyn Institute, Memphis, Tennessee. *Library Journal*, January, 1917.

"Can you give me a good human interest story for the Commercial Appeal?" The new, young reporter leaned hopefully over the information desk of Goodwyn Institute Library in Memphis, Tennessee. As he spoke, a handsome Hindu, with melancholy dark eyes and polished address, came up beside him, and asked the privilege of seeing the library's resources on river control. This interesting visitor identified himself as a student of engineering at the University of Illinois, an institution which attracts so many aspiring Orientals. In a year more he would return to Calcutta to teach American engineering methods to his countrymen. On his summer vacation travels, he had come to Memphis to learn something of river and drainage engineering in the lower Mississippi Valley, a region which has many natural problems in common with his own.

"Have you also the works of my countryman, Rabindranath Tagore?" he inquired. As they were laid beside the engineering books on his table, he settled to a day of blissful research, mingled of drainage, poetry and philosophy.

Two American lads, one short and stocky, the other slim and tall, were waiting a bit sheepishly for next chance at the information desk. "Can you tell me,"—this from the stocky one—"how tall a man has to be to join the National Guards?" "And how much he has to weigh?"—from the slim one—"and for the regular Army too?" It took an Army Regulations handbook, a recruiting circular, and finally a telephone call to the captain of the Chickasaw Guards, to solve this problem. Ultimately, the sons of two mothers who quite obviously had not raised their boys "to be a soldier," went off exultant in the conviction that neither height nor width nor lack thereof could debar them from their country's service.

The desk telephone buzzed, and an anxious voice at the other end besought the name of the German consul-general at Chicago; and might so august a personage be addressed in plain Americanese as "My dear Sir?" Another buzz, and a lumber office spoke: "What is the comparative of sappy?" The librarian was dazed for a moment, but gathering herself, ventured on sappier, to rhyme with happier, and turned to meet the perturbed gaze of a young deaf-mute.

On a tiny slip of paper his question was written and was now thrust forward with embarrassed eagerness. "Have you a book of love letters?" The librarian read, and down the long procession of epistolary lovers ran her mind, from Abelard and Heloise to Balzac and his Madame Hanska. She read again, and this time the authentic inspiration came. Forth from its sacred space she fetched "The new standard business and social letter-writer," and with sympathetic finger pointed to Section III, on "Love and marriage." Breathing a sigh of relief, the amorous youth withdrew to a corner, where he feverishly read, wrote and destroyed by turns, till a final draft permitted to survive, was folded safely into his breast pocket. Then he departed leaving in the library waste-basket and all about the chair where he had sat, mutilated fragments and scraps, beginnings and ends of "love letters" not lacking in the divine fire, but couched in the somewhat stilted terms of "The new business and social letter-writer."

Again the telephone spoke. The Farm Development Bureau would like a list of the six best books on country life—including one on diversified farming—for the little library at Kerrville. An interested friend had promised to give them. Also, had the library copies of the new Rural Credits and Cotton Futures Bills? The librarian said "This afternoon" to the list, and "Yes" to the bills, inwardly thankful that she had written for the latter promptly. Thankful, also, when another buzz followed, that she had heeded the slogan of "Cotton mills for the cotton states," and was ready for the Memphis capitalist who wished to investigate mill costs and machinery.

A committee of three determined looking ladies appeared at the desk. The city was in the throes of a summer struggle between the Board of Health, seeking to enforce pasteurization of the milk supply, and the Dairymen's Association, asserting that its product was already beyond fear and above reproach. The largest woman's club of the city was preparing to take a hand and its representatives had come for ammunition. Armed with latest reports of the American Medical Milk Commission, and the milk bulletins of Uncle Sam's never resting Department of Agriculture, they retired to a table. Meantime the librarian telephoned to a wise children's specialist who knows the milk supply as life or death to his charges. He summed the situation in a sentence: "Tell the ladies to tell the dairy-men if they will keep their milk down to 100,000 non-pathogenic bacteria per cubic centimeter in winter and 200,000 in summer, they will not need to pasteurize: certified milk is always under 10,000: I give all my babies certified milk."

A fair-haired foreign youth was waiting, as the librarian hing up the receiver. He had just come down the river from St. Louis; said the big policeman on the corner of Main and Madison had told him to come to

Goodwyn Institute and "the library lady" would tell him how to find a job. Said he was from Odessa, had been in this country two years, had good experience as a house-boy, but was willing to do anything. His frank and wistful countenance was most appealing. The library lady felt she must not fail. She looked about the room. At one of the tables a resourceful and sympathetic young rabbi was looking over the latest sociological books. It needed but a word to bring his resourcefulness into play. In a trice he had the head of the Jewish Charities on the 'phone and in possession of the story. "From Odessa, did you say? Why, that's the town where I was born. Send the boy along. Sure I'll get him a job." And once more the receiver clicked with the joy of achievement, as it hung up for a brief rest.

The young reporter was still waiting, but watchful. His pencil scratched intermittently. "Strikes me you get lots of human interest up here," he volunteered. "Quite a good deal in the last twenty minutes. If you don't mind, guess I'll call my story 'Thirty minutes at the Library Human Interest Desk.'"

Great Reasons to Go to the New SF Main Library

Library Offers Wisdom to Knowledge Seekers
There Isn't Any Subject One Can't Get Facts About Among Books

San Francisco Examiner, Feb 18, 1917.

Is your mind a series of empty rooms in which a few lonely ideas rattle around with no company except an echo? Have you dragged them out in all sorts of company and batted them around conversationally until they are worn to fringes? If so—then now is the time to furbish up the blank spaces with full grown thoughts, practical, ornamental, witty and heavy. Go to the clearing house of ideas, the new City Library in the Civic Center, where there are 182,000 volumes and get yourself a new set.

If you have grown to be a chronic quotation mark, constantly repeating the opinions of your friends, adapting them to your own uses it is time for you to spend an hour in the reading room with the 399 people who are crowding there daily. Don't condemn a political candidate, a presidential policy, a crusade or attempt to discuss international affairs until you have stored away genuine information. There is no easier way to tincture your words with foolishness than to speak when half-informed.

Room for Music Lovers

A great room, drenched with south sun, has been set aside for music lovers. The shelves are loaded with scores of operas and sheet music, critical orks and the complete scores so that no one need attend a musical programme without a complete understanding of the numbers. Should you care to run over a song alone then there is a sound-proof music room and a piano for your convenience. It was Victor Herbert, the composer, who is supposed to have ordered a sound-proof studio in New York and discovered that it was also air-proof. This one has the advantage of perfect ventilation.

For the domestic soul who is content without dabbling in "cultchaw" there are excellent books on balanced menus, dietetics, and the dispensation of the household budget. Should she be puzzled about a point of dinner service or the ingredients of a salad dressing then the library is the place to go at once.

Books for All Desires

If she desires to make over her house in keeping with the best taste of the time there are books on interior decorating which plan the furnishings of an average home from curtains to carpets and design the rooms from kitchen to sun porch.

Engineers are to have a gathering place of their own, a sort of club room reserved for books about kilowatts and ions, suspension bridges and tunnels. Under lock and key a wonderful collection of art books are kept sacred for young painters and architects. You will find them there with their cameras taking time exposures of engravings for permanent use.

In spite of the fact that this library is only ten years old it is a rendezvous for collectors of California data. Tier upon tier of shelves hold copies of newspapers dating from the fifties. One entire set is given over to those which dealt with the fire of 1906. It contains the Eastern editions in which appear the ludicrous exaggerations which represented the city as sliding into the sea on the crest of a tidal wave. The collection of city directories begins with 1850, a tiny dot of a book hardly larger than a pamphlet.

According to Robert Rea, the librarian, and a State inspector of libraries, the local institution is a meeting place for what he terms "real Bohemians." He does not mean the variety who prove their ability in juggling strings of macaroni washed down with red paint, who soulfully look into each other's eyes and exchange long passages from Swinburne and Oscar Wilde. He refers to a set of writers and artists who already wearing the mantle of fame make frequent pilgrimages to consult greater masters.

20,000 Daily Visitors

During one day the library received 20,000 visitors who set their approval upon the city's latest achievement. On the same day, in spite of the natural confusion of settling down, 4,000 books were "borrowed." The conveying of volumes between departments is done by machinery which minimizes the rushing about of employees which in some libraries has become a nuisance. Cork floors deaden every footfall. Enormous windows give the maximum of light.

For the forty women employees there is a group of delightful rooms, a rest room in brown wicker and cretonne; a dressing room with a shower bath in case some girl wishes to dress there for a dinner party or the theatre without first going home; a cunning kitchen and a cheery dining room looking out over the prim little park.

Get Library Habit

With such a wonderful library, a room with 50,000 volumes in which you may amble about until title catches your fancy; a children's section which some day will be decorated with murals of Mother Goose characters and another room of 100,000 reference volumes there is no excuse for such conversation as "I gained a pound last week," or "I lost a pound last month," and the many other standard forms of inanity.

Get the library habit so that you do not have to say "I don't know" about the same thing twice.

Get it and when you open your mouth to speak you will always be able to say something.

Libraries Should Provide for the Reader Who Smokes

San Francisco Examiner, February 20, 1919. p. 20.

Many a man has gotten the inspiration which shaped his life-course while reading a paper or magazine or book that he had picked up because he had nothing else to do.

We are not speaking now of spiritual regeneration, but of something of value in this workaday world.

Many a man has spent minutes or hours in saloons drinking and chatting with friends which he might better have spent over some newspaper, magazine or book. After next July the saloon will be done and finished with. But there will be just as much time in the circle of the clock. It will be incumbent upon the community, as a public matter perhaps, to find an opportunity for the spending of some of the leisure time which heretofore has been spent by many in the saloon.

How about the libraries?

The question was recently brought up in the Book Review section of the New York "Sun." They must be made more clubby, the writer said. The old idea that libraries are storehouses of knowledge for folks already well-read and cultured must go by the board. The libraries must be made "reading clubs" and made especially comfortable for all the plain people who might be induced to use them if they were made more inviting to them in particular. In other words, the library folks have got to get away from the notion that they are an ultra-cultured set whose ministrations are meant only for similarly ultra-cultured folk. And the writer in the "Sun" made on smashing suggestion, which, we will wager, strikes many of the readers of this editorial right between the eyes. He suggested that libraries allow smoking in specially designated reading rooms.

One can imagine the faint screams of astonishment with which this suggestion will be greeted by some of our librarians. Of course, smoking in the reading rooms. Those of us men folks fortunate enough to have homes, whenever we sit ourselves down in them for an evening with a book, never think ourselves quite fixed for it until there is a smoke going. Why not similar comfort in the libraries?

Doesn't it sound meet and proper for the reader to be equipped with smoking material when he opens a volume of Anatole France or of Flaubert, or let us say, Rabelais? Even Emerson, for all his abhorrence of the weed, is more easily digested, we think, if the reader gets an occasional lift from a whiff of smoke. And as for such a chap as Henry James, we verily believe a smoke is a first aid to comprehension.

And this writer in the "Sun" goes further and says we ought to install soda-fountains in the libraries. A chocolate soda or a nut-sundae might be more agreeable to break up an evening's or afternoon's reading than plain water in those spurty faucets they supply in our San Francisco libraries.

In the main library at the Civic Center and in all the branches there is no regard for the smoking reader. If he insists upon a smoke, he must needs pace the sidewalk outside. Up in the Mechanics' Library the only place he may smoke is in the room where congregate those genial one-idead gentlemen who interminably play chess and checkers. Out in the reading rooms a cigarette would be the signal for getting pitched out into Post street.

By all means, we think this matter of supplying a reading room devoted to the cause and comforts of folks who like to smoke while they read should be taken up seriously by the authorities on both the public and the Mechanics' libraries.

Maybe the soda-fountain might be good, too.

Ankles of Library Girls Seized as They Stack Books

San Francisco Examiner, December 5, 1920, p. 90.

Mysterious hands that grab girls' ankles have caused consternation among some of the feminine attaches of the public library.

Women members of the library staff whose duties call them among the book stacks have experienced the startling grasp of the hands.

Strange men have been seen disappearing into the corridors simultaneously with the molestations, which have led John Rea, the librarian, to appeal for police protection.

Complaints have been made of late to Rea from several of the women assistant librarians that they have been subjected to sudden attacks of that sort.

Copyright and the Publishers: A Review of Thirty Years (and Reply)

By M. L. Raney, Librarian, Johns Hopkins University, Baltimore, Maryland, and Frederic G. Melcher, Executive Secretary, National Association of Book Publishers. ALA Annual Conference, Detroit, Michigan, 1922. *Papers and Proceedings of the Fifty-Fourth Annual Meeting of the American Library Association*, pp. 110-117.

We are here to consider a copyright measure introduced (by request) in Congress April 28 by Mr. Tincher, of Kansas (H. R. 11476). Its titular author is not committed to it and has yet to make the necessary studies for the determination of his own attitude.

The bill's putative origin is the so-called Author's League of America. "So-called" I say, for such copyright organizations in America have always been but parade bunting hung on publishing fronts, to be discarded after the parading was over. The reason for such carnivals when the legislator comes to town is a little lone paragraph in the Constitution of the United States which says not a word about the manufacturers and sellers of books, but speaks only of authors and their public. Thus runs a part of ARTICLE I, SEC. 8. The Congress shall have power: To promote the progress of science and useful arts, by securing, for limited times, to authors and inventors, the exclusive right to their respective writings and discoveries.

The old time publisher has a poor opinion of that subsection and a worse one still of its English mother, the Statute of Anne. He would amend it if he could, but there is not the slightest chance. Copyright legislation remains the concern of authors and their public. As a class, however, authors are a timorous folk and slow to unite, while the public, in Mr. Roosevelt's lament, will not take its own part. Rarely, therefore, has either of these principals functioned constructively in drafting the measures definitive of their relations. In the one great historic instance of their conjunction, above noted, the publishers lost perpetual monopoly, and the author's copyright was won. That eclipse of 1710 will never be forgot. But while the sceptre had passed from Stationers' Hall, the role of Warwick remained ever a possibility. And so, what with the diffidence of authors and the confusion of the people, publishers, busy and indeed indispensable scribes that they are, together, in the United States, with the printers, have played conspicuous parts suggesting claims and formulating terms. The present bill is no exception. The typographers announce their willingness to forego an (unproductive) privilege—for increased tariff protection. Two publishers draw up the stipulations, and the document is taken to Washington by the secretary of the Authors' League. The measure has great capabilities for good, but the zealous scribes could not forego the temptation of slipping in a clause to the fattening of their own pockets at tremendous cost to the public and no advantage to authorship—"not emphasized by authors," as they once expressed it. Will the people's representatives sign? If the past is any criterion, they will not, for the publishers have essayed such a rider four other times in the past thirty years, and suffered four defeats—two on the floor of Congress, two in committee. The bill itself has the worthy purpose of qualifying the United States for membership in the International Copyright Union, from which, save Russia, we are the only conspicuous absentee among the powers of the first rank. We do hold place in the Pan American convention, founded on the same general principles, but our literary relations are much more intimate with Europe, especially Great Britain because of common language, than with South and Central America. We should without question enter the larger fellowship also, as Brazil has set out to do. The fundamental principle of this association (called the Berne Union from its place of birth in 1886) is that copyright once secured in any Union country has validity, without further formality or cost, throughout all the countries of the Union. From this family of nations we have been barred for thirty years because of a provision in our law, known as the "manufacturing clause," which denies copyright to the foreigner unless his book is made here. This was the price paid to printers in the Act of 1891 for any protection at all to foreigners other than resident here. Previous to that, literary piracy was legalized and constituted the national sin, for the remission of which a host of men and women of high repute in and out of Congress struggled for a half century before attaining any degree of success.

It is but fair to say, however, that in this particular the United States were but following European precedent. Our first federal act, which established the nation's policy for a century, was passed in 1790. This was three years before France set the precedent of granting, irrespective of residence of nationality, copyright to anyone publishing a book on her soil, though in 1852 she took a longer lead by decreeing against republication (though not against performance) of works first published abroad, without regard to reciprocity. As for Great Britain, her law was not superior to ours when the famous petition of fifty-six British authors was presented to the Senate by Henry Clay in 1837. It took a court construction of 1868 to establish the applicability to non-residents of the Act of 1842, which allowed a book first published in the United Kingdom (England, Scotland, Wales, and Ireland) to bear copyright throughout the British dominions, while it was not till 1886 that such protection was given a book first published elsewhere in those dominions. And even since 1887, when the Berne convention went into effect, it must be remembered that an American author, to attain copyright in the Union countries, must publish there first or simultaneously, just as much as a British author must since 1891 do in the United States to get legal protection here. Publication twice in each case is necessary.

Finally, in the interest of fairness and sound action, let it be clearly recognized that American publishers cannot nowadays be charged with the habit of pirating foreign authors' works as was true before the Act of 1891. There is no National Sin crying out now for expiation. A very striking proof of this lies in the fact that, though English authors can since 1891 get under our law by publication here, less than one per cent, according to a published statement of the Register of Copyrights, have felt the necessity of doing so.

So that, while the nuisance of double publication should be abated, public law substituted for private agreements, and the temptation to Canadian retaliation removed, yet the international situation is not such as to justify the purchase of such advantages at any price. There is abundant time for deliberation, and the opportunity for action alike uncompromising and distinguished. In such unhurried and critical tember, we may now pass from the bill itself to an examination of Sinbad, the Publishers' Rider. The proposal is that with the repeal of the manufacturing clause shall go another, viz., revocation of everybody's right to acquire a foreign book from any source except the publisher of its American edition. No matter how shoddily the reprinter might do his work (and there would be no object in a reprint, except a cheaper one), he would thereby gain monopoly of all originals shipped here, and could charge at his pleasure. But this is to state the case in its most innocuous form. Printing here would not, under the new conditions created by the Act, be requisite to the establishment of an American edition. The foreign original might be made to serve the purpose. Three words—Copyright, John Smith, 1922—behind the title page of two such copies, when registered and deposited in Washington, would constitute an American edition. The Register of Copyright would not ask whether there were any more like these. All dealings must be with the new owner, under the dire penalties of infringement. The inscription of the magic words would be a matter of arrangement between the jobber here and the publisher there, or between the east and west sides of the same house.

The first beneficiary of this scheme would be the international publisher. Through our membership in the Berne Union, all his European issues would automatically have the protection of our laws against piracy, while only compliance with the simple formalities above mentioned, with payment of a dollar per title, would be necessary to qualification as publisher of an American edition. We could not then order such London books from London Agents, but must deal instead with the New York house and pay its prices or do without. What those prices would be is not a matter of conjecture. For example, one half the titles handled here by The Macmillan Company are importations; that is, books not printed or reprinted in the United States. The average rate at which they are priced on this side is 38.3 cents a shilling (which has an actual value at present of 22.5 cents). Now, as always heretofore, a buyer, whether individual or institution, can escape such charges by importing from England. The rider to subsection (a) of Section 6 would block that escape, and exact the higher toll.

The second beneficiary would be the importer of books from countries with broken down currency, especially Germany, and to a less extent Italy and France. What a harvest awaits the copyright manipulator in this field. The German mark has fallen to about one-sixtieth of its ante bellum value, but the domestic price of books has increased five fold. Under the rules of the trade, enforced by the Government, this price is trebled in sales to most foreign countries, including the United States. Even so, that has made German books cost us about one-fourth as much as in 1914. For the profiteer, who is already finding a way to operate, here is a golden opportunity, through employment of the American edition fiction, to double or treble the price of sure sellers—which will mean the first rate manuals of science and philology exploited at the expense of American investigators and students.

From the operations of this pair, the bill provides six exemptions—the Government, the blind, the traveler, imported libraries, whether bought en bloc or brought in by the immigrant, foreign newspapers or magazines, and the imported originals of English translations copyrighted here. In this line of eight beneficiaries, one misses two faces—the author, who gets not an added penny, and the general public for whom his work is done. These two would like to meet. The Constitution would have them do so freely. The bill says they may, provided the buyer is a Government official, or bereft of eyesight, or content with a periodical, or has money to take a trip to Europe, or to buy a whole library at once. But the searcher after truth in study and laboratory, the cultivated reader at home, the impecunious student who has not the price of an ocean voyage—they will pay heavily for the meeting, if the rider reaches his goal. The profiteer in foodstuffs for the body is held in execration. What more can be said of him who would corner the supplies of the brain?

And so, if the rider pulls rein at the White House, it will come to pass the librarians and bookbuyers of every degree will go very charily about their foreign acquisitions, for the penalty of a misstep is ugly. Never knowing what the registry of copyrights in Washington might show, they will in every instance first inquire whether some monopolist has beat them there. Is it thus we shall "promote the progress of science and useful arts?"

History of the Project

This offering of the publishers is not a new one, though the law of other countries knows it not. By it they attempt to retrieve one of their two historic defeats of the past thirty years—the first, suffered in the At of 1891 when victory by ambush seemed certain till a month before the Session's end Senators Sherman and Carlisle discovered the stratagem and plucked the invaders; the second, suffered in three successive adverse verdicts in the Supreme Court of the United States, in 1908 and 1913. As both these contests were waged in adherence to false theories of copyright, it is well to review them.

Copyright is the exclusive privilege of multiplying and first disposing of literary and artistic works. It is not a natural right, but one fixed by statute, as all rights in human society are. A natural right would be an absolute right, but absolutism is dead; one has not an absolute right to life itself. A criminal may be sentenced to death and a patriot yield his life at his country's command in its defense.

This grant is of distinctly modern origin and its entire development can be traced. The idea was unknown before the invention of printing, though there was a lively manuscript trade during the Middle Ages and copyists abundant—no less than 10,000 in Paris and Orleans alone, it is said. By the end of the sixteenth century it was coming to be seen that if authorship, with its attendant advantages to the public, was to flourish otherwise than at the precarious pleasure of wealthy patrons, the author should for a limited term have the monopoly of production and sale. It was a national affair, however, the foreigner was not recognized, and the native author was protected against importation of the foreign imprint. Such was the typical situation in the United States when in 1891 Congress concluded at last to grant the foreigner copyright if he had his book made here. The publishers lay low, thinking to draw the old non-importation clause to prevent the customary sale of the original which they would then undertake to reprint under

American copyright. While there is good reason to suppose that the attempt in court to prevent importation for use as against sale would have failed, yet the threat of such litigation might have proved a deterrent to libraries especially. So after mature deliberation, involving a distinguished Senatorial debate, Congress passed the Act with a specific proviso insuring to institutions and individuals the continued right of importation for use, though restricted to two copies.

This decision greatly upset the publishers and they have made repeated efforts at its repeal, the present being the fourth in thirteen years. It is not generally known that they tried it twice during the war—Jan. 8, 1915 (H. R. 20695) and Jan. 27, 1916 (H. R. 10231)—when public attention was focused elsewhere, but these bills did not emerge from committee, since the American Bar Association's Committee on Patent, Trademark and Copyright, under the chairmanship of R. H. Parkinson, of Chicago, was awake and made efficient protest. The most ambitious drive, however, came in connection with the Act of 1909. This campaign really ran over nearly a decade. Learned counsel was employed, and elaborate preparations carried through. On May 1, 1901, the American Publishers' Association and the American Booksellers' Association, recently formed for the purpose, put into effect a joint pact placing most classes of books on a net basis, except for a discount of ten per cent to libraries.

Article III of the Publishers' program ran as follows: That the members of the Association agree that such net copyrighted books and all other of their books shall be sold by them to those booksellers only who will maintain the retail price of such net copyrighted books for one year, and to those booksellers and jobbers only who will sell their books further to no one known to them to cut such net prices or whose name has been given to them by the Association as one who cuts such prices, etc.

The Booksellers, on their part, voted "not to buy, not to keep in stock, nor to offer for sale, after due notification, the books of any publisher who declines to support the net price system"; to expel any member reported by any three of his fellows as having had commerce with a denounced publisher; to refuse such expelled member or a denounced dealer all discount. Here was an agreement to destroy the business of anyone who refused an oath to support whatever retail price a publisher might set and join in punishing those who did not. Here was plain combination in restraint of trade. One need not necessarily condemn maintenance of price in order to condemn the coercive methods here employed. The defense lay in the nature of copyright as a monopoly, which was alleged to place the proprietor beyond the reach of anti-trust laws, and as sole vendor to control resale.

Two results followed swiftly. First, libraries found their prices advanced about twenty per cent. The American Library Association, joined by the National Education Association, protested. Second, R. H. Macy & Company, blacklisted and blockaded for retailing at $1.24 a net copyrighted $1.40 novel, purchased by them at forty per cent discount, brought suit Dec. 3, 1902, against both Associations and others. On Feb. 23, 1904, the New York Court of Appeals declared the combination illegal so far as it sought to control uncopyrighted books. In March the agreement was changed to cover copyrighted books only, and two publishers instituted suits against Macy's shortly afterward. The Bobbs-Merrill Company printed, under the copyright notice of The Castaway, the following in each copy: "The price of this book at retail is one dollar net. No dealer is licensed to sell it at a less price, and a sale at a less price will be treated as an infringement of the copyright." Macy's price was $.89.

Scribner's sought to attain the same end by printing in their catalogs and bills the following notice: "Copyrighted net books published after May 1, 1901, and copyrighted fiction published after Feb. 1, 1902, are sold on condition that prices be maintained as provided by the regulations of the American Publisher's Association." In both these instances, the attempt was being made by reason of copyright monopoly to impose by notice a retail price on a dealer with whom there was no privity of contract. The United States Circuit Court, Southern District of New York, found for Macy's July 11, 1905, and these verdicts were affirmed June 16, 1906, in the United States Circuit Court of Appeals for the Second Circuit.

This sequence of events is of the greatest significance to the case which we have in hand today, for it was in June and November, 1905, and March, 1906, that the three conferences to lay the basis for a bill "to amend and consolidate the acts respecting copyright," as requested by the Chairman of the Senate Committee on Patents, were held. The publishers swarmed over the place, for here was the chance of a lifetime tow in in Congress a battle they were losing in the courts. Despite the substantial labors of the Copyright Officer, an amazing strand of privileges, filched from author and public for the aggrandizement of the publisher, was woven into the fabric of the draft. Here they inserted absolute prohibition of importaiotn unless with the reprinter's consent. Continued control after sale was covered by this astounding clause: That the copyright secured by this Act shall include the sold and exclusive right: (b) To sell, distribute, exhibit, or let for hire, or offer or keep for sale, distribution, exhibition, or hire, any copy of such work. A purchaser could not even show a book he had bought, let alone sell it at will, unless the publishers gave written consent, and a violation would incur the fine or imprisonment fixed for infringement.

And there was much else of the same ilk. So deftly, however, was the work done by counsel and so assured the client's manner that the Congressional committees were at first taken in and spoke for a brief space the approved patois of the publisher. The trend of events thereafter cannot more certainly be gauged than by reading side by side the two reports of Chairman Currier dated respectively Jan. 30, 1907, and Feb. 22, 1909. The primary rights of the public were the keynote of the latter. His eyes and those of the Senate Committee, which also adopted it, had been opened by the pleas of the American Library Association, and the Library Copyright League, organized for the purpose by W. P. Cutter, but especially through the appearance of a brilliant protagonist of the cultivated reader, at the Hearings of March, 1908, in the person of William Allen Jenner, a New York lawyer, speaking in his own name. Mr. Jenner had already got the ear of Congress by the private publication in 1907 of a masterly analysis of the bill entitled *The publisher against the people, a plea for the defense*, to be followed after the Hearings by *The octopus*, similarly issued. Under his penetrating probe, the proceedings broke up and turned into a general rat-hunt by all aboard. At the end, the importation right was back where it ought to be, the disposal section resumed its traditional tenor in the grant, "To print, reprint, publish, copy, and vend the copyrighted work" and many other nests were cleared out.

One last stand was yet to be made. The Supreme Court on June 1, 1908, had affirmed the lower court decisions in the Bobbs-Merrill and Scribner cases, even though in January, 1907, the publishers had changed their "agreement" into a "recommendation," without, however, altering coercive practices. Thus the publisher could not by mere notice limit the price of resale, nor after the first vending exercise any further right. The final drive, made at the critical Hearing of Jan. 20, 2909, was in the effort to insert the following clause:

That subject to the limitations and conditions of this act copyright secured hereunder shall be entitled to all the rights and remedies which would be accorded to any other species of property at common law.

Here again appeared Mr. Jenner for the public, joined by Mr. Parkinson, who, as already seen, was still keeping his vigil in 1916.

This clause was to revive an old claim of the Stationers' Company of London, which, under the aegis of the Star Chamber, carried so high a hand for a century and a half from its charter in 1556. Since 1710 when the Statute of Anne, the first copyright act, went into effect, all copyright in published works has been statutory. So finally decided the House of Lords in 1774. In this spirit the American Constitution wsa written and the Act of 1790 so construed by the Supreme Court in 1834 and repeatedly since. The effect of the clause would probably have been to upset the Bobbs-Merrill verdict. It failed, and the bill only when so amended was signed by President Roosevelt on the last day of his second term in 1909.

The end of the American Publishers' Association came in 1914 with the payment of $140,000 in damages following the third unanimous verdict of the Supreme Court Dec. 1, 1913, in favor of Macy's. And now after all this history, with the fate of its sire full before its eyes, the young National Association of Book Publishers, our nativity greetings hardly dead on the air, dashes up on the old steed, with the prettiest trappings the best copyright saddler in America could give him, determined once more to stay the free flow of the world's through our way, thus beggaring American art, science and scholarship to fill a private till.

Copyright—Reply to M. L. Raney

By Frederic G. Melcher, Executive Secretary, National Association of Book Publishers Fourth General Session

I have asked President Root for the opportunity to make reply to Dr. Raney's discussion on copyright in the earlier session, not so much to argue the details of the Copyright Bill as to criticize the spirit in which his comment on the book-trade was offered.

His speech was called "A Primer of Copyright." This suggested to me, while being delivered, the following paraphrase of Kipling's well-known verse:

"If the book-trade were as here it seems,
And not the book-trade of my dreams,
But only intrigue, graft and taint,
If the book-trade were,
But—the book trade ain't."

Like Mayor Hylan in his attitude toward the transportation interests in New York, Dr. Raney believes that all who have had to do with copyright from the publisher's angle are to be under suspicion at every turn and ranked with the sinister interests.

In order to paint the publishers in darkest colors, it seemed necessary in his argument to explain the Authors' League's connection with the Bill. This he did by stating that the Author's League was but parade bunting stretched out in the publishers' interests, to be taken down when the issue was over. This unfair and inaccurate criticism of the Authors' League is entirely out of agreement with the facts as known to all. The Authors' League is a large independent organization with an effective record, and no publisher is on its committee. In the preliminary work of arranging for a revision of copyright, the hard work done by Eric Schuler, secretary of the League, who should be given all praise, and the first draft of the Bill was drawn by the attorney of the League.

The inaccuracy of the statement that the publishers molded the new Copyright Bill is shown by the fact that three out of the four principal workers in the drafting of the Bill were not publishers at all. One of Mr. Raney's friendly little references to the people who did this work is in one of his letters where he refers to Major Putnam and Mr. Bowker as the "Gold Dust Twins" of copyright. Perhaps I will accept that reference, because, if it comes to copyright matters, these men have done the hard work and they have done clean work.

Lest it be considered that there is something eccentric in believing that the present Bill has been drawn with an attempt at justice to all parties, it should be pointed out that after very careful examination, Dr. Rothlisberger, Secretary of the Berne convention, approved the phrase under criticism, and in fact said that he had suggested the same solution to the Canadian Legislature in a comment on the new Canadian law. Dr. Raney seemed to believe that the publishers do not like the reference to copyright in the American Constitution, but this point in his argument did not seem clear. Publishers are not mentioned in the Constitution, neither are booksellers or libraries, and the Copyright Bill is merely intended to give all parties their proper protection in order that the author and public may be well served. In a recent letter to our office, Dr. Raney wrote: "As to the washing of dirty linen, my reference was to the necessary review of the record of the American Publishers' Association, which in its struggle for monopoly, suicided to escape the gallows. To me that is dirty linen, but if it is shoved under our noses we willw ash it." This he has presumably attempted to do in his brief history of the American Booksellers' Association and the original American Publishers' Association in their attempt to put stability into the American book distribution machinery, by finding some method of standardizing prices. If that is a culpable effort, the publishers cheerfully take the responsibility. Everyone in this audience who is familiar with book-trade conditions twenty-five years ago will know how necessary some such action wsa. Bookstores were blinking out under pressure of cut-throat competition and new ones were not starting to take their places. Certainly there was nothing for author or public to gain from such a condition, and it is worth recording that, although the effort finally came to a legal disaster, the atmosphere was clarified during the discussion and that, in spite of the cost, the effort was worth making. If legal defeat is a proof of sinister intent, then those who have been favoring the Child Labor Law in Washington should also be under fire.

Dr. Raney has a good deal to say about monopoly, as if that very word proved that there was a plot against the public. He should keep in mind that the very essence of copyright is monopoly and that, as authors continue to need publishers and seek for them, and, as probably half the books published are conceived in publishing offices, monopoly is a necessary part of the situation. Libraries on their part have monopoly, even though bookstores do not. Authors sometimes avoid having publishers, but it has not yet been claimed that they find advantage in the other system. Nine-tenths of the books that libraries buy—probably more than nine-tenths—are of American origin and their copyright gives some publisher a monopoly. The justice of this has not been questioned in Dr. Raney's report.

It should not be forgotten that it may matter to the author whether the book is bought in the English edition or bought here—the author's income does not depend upon the percentage he gets on one sale but on the total number of sales. If an English author can get five times as many sales in this country by having a publisher actively interested in this success, he is better off than if a small number of orders came from those libraries most actively following the English announcements. This curtailment of the English author's opportunity is just what this "buy in England" campaign brings about. The owner of a patent in the American market does not suffer competition from the same machine made in England. The purchaser of the dramatic or movie rights for the American market does not suffer because of importations. But the American publisher is questioned because he argues that it is better for all hands that there be someone with full authority to promote a given item in this area. We should not forget that American authors are also anxious to get substantial hearings in England, and tthat these hearings are obtained by an English publisher's promotion and not by casual hearings of a few copies going to that country.

That authors appreciate the importance of having the undivided support of publishers and do not stand suspicious of every business house is shown in a recent signed statement by a group of English authors, who, in commenting on the situation that developed in connection with Tolstoi's works, maintained that no author could get a proper hearing wihtout a publisher and that "it is practically impossible to engage modern capital in publishing or any other enterprise without property rights."

Just what the Bill provides in the way of free access to the other markets for the libraries should be noticed. Only books in English fall under this restriction, and only those books in English which are registered at Washington by an American publisher as having been duly published in this country. These might perhaps be ten per cent of the English publications at most. The book thus being registered, the library can still obtain the English edition by filing its request with the American publisher, and if the publisher does not acknowledge and file the order within ten days, the library can order direct. This English edition would be supplied by the American publisher at a price equivalent to the English price.

At a hearing before the Senate Committee last December, Dr. Raney gave figures showing the comparative cost of twenty-five books in England and America. These prices, he stated, were supplied by a western library of fifty thousand volumes. Investigation proved that while the English prices were so supplied, the American prices had been obtained by Dr. Raney by writing to the individual publishers, who on such orders quoted the books at ten per ent off, plus postage. This figure would constitute about as high a price as could be given in any showing, with the natural result that the comparison was as bad as possible. Certainly there is nothing in the present discussion of one small phrase of an important Bill which need lead to arguments of such a nature.

The new Bill has the approval of the leading world authority on copyright, the friendly comment from England and Canada, and has had the advantage of being drafted by four recognized experts in copyright law. Under the circumstances, the publishers are surprised at an attack of such bitterness on their standing. American publishing is making good strides forward in the character and variety of books and the ability with which the needs of this great market are met. In fact, the publishers take pride in being publishers, as they also take pleasure in their relations with all groups who have to do with book distribution. I wish to say finally in the phraseology of Christopher Mornley that "We may be inept, but we are not sinister."

Editor's note: The copyright bill of 1922 did not pass. The U.S. did not become a party to the Berne Convention until 1989.

Index

A.L.A. Bibliothecal Museum, 64
A.L.A. Index to General Literature, 101
Abbot, Ezra, 22, 33
Accession book, 29,
The Age of Reason: From Bryant to F.D.R., 3
Alexandria, 143
Alexandrine MS Greek Bible, 149
Ambrose, Lodilla, 101-104
American Association for International Conciliation, 178
American Library Association, 6, 7, 8, 71-77, 85, 93-94, 96, 179
American Library Association conferences, 71-74, 89-96, 101, 104, 105, 111, 137, 135, 143, 173, 181, 209, 231
American Library Association headquarters, 105-107
American Library Association, Presidential Address, 89-96
American Library Association, *Proceedings*, Fourteenth, 71-77
American Library Journal, 7
American School Peace League, 179
American thought, 189-198
American Woman: Images and Realities (1933), 5
Ankles seized (of library girls), 229
Anonymous works, 26-27
Aristophanes of Byzantium, 145
Assur-Bani-Pal, (Assurbanipal, d. 626 B.C. Nineveh), 112
Atlantic Monthly, 17
Authority control, 24-25

Baker, Paula, 5
Baker, Thomas, 80
Balkin, Richard R., 7
Bentley, Richard Sir, 149-150
Berne Convention, 232, 242
Berne Union
 See Berne Convention
Bettinelli, Saverio, 115
Biagi, Guido, 111-123

Bibliographic Society of Chicago, 104
Bibliothèque Mazarine, 146
Billings, John Shaw, 41-42, 104
Black, Miss (People's Palace, London), 81
Blair, Karen J., 4, 6
Bobinski, George, 3
Bodleian Library, 146, 148-149
Bodley, Thomas, 113, 148-149
Bohemians, 224
Bonfire of the Vanities (1497), 118
Book selection, 87-88, 135-136
Boston Athenaeum, 36
Boston Medical Library
 See Medical Library of Boston
Boston Public Library, 2, 182
Bostwick, Arthur E., acknowledgments, 157-165, 189-198
Bowerman, George F., 173-180
Bradford, William, 53
Braille, 114
Breckinridge, Sophonisba P., 5
British Museum, 40, 97, 102, 135, 151-156
Brooklyn Public Library, 178
Brosses, Charles de, 144
Brosterman, Norman, 9
Bowditch, Dr. Henry Ingersoll, 35
Bowerman, George F., 11
Bowker, R.R., 64

Cadwalader, Thomas, 53
Calcography, 113
Card catalog/catalogue, 21-23, 117
Carichael, James V., 10
Carnegie, Andrew, 3, 104, 126
Carnegie Libraries across America: A Public Legacy (1997), 6
Carnegie Libraries, 6
Carpenter's Hall, 56
Cary, Henry Francis, 152-153
Cataloging/cataloguing, 17-18, 122

Cato Major or His Discourse of Old Age (Cicero), first classic published in America, 57
Casaubon, Isaac, 131, 145-146
Catherine the Great of Russia (Sophie Fredericke Auguste von Anhalt-Zerbst), 147
Caxton, William, 113
The Century, 53
Chicago Woman's Club, 157
Children, 90-91, 127
Chronic fussers, 155
Circulating art exhibitions, 106
Circulating libraries, 51
Circulation, 88
Civil War, 3, 4
Clark, George T., 7-8, 85-88
Classification, 122
Clay tablets, 111
The Clubwoman as Feminist: True Womanhood Redefined, 1868-1914 (1980), 4
Codex Bezae, 150
Codices, 113
Coes, E.M., 71, 75
Collating, 18-19
Collection development, 31-33, 85-88
Columbia College, 8
Columbia Library School, 64-69
Commercial traveler, 157-158
Concilium Bibliographicum of Zurich, 117
Cooperation
  See Library cooperation
Copyright, 51, 231-242
Countryman, Gratia Alta, 125-128
Cultural Crusaders: Women Librarians in the American West, 1990-1917 (1994), 8.
Cutler, Mary S., 71
Cutter Expansive Classification, 122

Dana, John Cotton, 10, 89-96, 125
Democracy, 165
Denver Public Library, 89
Descriptve cataloging, 28
Dewey, Annie, (Mrs. Mevil), 71, 77
Dewey decimal classification, 122
Dewey, Melvil, 9, 59- 61, 64-69

The Dial, 101, 137, 139, 141
Dickinson, John, 54
Diderot, Denis, 147
Diner, Steven J., 7
Don Quixote, 37
Dorr, Rheta C., 4
DuBois, Ellen Carol, 3
Duche, Jacob Rev., 55

Edinburgh, Faculty of Advocates, 151
Education, 6
Electricity, 97
Ellis, Henry, 153
Encyclopedia, 122
Enrichment: A History of the Public Library in the United States in the Twentieth Century (1998), 11
Everyday Life in America (1991), 7

Faculty of Advocates, Edinburgh, 151
Fairchild, Mary Salome Cutler
  See Cutler
Fiction, 15, 127, 135-136
Fiske, John, 17-34
Fitzgerald, F. Scott, 10
Foundations of the Public Library (1949), 2
Franklin, Benjamin, 2, 53-58
Frederic, Duke of Urbino, 113, 115
Freeman, Marilla Waite, 219-221
From Altruism to Activism: The Contributions of Women's Organizations to Arkansas Public Libraries (Ph.D. diss, 1993), 5, 8
From Pedestal to Platform: The American Women's Club Movement, 1800-1920 (PhD diss., 1993), 5.
Fust, Johann, 113

Garnett, Richard, 97-99, 154-156
General Federation of Women's Clubs, 5
Germantown Quakers, 8, 15
Godfrey, Thomas (the mathematician), 54
Grace, Robert, 56
Graphophone, 114
Great War
  See World War One
Green, H.E., 77

INDEX

Greene, Charles S., 109
Grotzinger, Laurel A., 10

Hague Peace Conference, 179
Handwriting, 67
Hannah, George, 64
Harris, Michael, 2
Harvard College Library, 17-34
Heim, Kathleen M., acknowledgments, 8
Henry, W.E., 199-207
Hildenbrand, Suzanne, 8, 9
History of Libraries in the Western World, (1999), 2
Hofstater, Richard, 3, 7
Holmes, Oliver Wendell Sr., 35-49
Homeless, 89
Homer, 158
Human interest, 219-221
Hume, David, 151-152

Iles, George, 101, 105-107, 117
Improper books, 85
Incunabula, 37-38, 113
Index to Periodical Literature, 39
 See Also Poole's *Index to Periodical Literature*
Indolent, 89
Indexes, 38-42
Information desk, 139
Institut de Bibliographie of Brussels, 117
Inventing Kindergarten (1997)
"It's Your Misfortune and None of My Own": A History of the American West (1991), 4

James, H.P, 77
James, William, 173
Jesuits, 144-145
Jewett, Charles Coffin, 33-34, 47
Johnson, Dr. Samuel, 155
Jones, Theodore, 6
Josephson, Aksel G.S., 131

Keeper of Printed Books (British Museum), 152-156
Kindergarten, 9

King's Library (England), 153
Koch, Theodore W., 143-156
Larned, J.N., 106
Legler, Henry Eduard, 133, 137
Lessing, Gotthold, 147-148
Lewis, Sinclair, 5, 10
Librarians
 Community involvement, 216
 Education of, 64-69, 82, 205-207
 Profession, 199-207
 Torchbearers, 187
 Work of, 17-34, 47, 93-96, 133-135, 139, 141, 143-156, 181-187, 199-207
"The librarian who reads is lost," 118, 131, 145
The Library, 79
The Library and Society: Reprints of Papers and Addresses (1921), acknowledgments
Library as social centre, 125
Library Assistants' Association, 168
Library Association (England), 73, 80, 168
Library Boards, 10, 87
Library Bureau, 64
Library Company of Philadelphia, 2, 53-58
Library cooperation, 101-104, 117
Library extension, 106
Library future, 111-123
Library history, 1, 35-49, 53-58, 111-123, 143-156
Library Journal, 71, 157, 199, 219
Library Notes, 59, 64
Library of Congress, 20, 101-103, 117
Library of Congress Printed Cards, 103-104
Library of libraries, 105-107
Library School at Albany, 79
Library World, 167
Lloyd, Thomas, 56
Logan, James, 56
London Institute, 151
Lorenzo de' Medici, (Lorenzo the Magnificent), 113

Maack, Mary Niles, 10

McCook, Kathleen de la Peña, acknowledgments
McKean, Governor Thomas, 54
Magliabecchi, Antonio (librarian to Cosimo III de' Medici), 113, 122, 144-145
Manuzio, Aldo (Aldus Manutius), 113
Marucelli, Francesco, 122
Massachusetts Medical Society, 36
Martin, Lowell A., 11
Martin, Marilyn J., 5
Martin, Penny Theodora, 4
Matthews, Glenna, 4
Mazarin, Jules Cardinal, 146
Mazarin Library (Paris), 146
Medical Improvement Society, 36
Medical Library of Boston, 35
Medical Observation Society, 36
Melcher, Frederic G., 239-242
Middleton, Conyers, 150
Minnesota Library Association, 125
Missouri Library Association, 189
Montaigne, Michel de, 144
Musmann, Victoria Kline, 5
Myers, Sally A., 5

The Nation, 15, 51, 131, 133
National Association of Book Publishers, 239
National Education Association, Library Department, 94
National Medical Library, 41
Natural Allies: Women's Associations in American History (1992), 4, 5
Naudé, Gabriel, 146-147
New York Library Association, 189
New York Public Library, 134
North American Review, 143
Northwest Ohio Women's Literary Clubs as Arbiters of Culture: 1880-1918 (PhD. diss., 1995), 5

Oakland Free Library, 109, 129
Ostendorf, Paul John, 5

Panizzi, Sir Anthony, 153-154
Passet, Joanne E., 8, 9
Pattison, Mark, 117, 131, 145

Peace, 173-180
People's Palace, London, 81
Pepys, Samuel, 150
Pergamum, 112, 143
Perry, Bliss, 165
Petrie, W.M. Flinders, 185-186
Philadelphia, 2
   See Also Library Company of Philadelphia
Photography, 120
Platina, Bartolomeo, 143-144
Plantin, Christopher, 113
The Politics of an Emerging Profession: The American Library Association, 1876-1917 (1986), 7
Pollio, Asinius (est. first library for the public in Rome- Atrium Libertatis), 112
Poole, William Frederick, 39
Poole's Index to Periodical Literature, 101
Porson, Richard, 151
Printing, 113-114
Ptolemy (Alexandria), 112
Printed catalog, 33
Professionalism, 6
Progress, 112
Progressivism, 3, 4, 10
Pseudonymous works, 26-27
Public library, 25
   Children's Services, 90
   Economic value, 213
   Educational role, 85-86, 91, 187
   Finance, 158
   Governance, 157-165
   Italy, 111
   Publicity, 209-217
   Recreational role, 86-87, 187
Putnam, Herbert, 101-103, 143

Quaas, Eduard, 51
Quirini, Cardinal Angelo Maria, Bishop of Brescia, 144

Raney, M.L., 231-242
Rea, Robert, 224
Reading, 15, 115-116, 133-134
Reclaiming the American Library Past: Writing the Women In (1996), 9

INDEX

Renaissance, 114
Revolutionary war relics, 56
Richardson, Miss, 79-83
Ridgeway Library (Philadelphia), 57
The Rise of Public Woman: Woman's Power and Woman's Place in the United States, 1630-1970 (1992), 4
Role of Women in Librarianship: 1976-1976: The Entry, Advancement and Struggle for Equalization in One Profession (1979), acknowledgments
Robinson, Patricia Dawn, 5
Royal Laurentian Library, Florence, 111
Royal Library (St. James Palace, England), 149-150
Royal Library (Paris), 145
Royal Society of London, 117
Rush, Benjamin, 54
Rush, James, 57-58

St. Louis Public Library, 159
Samuel, Bunford, 2, 53-58
San Francisco Public Library, 223-225, 229
Sanders, M.R., 74
Sargent, M.E., 74
Savonarola, Girolamo, (Bonfire of the Vanities, 1497), 118
Schlereth, Thomas J., 7, 9
Schoeffer, Peter, 113
School of Library Economy, Columbia, 9
Scott, Anne Firor, 4
The Search for Order, 1877-1920: Making of America (1967), 3, 4
Shelf catalogue/shelf-list, 20
Shera, Jesse Hauk, 2
Smokers, 227-228
The Sound of Our Own Voices: Women's Study Clubs, 1860-1910 (1987), 4
Southey, Robert, 43
The Status of Women in Librarianship: Historical, Sociological and Economic Issues (1983), 8
Stereotype plate, 33-34
Subject catalogue/catalog, 22-24, and 30-31
Swedenborg, Emmanauel, 42

Sydenham, Thomas, 37

Telautograph, 98-99
Telegraph, 98
Telephone, 97, 129
Templeman, Peter, 152
Thomson, Charles, 54
Thou, Jacques Auguste de, 145
Title page, 26
Transformations in Everyday Life, 1876-1915 (1991), 7
Traveling library, 101, 106
Treadwell Library at the Massachusetts General Hospital, 36
Turin, library fire (1904), 119
Typewriter, 114

Underwood, June O., 5
United States after 1865 (2000), 3
U.S. Bureau of Education Report on Public Libraries (1876)

Van Slyck, Abigail A., 5, 6, 8, 9
Vatican Library, 143-144
A Very Different Age: Americans of the Progressive Era (1998), 7

War, 167-172, 173-180
Watson, Paula D., 6
Weibel, Kathleen, acknowledgments
Wellman, Hiller C., 181-187
Welter, Barbara, 5
What Eight Million Women Want (1910)
Wharton, Edith, 10
Wheeler, Joseph L., 209-217
White, Richard, 4
Wiebe, Robert H., 3, 7
Wiegand, Wayne A., 7
Wild flower show, 109
Williamson Report of 1920, 11
Winsor, Justin, 47, 131, 134, 182
Wolf, Miss F.J. de, 109
Wolfenbüttel, 147
Woman's Meeting of the American Library Association (1892), 71-77
Women and the Founding of Social Libraries in California, 1859-1910 (PhD diss, 1982), 5

Women in libraries, 3-10, 31, 59-61, 65-66, 71-77, 79-83, 137, 167-172, 229
Women in the Twentieth Century (1933), 5, 6
Women's clubs, 4-6, 94-95, 165
Women's Work, Vision and Change in Librarianship (1994), 10
World War One, 10, 167-172

Xylography, 113

www.ingramcontent.com/pod-product-compliance
Lightning Source LLC
Chambersburg PA
CBHW030617230426
43661CB00053B/2028